AF378887

THE LANGUAGE OF THE GODS

SANSKRIT KEYS TO INDIA'S WISDOM

By

JUDITH M. TYBERG

(JYOTIPRIYA)

M.A., M.TH., Ph.D. from Theosophical University
CALIFORNIA

M.A. in Indian Religion & Philosophy from Benares Hindu University
INDIA

In reverent memory of Sri Aurobindo

Published by

EAST-WEST CULTURAL CENTRE

2865, West Ninth Street
Los Angeles, Cal. 90006, U.S.A.

© *COPYRIGHT 1970*

EAST-WEST CULTURAL CENTRE

LOS ANGELES, CALIFORNIA 90006, U.S.A.

ALL RIGHTS RESERVED

SECOND EDITION 1976

Printed by
MARVIN SHEEN PRINTING
4531 Sunset Boulevard
LOS ANGELES, CALIF. 90027

THE LANGUAGE OF THE GODS

PREFACE

Sanskrit is the ancient language of thousands of sacred scriptures of the *Sanātana Dharma* or 'Eternal Truth' revealed down the ages in India. Because these Sanskrit writings are still the living guides for the moral, aesthetic, intellectual, and spiritual life of the Indian peoples, to be able to express and to understand the Sanskrit terms of this lofty wisdom is to discover the heart of the culture of this Eastern race, another part of our own nature and very being, another richly laden aspect of the Divine in manifestation.

Sanskrit is rich with words dealing with the inner mysteries and workings of the mind, heart, soul and spirit, with the many states of consciousness in waking, sleeping and after-death life, with the origin, evolution and destiny of beings of all realms, and with the glorious descriptions of the Divine and Its infinite manifestations. These words have been ringing with these high meanings for many ages for they have been kept alive with truth by an unending series of seers and sages and realized souls, called in India by many a name: *Swāmīs, Āchāryas, Sādhus, Sannyāsins, Mahātmans, Yogins, Avatāras,* and *Ṛishis.*

In this age when men are responding to a spiritual need for unity and brotherhood among all nations of the world, we find a spiritual vocabulary being drawn from the rich treasury of Sanskrit terminology because these words are already mature and ripe with truths divine. Even our Western sciences have adopted words from the Latin and Greek in order to express more clearly their conceptions. Why have they done this? Because modern languages were seemingly inadequate and the Latin and Greek languages already possessed appropriate roots and expressions for these ideas. The initial difficulty of learning the technical scientific terms is nothing compared to the vast fields of information open to us once we have mastered this terminology. So it will be with these Sanskrit mystical and philosophical terms and their meanings — a great enlightenment will dawn with an ever increasing intuitive faculty as a result of being able to delve deeper into the wisdom-treasury of Divine Revelation. "To know truly is to be" is one of the old Vedāntic precepts helping the disciple on his path to God-Realization.

June, 1967 JUDITH M. TYBERG

I have great pleasure in introducing Dr. Judith M. Tyberg and her work, *The Language of the Gods*. I came to know of Miss Tyberg in the year 1947 when she came to Banaras Hindu University as a Seth Jugal Kishore Birla Scholar to join the M.A. Class in Indian Philosophy and Religion. I was then the Head of Departments of Philosophy and of Indian Philosophy and Religion and was also a teacher in these subjects. Miss Tyberg evinced a very keen interest in the subject and took her M.A. degree in Indian Philosophy and Religion in 1949 in Banaras University. Formerly she had taken an M.A. degree, an M.Th. degree and a Ph.D. degree from the Theosophical University in Point Loma, California, U.S.A. She had also been the Head of the Oriental Department of the University for some years and written text-books on the subject.

During Dr. Tyberg's stay at Varanasi she lived like an Indian and came to know much about Indian life and the religion of the people. She was impressed with the vast and profound aspects of Hinduism and studied them closely and with appreciation and admiration. She picked up some Hindi, the language of the people, and acquired a fair acquaintance with Sanskrit, the language of the sacred scriptures of India.

When Dr. Tyberg returned to her home in California after three years in India, she took up the task of making her people acquainted with the Sanātana Dharma, the Eternal Religion of India, and also developed methods of teaching Sanskrit to the people of the West. In her training of the American students in the American Academy of Asian Studies and at the East-West Cultural Center which she founded in 1953, she combined with her creative genius the teachings of Sanskrit and Hinduism in a unique manner. Her presentation of Sanskrit and the great truths that its writings contain is quite original. It is a more or less direct method of teaching truths through a language, and deserves to be followed by both Eastern and Western teachers of the subject. Through her text-book students have become quite familiar with Sanskrit or *Devavāṇī*, the 'Language of the Gods' and its higher religious literature such as Vedas, Upanishads, and the Bhagavad-Gītā.

This book is not just an introduction to the Sanskrit language, it is a very good introduction to the literature and spiritual teachings of the Eternal Religion of India, a religion or Dharma which has known no beginning and no end. It is hoped her book will help other writers and thinkers in their efforts to make Indian Culture better known and understood in foreign lands. Her work deserves great congratulations. May Dr. Tyberg long continue to serve the country where she received her highest education.

B. L. ATREYA
(Padmabhushan)
Knight Commander Darshanacharya
8th August 1967

INTRODUCTION

Dr. Judith Tyberg, founder-director of the East-West Cultural Center, Los Angeles, U.S.A., has been a leading exponent of the East to the United States. During the last twenty years and more, to numerous pupils that joined her Center year after year, she has served as an outstanding teacher of Sanskrit which she herself learnt the hard way in the States and then in the environs of Benaras University. She has unlocked to her pupils the treasures of the ancient Indian wisdom enshrined in Sanskrit.

This book is the fruit of a life-time of labour and of a ceaseless search for Truth. Dr. Tyberg found in the literature of the ancients and in modern Indian interpretations of their vision, particularly Sri Aurobindo's, what she had been seeking all the time. It is the burning desire to communicate to other aspirants what vision of Reality she herself attained through her study of ancient and modern Indian philosophy that has sustained her in her work on this book, *The Language of the Gods*. Her book is a comprehensive guide to the manifold aspects of Indian religion and philosophy. It is her faith that a richly laden aspect of Eternal Truth has been revealed to mankind through the sacred texts in Sanskrit.

Dr. Tyberg is concerned in this book, not so much with literary and classical Sanskrit as with spiritual vocabulary: the mystical and philosophic terms in Sanskrit and their entitled meanings which help us to map out precisely the realms of the superconscient in man.

She has grouped the spiritual vocabulary in a manner which facilitates the understanding of the main Sanskrit texts. Chapter I deals with essential religious terms. The third Chapter sets forth the philosophic terms that one encounters in a study of the Bhagavadgītā. This is the simplest and the most comprehensive of the sacred texts in Sanskrit, setting forth as it does the essence of the teachings of the Vedas and the Upanishads. The Seventh Chapter introduces the student to Upanishadic terms. The Eighth Chapter deals with the systems of Yoga and the philosophic terms that one comes across while studying the yogic texts. The Ninth Chapter deals with the philosophic meanings of the terms used in the Vedas. The Tenth Chapter deals with various philosophical schools and the philosophic terms found in the literature of these schools. The Eleventh Chapter is devoted to the terms and the names that one encounters in the Buddhistic texts.

Around these clusters of words Dr. Tyberg has woven an illuminating account of the Mantric power of Sanskrit, Vedic and classical Sanskrit literature, the Upanishads and Yogic texts, the systems of Yoga, the various philosophical schools and Buddhism. The Twelfth Chapter gives an outline of Sanātana Dharma. It presents an acute analysis of the inter-connections that exist among the various spiritual movements in India.

Valuable assistance is given to the reader by devising a number of reading lessons. The clusters of words are used in relevant contexts with roots and prefixes, and brief explanatory notes on important words, the passages are also followed by translations into English. This helps to fix the words in the reader's memory. There are also apt quotations from the Sanskrit texts by way of brief comprehension exercises.

There are a number of indices in the body of the book and at the end which enhances its value in a great measure. The note on the Devanāgarī alphabet with rules on the pronunciation of Sanskrit is very helpful to the foreign reader.

The Indian student of Sanskrit also can benefit greatly by a study of Dr. Tyberg's book. I have not come across any single publication which narrows down the range of study to the requirements of the spiritual seeker and attains a rich comprehensiveness in fulfilling these requirements.

The East is doing its best to absorb all the science and humanism which the West has gifted and is gifting to mankind. Dr. Tyberg and her associates have embarked on another adventure which is equally significant — that of enabling the West to apprehend the Eternal Truth that lies hidden in the sacred texts of India and in the literature that has grown around them. This is a great task and I sincerely wish Dr. Tyberg the richest fulfilment in it.

Bangalore   V. K. GOKAK
8th August 1967

NOTE OF GRATITUDE AND APPRECIATION

I wish to express my gratitude and deep appreciation to those who have helped me in the preparation of this book: to Dick Shive and Clay Barton, two of my Sanskrit students who helped with the checking and typing, to Mrs. Katherine Doran who helped with mimeographing, and to Ina Selin, who helped with typing and photostatic work for the book. All these friends gave their kind help freely and graciously.

To Sri A. A. Inamdar, President of Fellowship School in Bombay, to Vidvan B. V. S. S. Mani, Honorary Secretary of the Swadharma Swarajya Sangha of Madras, and to my friends, Deborah Smith and Helen Harris, all of whom have so generously made the printing and publishing of this book possible, I offer my *pranāms* and deep gratitude.

Finally to all the Great Sages of India who have revealed and passed on this wisdom to me for instructing and offering to others, I offer my heart-thanks and *Namaskāras*.

JUDITH M. TYBERG
January 30, 1971

This book has been written for students who would like to become familiar with the meaning and symbolic truths contained in the many Sanskrit words used in books on India's religions, philosophy, and Yoga, and in translations of Hindu and Buddhist sacred scriptures. Its lessons have been made suitable for students of Sanskrit Grammar as well as for those only wishing to recognize and understand the Sanskrit terms so frequently found in books on Eastern culture.

For those wishing to master the fundamentals of Sanskrit Grammar, my book, *First Lessons in Sanskrit Grammar and Reading*, recently printed at Sri Aurobindo Ashram Press, will be very helpful along with this book, *The Language of the Gods*. These two books do not give an exhaustive study of Sanskrit for they are intended to aid the Western student with India's spiritual teachings and practices as given down the ages by the Sages and Seers in their sacred Sanskrit scriptures.

In this book a stress has been given to the verb-roots of the words, for they are the essential carriers of the meaning of the words as originating in the spiritual element of the Universe. To recognize the verb-root with its prefixes is to get at the real meaning of the word, free from the loaded implications that so many words have come to possess because of religious dogma and a misunderstanding due to lack of spiritual experience.

The law of Sanskrit vowels is very basic in the formation of words from verb-roots. If one can trace a word to its verb-root it will aid in using most Sanskrit dictionaries where the words are grouped according to verb-roots and not according to the first letter of the word. Observe the following development of vowels and words:

Root-Vowel	Guṇa Form	Vṛiddhi Form	Verb-root	Noun	Adjective	Verb-meaning
a or ā	a or ā	ā	man	manas	mānasika	think
i or ī	e or ay	ai or āy	div	deva	daiva	shine
			lī	laya	lāyika	dissolve
u or ū	o or av	au or āv	budh	bodha	baudha	know
			bhū	bhava	bhāva	become
ṛi or ṛī	ar	ār	kṛi	karma	kārmika	to do or act
lṛi	al	āl	klṛip	kalpa	kālpika	be in order

Each of the first three chapters is carefully planned for mastering the most frequently used Sanskrit terms. Each lesson first gives an explanation of the words arranged as to meanings rather than by alphabet. Then a Sūtra or little essay stringing together the words just explained is presented with its very succinct meaning either below or on the opposite page. This Sūtra is good for reading aloud after the teacher in order to grasp the correct pronunciation. If any accent is given a word one gives a slight stress to the verb-root. One should learn to give the English meaning of the Sūtra without looking at the English translation. Then with the Sūtra mastered, turn to the next pages giving the alphabetical list of the words and see if the meaning can be given quickly. Then for the Grammar students the list of verb-roots can be checked and a Sanskrit term derived from the verb-root should be given. After the first lesson is perfected some 90 words will belong to your Sanskrit vocabulary, after the second lesson some 60 more words, and after the third lesson some 375 more terms and names, hence a total of 525 important words and famous names. Words once given are not repeated in another chapter unless a variation or addition in meaning is necessary. By the end of the book some 2,000 words are presented.

Starting with Chapter Four the Sūtra and verb-root lists are omitted. The verb-roots are given when necessary in the explanation of the word. Many of the words in the Chapters on Literature and Philosophy will require further research. The Tables and Charts given in some of the Chapters will reveal the many variations that exist in the vast fields of the

Sanātana Dharma. They will also provide very interesting material for comparative study in both Eastern and Western philosophy and religion.

The final Indexes will give the serial page on which each word and its explanation or use may be found. May this study and its contents enlighten you on your pathway in search for TRUTH!

JUDITH M. TYBERG

RULES FOR THE PRONUNCIATION OF SANSKRIT

a	—	like a in org*a*n or the u in b*u*t
ā	—	like a in f*a*r but held twice as long
i	—	like i in p*i*que
ī	—	same as i but twice as long
u	—	like u in r*u*le
ū	—	same as u but twice as long
ṛi	—	like ri in *Ri*ta
ṛī	—	same as ri but twice as long
lṛi	—	pronounced lree
lṛī	—	same but twice as long
e	—	like e in th*ey*
ai	—	like ai in *ai*sle
o	—	like o in g*o*
au	—	like ow in h*ow*
ṁ	—	anuswara is a resonant nasal pronounced with open mouth
ḥ	—	visarga is a final h-sound uttered in the articulating position of the preceding vowel: thus kaviḥ is pronounced kavihi, etc.
k	—	as in *k*ite
kh	—	as in Echkart
g	—	as in *g*ive
gh	—	as in di*g-h*ard
ṅ	—	as in si*n*g
ch	—	as in *ch*air
chh	—	as in staun*ch-h*eart
j	—	as in *j*oy
jh	—	as in hedgehog
ñ	—	as in se*ñ*or
ṭ	—	as in *t*ub with tongue to roof of mouth

PRONUNCIATION CHART

ṭh	—	as in ligh*t*-*h*eart tongue to roof of mouth
ḍ	—	as in *d*ub tongue to roof of mouth
ḍh	—	as in re*d*-*h*ead tongue to roof of mouth
ṇ	—	as in *n*ut tongue to roof of mouth
t	—	as in *t*ub with tongue against teeth
th	—	as in ligh*t*-*h*eart tongue against teeth
d	—	as in *d*ub with tongue against teeth
dh	—	as in re*d*-*h*ead with tongue against teeth
n	—	as in *n*ut tongue against teeth
p	—	as in *p*ine
ph	—	as in u*p*-*h*ill
b	—	as in *b*ird
bh	—	as in ru*b*-*h*ard
m	—	as in *m*other
y	—	as in *y*es
r	—	as in *r*un
l	—	as in *l*ight
v	—	as in *v*ine
ś	—	as in German word *s*prechen (sh in palate)
sh	—	as in *sh*ine
s	—	as in *s*un
h	—	as in *h*omo

TABLE OF CONTENTS

CHAPTER

CHAPTER I

ESSENTIAL RELIGIOUS TERMS

The sacred language of India; the language of much of the holy literature, philosophy and religion. It is supposed to have originated from a very early Aryan tongue which was perfected and polished to express the truths of the seer-sages of ancient India. Hence its etymological meaning 'perfected', 'polished', from the verb-root *kri* plus the prefix *sam* meaning 'to make perfect, complete'.

Saṁskṛita (Sanskrit)

The Sanskrit script. 'Divine-city' writing or temple script. (From *deva* — god, *nagara* — city.) Several of the modern languages of India use varied forms of the Deva-nāgarī. Hindi, now the national language of India uses the original Devanāgarī.

Devanāgarī

A holy man; a man of the highest aspiration, noblest religious dispositions along with an undaunted courage in the upward march of the human race, and one with self surrendered to the Divine Will. (From the verb-root *ṛi* — to rise upward.)

Ārya

Āryāvarta 'Land of the Holy' an ancient name of India.

Āryāvarta

Unholy, unaspiring (*an* — not).

Anārya

The land (*varsha*) of the Bhāratas (the descendents of the great Bharata); a name for India. Bharata was a celebrated hero and monarch of ancient India. Sometimes the people of India are called 'Bhāratas'. (From the verb-root *bhṛi* — to support.)

**Bhāratavarsha
Bharata
Bhārata**

Duty, righteousness, law, order. (From verb-root *dhṛi* — to hold, to establish.) Used in the plural, 'Dharmas' means the ordained duties of religious and social life.

**Dharma
Dharma(s)**

"Dharma in the Indian conception is not merely the good, the right, morality and justice, ethics; it is the whole government of all the relations of man with other beings, with Nature, with God. Dharma is both that which we hold to and that which holds together our inner and outer activities, and in this its primary sense it means a fundamental law of our nature which secretly conditions all our activities, and in this sense each type, species, individual, group has its own dharma.... Dharma is all that helps us to grow into the divine purity, largeness, light, freedom, power, strength, joy, love, good, unity and beauty." — Sri Aurobindo.

Sanātana Dharma   The 'Eternal Religion or Truth'.

Not-righteousness; the shadow and denial of truth and divine values; the reactionary force which makes for evil, ignorance **Adharma** and darkness and resistance to growth. One's **Svadharma** own (*sva*) law of action and being in harmony with the Divine intent.

Satya   'That which IS', Truth, Reality. (*Sat* is the present participle of the verb-root *as* — to be.)

'Holding on to Truth'. (From verb-root *grah* — to seize, hold.) Mahātmā Gandhi instituted a campaign of Satyāgraha **Satyāgraha** or 'Insistence on Truth'. One aspect of his Satyā- **Mahātmā** graha movement was the non-violent disobedience **Gandhi** to unjust laws.

Non-injury, non-violence. Mahātmā Gandhi interpreted this age-honored virtue of Ahiṁsā to basically mean 'Love'. He **Ahiṁsā** endeavored to bring about justice, peace and freedom for his country through non-violent methods, non-violence in thought, word and deed. (From *a* — not, and verb-root *hiṁs* — to injure.)

A Truth-Seer, a Seer-Sage (from verb-root *dṛiś* — to see); one who sees the true law of being directly by inner vision. The **Ṛishi** composers of the Vedic hymns are known as Ṛishis. Gandhi called Sri Aurobindo a Ṛishi.

**Āchārya
Śaṅkara
Śaṅkarā-
 chārya**
A spiritual guide; a teacher who invests the young student with the sacrificial thread and instructs him in the Vedas, the oldest wisdom writings of India, and teaches him in the laws of sacrifice and religious mysteries. (From verb-root *char* — to go, plus the prepositional prefix ā meaning 'towards'; hence to approach, for being led thither on the path). Āchārya is also a title affixed to the names of learned spiritual men like Śankara — hence Śankarāchārya.

**Bhakta
Bhakti**
A devotee of God, or of a representative or symbol of God. Bhakti is 'Devotion'. (From the verb-root *bhaj* — to love, to revere.)

Sādhu
A holy man, a saint. (From the verb-root *sādh* — to go straight to the goal.)

**Mahātman or
 Mahātmā**
A great Soul (*mahā* — great, *ātman* — self), a magnanimous, exceedingly wise man. Also a title of high respect and honor given to the noblest of the devotees of the Spirit.

**Svāmin or
 Svāmī**
A lord, owner, a spiritual preceptor, a learned Brahmin. (From *sva* — own.)

**Guru
Gurudeva**
A spiritual preceptor or guide. (*Guru* — heavy, venerable, from verb-root *gṛī* — to invoke, to praise.) A Guru in India is one who has the capacity to pass on his realizations to those who seek him for wisdom. There may be the outer Guru or Guide who removes ignorance by the radiant light of his divine wisdom or the inner Guru or Ātman (Self) who is the spiritual Guide working through the intuitive part of man. The Divine Teacher, a divinely illumined being. (From *deva* — god.)

Deva
A god, a higher being, a being of light. (From verb-root *div* — to shine.)

A renunciate; one who renounces all external and worldly bonds in order to devote one's life to the higher intellectual and spiritual self-culture and service of humanity; an ascetic; the

renouncer of worldly values; one who is a free super-social
man. From verb-root *as* — to throw, plus the prefixes *ni* — down and *sam* — implying 'completely' hence meaning 'to throw' aside completely, to renounce.)

Sannyāsin or Sannyāsī

Excellent, venerated, splendid. As a noun it means 'wealth', 'radiance'. (From verb-root *śrī* — to flame, diffuse light.) Śrī is often used as a spiritually venerable title or as a prefix to the names of the great Seer-Sages.

Śrī

A Divine Incarnation or the Descent of God in the world. (From verb-root *tṛī* — to cross, and the preposition *ava* — down.) An Avatāra is a revelation of Godhead in humanity. He comes down to reveal the divine nature in man and to show him the nature of divine works and with his divine love and power draws men to the being, wisdom and bliss of God. Hence each Avatāra has his unique work in fulfilling the divine intent in the world. Each leads towards the unfolding of ever higher potencies.

Avatāra

Some of the well-known Avatāras of ancient India are Rāma, Krishṇa, Buddha Siddhārtha and Śankara, also called Śankarā-chārya.

Rāma, Krishṇa, Buddha Siddhārtha, Śankarā-chārya

(Rāma comes from verb-root *ram* — to delight in. Krishṇa means 'black' or the 'dark-blue' of the infinite spaces. Buddha means 'the enlightened' from verb-root *budh* — to enlighten, know. Śankara comes from verb-root *kri* — to make, and *śam* — auspicious. Siddhārtha means 'attained purpose' from the verb-root *sidh* — to attain and *artha* — purpose.)

Ātman or Ātmā

The Divine Self in man, the God within one with the Brahman or God, the Infinite Divine. (From verb-root *at* — to breathe.)

Īśvara

The Divine as Lord and Ruler of the Universe; the so-called Personal God of the Yoga systems of India. (From the verb-root *īś* — to rule.)

Brahman or Brahma — The Divine, God, the Absolute, the Infinite Spirit which pervades All. (From verb-root *bṛih* — to expand.)

Brahman — Infinite Divine, Iśvara — Universal Divine, and Ātman — the Divine Self in man. All three are ONE.

Trimūrti
Brahmā
Vishṇu
Śiva
Rudra

The Hindu Trinity of Brahmā, Vishṇu and Śiva. (From *tri* three, and *mūrti* — form or aspect, from verb-root *mur* or *murch* — to form.) Iśvara or the Universal Lord is known through his three aspects of power: as Brahmā, the Evolver, creator or Emanator (from *bṛih* — to expand); as Vishṇu, the Preserver and Sustainer (from *viś* — to enter, pervade); and as Śiva, the Destroyer and Regenerator. Śiva means 'kindly, auspicious'; thus Śiva is often called 'the Propitious One', because he destroys the old and worn out and degenerate and awakens something higher and more spiritual. In his destructive aspect he is often called Rudra (from verb-root *rud* — to cry, howl).

"The Infinite creates and is Brahman [Brahmā]; it preserves and is Vishṇu; it destroys or takes to itself and is Rudra or Śiva." Sri Aurobindo in 'Defence of Indian Culture'.

Brāhmanism
Yajña
Vedānta

Brāhmanism is a religious system based on the Veda or ancient wisdom writings. It consists of sacrificial ceremonies known as *Yajña* (from verb-root *yaj* — to sacrifice), worship of God as Iśvara, and the wisdom which is known as Vedānta (from *veda* — wisdom, and *anta* — end or essence).

Veda
Brāhmaṇa
Upanishad

The Vedas, Brāhmaṇas and Upanishads are the principle scriptures of Brāhmanism. The Vedas (from verb-root *vid* — to know) are collections of illuminating hymns to gods and the goddesses of inner and outer Nature. the Brāhmaṇas contain the Vedic ritual along with myths and traditional matter. The Upanishads are treatises in poetry and prose on spiritual and philosophical subjects. (From verb-root *sad* — to sit, plus the prepositional prefixes *upa* — near, and *ni* — down; hence implying 'to sit down near' the spiritual teacher). (See Literature, Chapter VI.)

Vaishnavism is the religious worship that regards Vishnu as the Supreme Being. He presides over All. Followers of
Vaishna- Vaishnavism worship the Avatāras or divine
vism manifestations of Vishnu, such as Rāma and Krishna.

Śaivism is the religion wherein Lord Śiva is worshipped as the Supreme Being. As Lord of reproduction and regeneration,
Śiva is worshipped in the symbol of the Linga or
Śaivism 'Phallus' in temples and homes all over India. As
Linga Om is the Word of God, Linga is symbol of the
Kāla Form of God. In his destructive aspect Śiva is
Kālī called Kāla or 'the Black One' or 'Lord of Death or Time' (from *kal* — to count, to impel). However, the active destroying function of Śiva is usually assigned to his wife — Kālī, also 'the Black One', or 'the Mother of Time and Death'. Hence images of this formidable destructive character are worshipped all over India to this day.

The Principal scriptures of Vaishnavism and Śaivism are the Purāṇas, the legendary histories of ancient India. (From the
verb-root *pur* — to go before, precede.) The Āga-
Purāṇa
Āgama mas are their ritual scriptures. (From verb-root
gam — to go and the preposition *ā* — towards.)

In Tantra or Śaktism the power of God is called Śakti or the Divine Mother (from verb-root *sak* — to be able). This Mother-
Tantra or Power is worshipped as the Universal Energy made
Śaktism individual as a Goddess of many names and aspects.
Śakti The Tantras are the sacred writings of Śaktism.

A seeing, perceiving, a vision of a holy or great being or of God or the Divine Mother. (From verb-root *dṛiś* — to see.) In
Indian religion Darśan usually applies to the behold-
Darśana
(Darśan) ing or inner communion of the spiritually great,
either human or God by the outer vision of the disciple or by the developing inner perception.

**Namas
Namaskāra
(Namaskār)
Namaste**

Internal and external obeisance and reverence. (From verb-root *nam* — to honor.) The making of obeisance or Namaskāra was a symbol of submission to the Divine. (From *nam* and *kṛi*, verb-roots meaning together 'to do reverence, make obeisance.) It further represents the self-surrender of all the faculties, lower and higher to the Divine Will-Force, so that, free from internal opposition, the soul may be let through truth towards a joy and peace and light in a divine life on earth. Namaskār, as well as Namaste or 'Honor unto thee!' are still greeting phrases in India.

Mandira

A temple, an abiding place. (From verb-root *mand* — to abide.)

**Karman or
Karma**

Action; also the law of action and reaction, cause and effect. (From verb-root *kṛi* — to act, do, make.) In Indian religions and philosophy Karma is the law of conservation of moral values, of merits and demerits of action. A man at any time is the sum-total of the results of his previous thoughts and acts, and at every moment is the builder of his future.

Akarma

Inaction. (*a* — not.)

**Prasāda
(Prasād)**

Grace, Divine blessings in any form. (From verb-root *sad* — plus prefix *pra* meaning 'to settle down, grace, favor'.)

**Punar-
janman**

Rebirth. (From *punar* — again, *janman* — birth, from verb-root *jan* — to be born.) Indian religion and philosophy teach that the perfection of man is not attained in one life, but is the crown of a long series of experiences in many lives. This belief in a gradual spiritual evolution is the basis of the almost universal Indian acceptance of the belief in reincarnation and Karma.

Every life is a step forward or backward, determined by Karma, that is, by one's thoughts, words, and actions. The Law of Karma holds as long as one directs his own life by desire, ego and mind; but when one surrenders all to the Divine guidance then God's Grace and Power take over.

Fire. In the Vedas Agni as 'God of Fire' is symbolic of the Divine Fire or Spark within, the Will of the Soul 'Psyche'.

Agni   It is the Flame of Divine Force and illumined Will destined to manifest all the divine possibilities latent within man.

Divine Union (from verb-root *yuj* — to unite). Yoga is some form of God-realizaton. Yoga is also a term used for the pro-

Yoga   cess or the discipline undergone by the aspirant seeking Oneness with God. There are many systems of Yoga.

Yogin or Yogī   One who practises or attains Yoga or 'Divine
Yoginī   Union' is called a Yogin or Yoginī. Yoginī is the feminine form of the word.

The Three-fold Path of Yoga; the three Yoga-paths known as Karma-Yoga, Bhakti-Yoga and Jñāna-Yoga. (From *tri* —

Trimārga   three, and *mārga* — path, from the verb-root *mārg* — to seek, to strive.)

Karma-Yoga   Karma-Yoga is union with God through dedicated action. (From the verb-root *kri* — to act.)

Bhakti-Yoga   Bhakti-Yoga is union with God through love and devotion and reverence. (From verb-root *bhaj* — to love.)

Jñāna-Yoga   Jñāna-Yoga is union with God through wisdom. (From verb-root *jñā* — to know.)

The Trimārga or Three-fold Yoga of Wisdom, Love and Dedicated Action is taught of in the scripture which has become so sacred all over India as well as in the West: the Bhagavad-Gītā.

Bhagavad-Gītā   'The Holy Song' wherein Krishna reveals to
Arjuna   Arjuna, his disciple, the Divine Wisdom of the Ages. (*Arjuna* means 'white'.) (*Bhagavad* comes from verb-

root *bhaj* — to revere, love; and *gītā* comes from verb-root *gā* — to sing.)

Śrī Rāmakṛishṇa Swāmī Vivekānanda
The great modern Vedānta Sages: Śrī Rāmakṛishṇa and his disciple Swāmī Vivekānanda also tread the Three-fold Path of Yoga. Rāmakṛishṇa experienced God through all religions and Yogas.

Hatha-Yoga is the system of severe discipline which trains the lower vital and physical nature of man to become a perfect instrument for sustaining Divine power and for conquering physical death. (From verb-root *hath* — to oppress.)

Haṭha-Yoga

Rāja-Yoga is a system of discipline for stilling the workings of the mind in order to unite with and know that which is beyond mind. It is considered as 'Kingly Union' with God because of the power and wisdom attained. (*Rāja* means 'king' coming from verb-root *rāj* — to reign, to illuminate.)

Rāja-Yoga

Patañjali's great scripture, the Yoga-Sūtras or 'Yoga Aphorisms' gives a full description of this method of stilling the mind for the attaining of the resplendent rule of the Divine. Sūtras are terse, aphoristic rules. (From verb-root *siv* — to sew. Sūtras are like pearls of thoughts sewn together on one string.)

Patañjali Yoga-Sūtras Sūtra

Kuṇḍalinī-Yoga is the discipline which awakens the sleeping divine power at the base of the spine, known as the Kuṇḍalinī (from verb-root *kuṇḍ* — to burn). This power or Divine Cosmic Energy must be raised through the six spiritual centers of the body to unite with the Divine or Lord Śiva at the crown of the head. This Yoga brings into activity all the Divine Powers latent in man. The union brings wisdom, power and joy.

Kuṇḍalinī or Tantra-Yoga

Pūrṇa-Yoga is Integral or Total Union with the Divine. It is a system of discipline forged by Śrī Aurobindo, the great poet, sage and Yogin of modern India. It brings about not

Pūrṇa-Yoga   only the Divine Union of all parts of man's
Śrī Aurobindo nature but also a Divine Transformation of his
whole being for a Divine Life on earth. (From *pūrṇa* — full.)
Śrī Aurobindo's teachings support the true and inner meaning
of the Veda which reveals a path to Divine Creation and Divine
Work in the world. His great scriptures are "The Life Divine",
"The Synthesis of Yoga", "Essays on the Gita" and his spiritual
Epic of "Savitri". These books are all in English.

Sādhanā is the act of mastering the Yoga. It is one's worship
or method of spiritual fulfilment, spiritual self-training and
Sādhana   exercise. (From verb-root *sādh* — to go straight to
Sādhaka   the goal.) A Sādhaka is one who undergoes the
Sādhikā   discipline and practise leading to some form of
Divine Union or Yoga. Sādhikā is the feminine form.

Śāstra   Scripture; a religious, scientific or philosophical
            writing. (From *śās* — to rule.)

A Mantra is a word or phrase of power; an instrument of
thought. (From verb-root *man* — to think.) A Mantra may be a
            sacred text or speech, a prayer or a song of praise
Mantra   to the Gods or God. All the Vedic hymns are
considered as Mantras, as vehicles of spiritual realization for
others and as words of power for attaining one's desires. Any
word or phrase that carries the Word, that is, Spiritual Truth,
has the creative power and the force to light the spiritual fire
within.

SANSKRIT READING LESSON

The Vedic Āryas of ancient Āryāvarta reverenced Agni as the
Gurudeva within. Their inspired Mantras to the Devas within
and without became the channels for the inner and outer Yajña
of Brāhmanism. Later the Bhāratas of Bhāratavarsha were
blessed with great Avatāras like Rāma, Kṛishṇa, Buddha and
Śankara who taught the Sanātana Dharma and Svadharma in
order to correct Anārya Akarma and Adharma. These Mahātmans were the inspirers of Vaishṇavism, Buddhism and Vedān-

ta. Gurus of all ages taught Yogins and Yoginīs the Sādhanās of various Yogas: Haṭha-Yoga, Kuṇḍalinī or Tantra-Yoga, the Rāja-Yoga of Patañjali's Yoga-Sūtras, the Jñāna-Yoga, Bhakti-Yoga and Karma-Yoga of the Bhagavad Gītā and the Upanishads.

Later Bhaktas of the Purāṇic Age did Namas to one of Īśvara's Trimūrti: Brahmā, Vishṇu and Śiva. Others, Sādhakas and Sādhikās of Śaktism or Tantra learned to raise the Kuṇḍalinī by worship of the Mahā-Śakti of Lord Śiva. Prevalent throughout India are the Mandiras of Lord Śiva where his Linga symbol is honored by all followers of Śaivism.

Today Bhaktas of Śrī Rāmakṛishṇa and Swāmi Vivekānanda follow the Trimārga and recognise all faiths as paths to Brahman. Bhaktas of Mahātmā Gandhi practise Satyāgraha and Ahiṁsā, and Bhaktas of Śrī Aurobindo tread the path of Pūrṇa-Yoga.

To have Darśana of any of these Mahātmans or Ṛishis is Prasāda.

Our Namaskāras to them all!

IMPORTANT WORDS AND PREFIXES

a	—	not (before consonants)
an	—	not (before vowels)
ā	—	to, unto, at
ava	—	down off
mahā	—	great
ni	—	down in, into
pra	—	before, away
punar	—	again
sam (san)	—	along, with, together, completely
sva	—	own
śam	—	blessing
te	—	thee, you
tri	—	three
upa	—	to, unto, near, towards

FROM THE UPANISHADS

Asato mā sad gamaya, From the Unreal lead me to the Real,
Tamaso mā jyotir gamaya, From Darkness lead me to Light,
Mrityor mā'mrtam. From Death to Immortality.
Om Śāntih, Śāntih, Śāntih, om.

— (III, 28, Brihad Āranyaka Upanishad.)

TRANSLATION OF SANSKRIT READING LESSON

The Ancient-Wise Holy Men of the ancient Land of the Holy
reverenced Divine Fire as the Divine Teacher within. Their
inspired Words of Power to the Gods within and without became the channels for the inner and outer Sacrifice of the religion of the Brāhmins. Later the Indians of the Land of Bharata
were blessed with great Divine Incarnations like Rāma, Krishna,
Buddha and Śankara who taught the Eternal Truth and the
Individual's Truth in order to correct the Unholy Inaction and
Unrighteousness. These Great Souls were inspirers of the Religion of Vishnu, the Religion of Buddha and the Religion of the
Essence of Veda or Wisdom. Spiritual Teachers of all ages
taught Seekers of Divine Union (masc. and fem.) the Spiritual
Disciplines of various Methods of Divine Union; Union
through Development of the Physical, Union through Awake-
ning the Divine Mother-Force, Union through Stilling of the
Mind of Patañjali's Yoga Aphorisms, the Union through Wisdom, Union through Love and Union through Action of the
Holy Song and the Spiritual Philosophical Treatises.

Later Devotees of the Age of Legendary Histories and Epics
did Honor to one of the Universal Lord's Three Forms: the
Evolver, the Preserver, and the Destroyer and Regenerator.
Others, Spiritual Disciples (masc. and fem.) of the Religion of
Mother-Power Worship learned to raise the Cosmic Force by
worship of the Great Power of the Blessed Lord. Prevalent
throughout India are the Temples of the Blessed Lord where his
Phallic Symbol is honored by all followers of the Religion of
Śiva.

Today Devotees of Śrī Rāmakṛishṇa and Swāmi Vivekānanda follow the Three-fold Path of Yoga and recognise all faiths as paths to the Divine. Devotees of the Great-Soul Gandhi practise Holding on to Truth and Non-Injury, and Devotees of Śrī Aurobindo tread the path of Integral Union with God.

To have Vision of any of these Great Souls or Seer-Sages is Grace. Our Reverent Greeting to them all!

THE AIM OF SRI AUROBINDO'S YOGA

"Perfection has to be worked out, has to be accomplished Imperfection, limitation, death, grief, ignorance, matter, are only the first terms of the formulary; they are the initial discords of the musician's tuning. Out of imperfection we have to construct perfection, out of limitation to discover infinity, out of death to find immortality, out of grief to recover divine bliss, out of ignorance to rescue divine self-knowledge, out of matter to reveal spirit. To work out this end for ourselves and for humanity is the object of our Yogic practice." — Śrī Aurobindo

SANSKRIT VOCABULARY

Āchārya	Bhakti-Yoga
Adharma	Bharata
Āgama	Bhārata
Agni	Bhāratavarsha
Ahiṁsā	Brahmā
Akarma	Brahman or Brahma
Anārya	Brāhmaṇa
Arjuna	Brāhmanism
Ārya	Buddhism
Āryāvarta	Darśana
Ātman or Ātmā	Deva
Avatāra	Devanāgarī
Bhagavad-Gītā	Dharma
Bhakta	Guru

Gurudeva
Haṭha-Yoga
Īśvara
Jñāna-Yoga
Karman or Karma
Karma-Yoga
Kāla
Kālī
Kuṇḍalinī
Linga
Mahā-Śakti
Mahātman
Mandira
Mantra
Namas
Namaskāra
Namaste
Prasāda
Punarjanman
Purāṇa
Pūrṇa-Yoga
Rāja-Yoga
Rishi
Rudra
Sādhaka
Sādhikā
Sādhanā
Sādhu
Śaivism

Śakti
Śaktism
Sanātana Dharma
Sannyāsin
Saṁskṛta
Śānti
Śāstra
Satya
Satyāgraha
Śiva
Śrī
Sūtra
Svadharma
Svāmin or Svāmī
Tantra
Tantra-Yoga
Trimārga
Trimūrti
Upanishad
Veda
Vedānta
Vishṇu
Vaishṇavism
Yajña
Yoga
Yogin or Yogī
Yoginī
Yoga-Sūtras

MAHĀTMANS

Śrī Aurobindo
Buddha Siddhārtha
Mahātmā Gandhi
Śrī Kṛishṇa
Patañjali

Śrī Rāma
Śrī Rāmakṛishṇa
Śrī Śankarāchārya
Swāmi Vivekānanda

VERB-ROOTS

as — to be

as — to throw

at — to breathe

bhaj — to love

bhṛi — to support

bṛih — to expand

budh — to know

char — to go

dhṛi — to establish, to hold

div — to shine

dṛiś — to see

gā — to sing

gam — to go

grah — to seize

gṛī — to invoke

haṭh — to oppress

hiṇs — to injure

īś — to rule

jan — to be borne

jñā — to know

kal — to count, impel

kṛi — to do, make, act

kuṇḍ — to burn

man — to think

mand — to abide

mārg — to seek, strive

mur or murch — to form

nam — to honour

pur — to precede

rāj — to rule

ram — to delight in

ṛi — to rise upward

rud — to cry, howl

sad — to sit

sādh — to go straight to goal

śam — to be peaceful

śak — to be able

śās — to teach

sidh — to attain

śiv — to bless

siv — to sew

śrī — to flame or diffuse light

tṛi — to cross

vid — to know

viś — to enter, or pervade

yaj — to sacrifice

yuj — to unite

CHAPTER II

THE MANTRIC POWER OF SANSKRIT

The Vedas are spoken of as the revealed scriptures, the foundation-truth of all later inspirations. The sacred character of the *Rig-Vedic* hymns (*riks*), their source of revelation, their power to illumine, the magic potency of their chanting or their mantric power are all traditional. This mantric power of the old Vedas is based on certain scientific, philosophical, and psychological truths concerning the power of words which was fully realized by the poetic seer-sages (*rishis*) of that ancient time.

The Sanskrit language is very potent in its linguistic expression because it is scientifically formed and co-ordinates with universal basic principles that build and unfold all manifesting things. Its very alphabet is a *mantra* (a sound or phrase of spiritual significance and power) revealing the song that was sounded in space when the world sprang into being. The Sanskrit language is constructed in harmonious relation with the very truths of existence, hence its power of illumination. The word *Saṁskṛta* means 'perfected', 'refined', 'polished'. Primitive language was born from imitating sounds of nature and from vocal expressions responding to physical and vital movements innate with their own essential sound-vibrations. This elemental language was developed and reformed in the light of intellectual and spiritual genius by the wise men of old and the result was the creation of the Sanskrit language.

In Sanskrit most words can be reduced to a verb-root (*dhātu*), a seed-sound which is unchangeable and reveals the origin of the word. This verb-root is expressive of action (*kriyā*) which is involved in all existences, for the teaching is that everything in its essence is Being or *sat* and in its expression is Becoming or *bhāva*. All things are in a state of flux. Even the word *jagat* (world) is from the perfect tense form of the verb-root *gam* meaning 'to go'. Every word has its radical and its conventional significance, hence we find one of the words for 'lotus' is *panka-ja*, 'born of mud', — its radical meaning may also conventionally signify a 'lotus'.

How did Sanskrit words first attain their root-meanings? Sanskrit grammarians hold that every word or sound (*śabda*) has a power (*śakti*). This intrinsic power always can convey the sense which is inseparably related to the sound. Even the urge to imitate sounds of nature in the early formation of words followed this natural law. Hence Sanskrit word-sounds have like any native language a natural power to convey the inner meaning. But in the sacred Sanskrit scriptures this power was not only intuitively expressed but consciously wielded. As the power was not only of the human mind but of the Spirit these Vedic chants can raise us to lofty heights of consciousness. As the world of objects is pervaded by the Divine Being, so are words; but only through a perfected object may the Divine fully manifest. These sacred hymns and mantras are such perfected word-forms, hence their power to evoke divine influences.

Every sound in Sanskrit is said to have two aspects, the more audible sound and the subtler essential sound-element behind, vibrant with the meaning natural to it. This vibrant sense-sound within is the real *śabda* or fundamental sound, also called *sphoṭa*. The outward audible sound, its instrument of expression is called *dhvani* or the external sound, a quality of *śabda*. The *Sphoṭa* arises in the indivisible, permanent Spirit, and is eternally luminous with power and when the *dhvani* or spoken word, its vehicle, is perfectly sounded within and without, it stimulates this inner vibrant activity with the result that the power within responds and illuminates. "Itself luminous like a lamp, it illuminates others", thus the great poet-grammarian Bhartṛihari describes *sphoṭa* in his treatise '*vākyapadīya*'.

What is the philosophical basis behind this concept? The world of sound is described in Sanskrit as the manifestation of *Brahman*, the Divine or Absolute Being. Actually the universe was sung into being according to the Veda: "*Vāgeva viśvā bhuvanāni jajñe*". "*Vāg* (*vāch*), the 'Logos' or the 'Divine Word', or the 'Divine Mother of Sound' became all the worlds. *Vāch* is the creative Word, the dynamic principle of Creation which manifests its *artha* or meaning. The word and its meaning are nothing without one another, just as Sun and sunlight, fire and heat have no absolutely separate existence.

This profound truth of existence — the inseparable duality of the static and dynamic aspects of all Nature — is transparent in this truth about the *Sphoṭa* concept. *Sphoṭa* has been described as the expressional aspect of the Soul, the Soul emergent with a purpose, a subtle voice which is the basis of all speech in mind-form, the inner indivisible permanent sound (*nitya-vāch*) of the *Ṛig-Veda*.* In the early Vedic language *Brahman* is the word for *mantra* or 'prayer of power'. In the later writings of the Upani-shads *Brahman* implies the 'Supreme Being' beyond which there is nothing, and *Śabda-Brahman* was used for the 'written Veda'. In the *Āgamas* or Tantric works inculcating the mystic worship of God and his Power (*Śiva-Śakti*) as well as in the *Purāṇas*, the 'legendary histories', we find *Parabrahman* des-cribed as the 'Supreme' and Śabda-Brahman as the Power in-herent in it.

The hymns of the *Ṛig-Veda* reveal worlds and souls in dyna-mic evolution or the Divine in His Cosmic Play. Thus the true Vedas are the eternal repository of the vibrating Intelligence at the Heart of all Being. The external Vedas may be used as one of the channels to contact this high source of truth for they are its outer harmonious expression, though of course in limited form. Thus *Sphoṭa* is *Vāch*, the subtle Voice of Power which is the basis of all speech, the dynamic or soul of sound. Thus Bhartṛihari further states that "*Sphoṭa*" is audible to the Yogin when he concentrates in the heart.

Hence the hymns of Veda are not only pastoral songs or in-vocations to nature-forces, but they are grand poetic mantras,

* See 'Sphota and the Spoken Word' by Kapali Sastri in Sri Aurobindo Mandir, August 15, 1945.

words of creative power, a means of spiritual progress for seekers of the Divine. The great Sanskrit Paṇḍit of South India, Kapali Sastri says:

"Religious scriptures teach us profound truths indeed ; they instruct us as to what is and what is not to our good; but they do it as the master commands his servant. Other subordinate texts and sacred legends of ancient times, instruct and advise; but they do it as friend advises friend. But Poetry brings about the same result in her peculiar way; she does not command like a master, as do the Scriptures; she does not advise like a friend, as do the *Puranas*; she accomplishes her object by an intimate appeal, as the beloved wins the heart of her lover, by her charm of address and resonant sense, by a pleasing tact of expression laden with suggestions, finding her way straight to the soul of her lover, for his acceptance and delectation. Such is the value and high purpose of Poetry according to Sanskrit rhetoricians."

The *Rishis* (seer-sages) of old understood this truth of Word-Power and resorted to it for finding the inspired speech to express their inner strivings, visions and realizations. Thus they sang their *mantras* carved by the heart (*hridā tashtān mantrān*). Hence the glory of the chants of the *Rig-Veda*. They are the truth-forms of the Eternal Word, of the Divine Mother of Wisdom. Thus the *Rig-Veda* I, 71, 2 translated by Sri Aurobindo reads: "Our fathers by their words, the Angiras seers, broke the strong and stubborn places; our fathers burst by their cry the rock of the mountain, made within us the path to the Great Heaven, discovered the Day and the sun-world and thought-vision and the herds of light." and from Verse I, 164, 39: "The hymns abide in the Immutable Supreme Ether where are seated all the Gods."

If the Vedic writings were destroyed their truths could be reproduced by *Rishis* from their Eternal sounding in the spiritual regions within the heart. Thus "*Rishiḥ sūktān paśyati*" or "The seer-sage sees the Vedic hymns." Each Veda has its own distinct power and light and may be discovered by the true service and offering within. As Sri Aurobindo so beautifully expresses it:

"The Divine Thinker becomes himself the sacred mantra; it is the Light of his being that expresses itself in the thought directed Godward and is effective in the revealing word of splendour that enshrines the thought's secret and in the rhythm that repeats for man the rhythms of the Eternal. The illumining Godhead is himself the Veda. He is both the knowledge and the object of the knowledge. The *Rik*, the *Yajur*, the *Sāma*, the word of illumination which lights up the mind with the rays of knowledge, the word of power for the right ordaining of action, the word of calm and harmonious attainment for the bringing of the divine desire of the spirit, are themselves the *Brahman*, the Godhead. The mantra of the divine Consciousness brings its light of revelation, the mantra of the divine Power its will of effectuation, the mantra of the divine *Ananda* its equal fulfilment of the spiritual delight of existence. All word and thought are an outflowering of the great OM, — OM, the Word, the Eternal. Manifest in the forms of sensible objects, manifest in that conscious play of creative self-conception of which forms and objects are the figures, manifest in the self-gathered superconscient power of the Infinite. Om is the sovereign source, seed, womb of thing and idea, form and name, — it is itself integrally, the supreme Intangible, the original Unity, the timeless Mystery self-existent above all manifestation in supernal being."*

All words are said to be varied forms of the One Sound — *OM*, the mystical syllable which is representative of the Divine and vibrant with God-Power. AUM portrays the threefold Divine, the outer, the inner and superconscient. *OM* is the sacred syllable chanted at the beginning of all sacrificial ceremony and mantra, thus reminding the aspirant to make the threefold offering to God. The *Bhagavad-Gītā*, that 'Holy Song' from the *Mahābhārata*, closes its chapters with the mantra '*OM TAT SAT*'. *OM* representing the Divine, *TAT* portray-

* See "Essays on the Gita" by Sri Aurobindo. (II, 291)

ing the inexpressible aspect of the Absolute ONE in the simple and yet profound word 'THAT', and *SAT* signifying 'Being', 'Reality'.

The sages of the Upanishads would ask of their disciples: "*Kas tvam asi?*" meaning "*Who art thou?*" and then instructed them: "*Tat tvam asi.*" meaning "That (the Infinite Indescribable Divine) thou art." They learned the deep mystery of Self (*Ātman*) as one with and identical with Divinity (Brahman) while chanting "*Aham Brahmāsmi.*" — "I am Brahman." God was revealed to them even as this manifested universe which in contradistinction to *Tat*, 'That Inexpressible Divine' was called *Idam*, 'This'. Thus they learned another of the great *Mahāvākyas* or 'Great Utterances' of the Vedas; "*Sarvam Idam Brahma.*" — "All this (the manifested universe) is the Divine." or "Brahmaivedam Sarvam." — "God is verily all 'This'." To reveal the truth of the Infinite Divine as the potential Seed-Self in man's being, which through evolutionary unfoldment may ever manifest more fully its glory, they also let the mantra "*Aham asmi Parabrahma.*" — "I am the Boundless Divine." ring in their hearts.

The aspiring human soul attuned to God is chanting these sacred formulas as a spontaneous vibration of his flowering spiritual nature. All sacred chants that have come down to us through the ages were originally the outpouring of divine experience, and hence may act as a light on our higher pathway.

OM TAT SAT

LESSONS IN SANSKRIT READING
AND TRANSLATION

OM

The Ṛishis of old, their Ātmans consciously one with Brahman, revealed the Sanātana Dharma in the Saṁskṛita Śāstras of the Vedas, Upanishads, Rāmāyaṇa, Mahābhārata and its Bhagavad-Gītā, the Purāṇas, Tāntrika Āgamas and Vedāntic

Sūtras. In Sachchidānanda these Mahātmans visioned in their Hridayas the Satya and poured it forth in Svara which unveiled the Śakti of Sphota and Dhvani. Thus the Nitya-Vāch inspired their Ṛiks, Sūktas, Gītās and Mantras.

We read in Devanāgarī the Ṛig-Veda, Yajur-Veda, Sāma-Veda and Atharva-Veda. With Swāmis, Sādhus, or Sannyāsins we study this Śabda-Brahman and learn the Arthas and Dhātus of all Śabdas. To the Āchāryas's Praśna: "Kas tvam asi?" we are taught the Prativachana: "Tat tvam asi." Then with Namas we chant other Mahāvākyas of Yogins: "Aham Brahmāsmi", "Sarvam idam Brahma" or "Brahmaivedam Sarvam", and "Aham asmi Parabrahma" or "Aham eva Parabrahma." From Avatāras on this Jagat we learn of Sat and Bhāva, of Karma and Punarjanman, and in our Kriyās follow the Dharma leading to Ātma-Vidyā.

OM TAT SAT

Translation of Above

The Seer-Sages of old, their Spirits consciously one with the Divine, revealed the Eternal Religion in the Sanskrit Scriptures of the Oldest Wisdom-Writings, the Mystical Philosophical Treatises, the Epic of Rāma, the Epic of the Great Bhāratas and its Holy Song, the Legendary Histories, the Ritual Scriptures of the Worshippers of the Mother-Power and Aphorisms of Vedic Wisdom. In a State of Pure Being, Consciousness-Power and Bliss these Great Souls visioned in their Hearts the Truth and poured it forth in Sound which unveiled the Power of the Imperceptive Eternal Sound and the External Sound. The Permanent Creative Sound inspired their Sacred Verses, Hymns of Praise, Songs and Chants.

We read in the Sanskrit Script the Wisdom-Scripture of illuminating Hymns, the Wisdom-Scripture of Sacrifice, the Wisdom-Scripture of Spiritual Song, and the Wisdom-Scripture of Magic Incantations. With Masters, Holy Men, or Ascetic Devotees we study the 'Divine's Revealed Word' and learn the

Meanings and the Roots of all Words. To the Spiritual Teacher's Question "Who art thou?" we are taught the Answer: "That (the Inexpressible One) thou art." Then with Reverence we chant other Great Utterances of 'Those One with God': "I am the Divine", "All This (the Manifested Universe) is God" or "God is verily all This" and "I am the Boundless Divine" or "I am verily the Infinite Divine". From Divine Incarnations on this Earth we learn of Being and Becoming, of the Law of Retributive Action and Rebirth, and in our Actions follow the Fundamental Law of our Being leading to Self-Knowledge.

OM THAT INEXPRESSIBLE ABSOLUTE REALITY

VEDIC QUOTATIONS

1. Vāgeva viśvā bhuvanāni jajñe.
2. Ṛishiḥ sūktan paśyati.
3. Hṛidā tashṭān mantrān (agāyan).

VERB-ROOTS

arth — to request the sense,
  point out
bhū — to become
chint — to set mind on
dhā — to create
dhvan — to sound
i (ay before vowels) — to go
mṛi — to die

nand — to rejoice
paś — to see
prach — to question
ṛich — to praise
śabd — to sound
sphuṭ — to expand, burst
svṛi — to sound
vāch — to speak

IMPORTANT WORDS AND PREFIXES

Words
eva — verily
kas, kaḥ — who
ko' or ka — who
nitya — daily, continuous

sama — equal, harmonious
tvam — thou
asmi — I am
asi — thou art
asti — he, she, or it is

Prefixes

para — beyond

prati — in reversed direction, back to

su (sv before vowels) — fine, well, good.

GĀYATRĪ

The Gāyatrī is a meter and verse of the *Rig-Veda* (III, 62,10) used as a sacred formula for initiation of the Sacred Thread.

> Om bhūr bhuvaḥ svaḥ!
> Tat savitur varenyam
> Bhargo devasya dhīmahi
> Dhiyo yo naḥ prachodayāt.

1	2	3		1	2	3
Om bhūr bhuvaḥ svaḥ!				Earth, Midworld, Heaven!		

4	5	6			9	4
Tat savitur varenyam					Let us meditate on that most	

7	8	9		6	7	8	5
Bhargo devasya dhīmahi				Excellent light of the divine Sun,			

11	10	12	13		10	13	12	11
Dhiyo yo naḥ prachodayāt.					That it may illumine our minds.			

VOCABULARY

Āgama	Dhātu
Aham	Dhvani
Amrita	Gītā
Ānanda	Hridaya or Hrid
Artha	Idam
Asat	Jagat
Atharva-Veda	Kapāli Śāstri
Ātma-vidyā	Kriyā
Aum	Mahābhārata
Bhartrihari	Mahāvākya
Bhāva	Mantra
Brahma	Mrityu
Chit	Nitya-Vāch

Om	Sarva
Paṇḍit	Sat
Paṅkaja	Sat-chit-ānanda
Parabrahman	(Sachchidānanda)
Praśna	Śiva-Śakti
Prativachana	Sphoṭa
Purāṇa	Sūkta
Rāmāyaṇa	Svara
Ṛig-Veda	Tantra
Rik or Rich or Ṛig	Tat
Śabda	Vāch or Vāk or Vāg
Śabda-Brahman	Vākyapadīya
Śakti	Yajus
Sāma	Yajur
Sāma-Veda	

MAHĀVĀKYAS of the UPANISHADS

1. Kas tvam asi
2. Tat tvam asi
3. Aham brahmāsmi
   (brahma-asmi)
4. Aham asmi Parabrahma

5. Aham eva Parabrahma
6. Sarvam idam brahma
7. Brahmaivedam sarvam
   (brahma-eva-idam)
8. Om tat sat

Chapter III

THE BHAGAVAD GITA—
PHILOSOPHICAL AND RELIGIOUS TERMS

Śrīmad Bhagavad Gītā — The Glorious Holy Song from the *Mahābhārata*.

Śrīmat — Glorious, excellent, venerated, splendid. (From verb-root *śrī* — to flame, diffuse light.)

Bhagavad-Gītā
Mahābhārata
Gita
Śri Krishṇa
Nara
Yuddha

The Holy or Celestial Song. A holy scripture which is an episode in the great Indian Epic, the Mahābhārata. (From *mahā* — great, and *bhārata* — descendant of Bharata.) The Gītā contains the spiritual instruction given by Śrī Krishṇa the Divine Manifestation and Gurudeva, to Arjuna, the *Nara* or Man on the battle-field before the *Yuddha* or war between the Kurus and Pāṇḍus or the Kauravas and Pāṇḍavas. Yuddha comes from the verb-root *yudh* — to fight.

Dharmakshetra — Field of Divine Law or Dharma.

Kurukshetra
Kuru
Kshetra
Kaurava

The battle-field on which the great war between the Kurus and Pāṇḍus takes place as related in the epic of the Mahābhārata. Kuru is the name of an ancient prince and ancestor of both the Pāṇḍus and Kurus; and *Kshetra* means 'field', from verb-root *kshi* — to abide, remain. Kaurava is the adjectival form of Kuru.

Pāṇḍu
Pāṇḍava
Yudhishṭhira,
Bhīma,
Arjuna,
Nakula and
Sahadeva

The father of the five Pāṇḍus or Pāṇḍavas. Pāṇḍava is the adjectival form of Pāṇḍu. The five Pāṇḍus are Yudhishṭhira (from *yudhi* — in battle and *sthira* — firm), Bhīma, the terribly strong (from verb-root *bhī* — to fear), Arjuna (meaning 'white'), and the twins, Nakula and Sahadeva (suggesting 'night' and 'day'). The Pāṇḍavas with Arjuna as the hero have the right on their side.

The blind brother of Pāṇḍu (from *dhrita* — firm, and *rāshṭra* —kingdom) and also the father of the Kauravas, the cousins

Dhṛitarāshṭra
Duryodhana
and the opposing forces of the Pāṇḍavas. The Kauravas are the evil usurpers. Although Kuru was ancestor of both Pāṇḍavas and Kauravas the patronym Kaurava (sons of Kuru) usually applies only to the sons of Dhṛitarāshṭra. Duryodhana (from *dur* — hard, and *yodhana* — fighting) was the eldest of the one hundred sons and one daughter of Dhṛitarāshṭra.

The wisdom or philosophical concepts given to Arjuna by Krishna as a basis for higher action. In the Gītā Sāṅkhya is

Sāṅkhya
equivalent to Jñāna-Yoga or Wisdom-Yoga and the term Yoga is equivalent to Karma-Yoga or the highest law of action leading to Divine Union. In later times Sāṅkhya became one of the six orthodox schools of philosopy teaching of the two eternal realities of Spirit and Substance. It was called Sāṅkhya (from verb-root *sam-khyā* — to enumerate) because it enumerated the ultimate objects of knowledge.

The characteristic nature; the spiritual principle of self-becoming (from *sva* — self and *bhāva* — becoming or 'state' from the verb-root *bhū* — to become). It is the

Svabhāva
essential law of one's nature; the pure quality of the spirit in its inherent power of conscious will and in its characteristic force of action; specific individuality; that seed of spirit which manifests itself as the essential quality in all becoming.

The four castes of Indian Society. These four classes of society were worked out in ancient India in order that the high laws and intentions of the Vedas could be made to

Chatur Varṇa
Brāhmaṇa
Kshatriya
Vaiśya
Śūdra
Purusha
Sūkta
Kshatra
fit into the natural life of man. The idea of a spiritualized typal society arose from the supposition that each man has his own essential nature or Svabhāva which reflects some element of the divine nature. Hence they divided man in society into the fourfold order of (1) Brāhmaṇa — the spiritual and

intellectual man; (2) Kshatriya — the dynamic man of will and rule and power; (3) Vaiśya — the vital pleasure-loving and economical or business man; and (4) Śūdra — the material man. Thus these four classes were supposed to represent the complete image of the creative and active cosmic Being and his powers as set forth in the *Purusha-Sūkta* of the *Ṛig-Veda*, the 'Hymn to the Spirit'. The Brāhmaṇas, symbols of men of knowledge, are said therein to spring from the head of the Universal God; the Kshatriyas, sometimes called Kshatras, men of power, from His arms; the Vaiśyas, producers and supporters of society, from His thighs; and the Śūdras, servants, from His feet. So the four orders of mankind were understood as: the Divine as knowledge in man, the Divine as power, the Divine as production, and the Divine as service and obedience.

Gradually as the spiritual ideals receded, ethical ideals developed and the honor of the Brāhmaṇa resided in purity, piety and in a high reverence for things of the mind and spirit along with a disinterested possession and pursuit of learning; that of a Kshatriya lay in courage, chivalry, strength, self-restraint, self-mastery and nobility of character as well as its obligations; that of a Vaiśya was maintained by rectitude in all his dealings; that of a Śūdra consisted in giving himself in service with disinterested devotion. But even these ideals gradually became noble conventions, mere traditions, and the outward signs of body and clothes became more important than the character and inner value and motive and finally the four orders became merely hereditary castes exaggerating outer differences out of all proportion. A Brāhmaṇa became a priest or pandit, good or bad; a Kshatriya became a king, an aristocrat or a feudal baron or warrior; a Vaiśya became the merchant, trader or money-getter; and the Śūdra became the laborer and servant. The system became degraded so much so that great leaders like Gandhi worked powerfully to entirely remove the system. Now it is a law in India that no discrimination based on caste can be made in social and civil life.

The four castes also had originally a relation to the spiritual paths of Yoga or God-Union: the Brāhmaṇas were followers of Jñāna-Yoga or the God-Path of Wisdom, the Kshatriyas of Rāja-Yoga or the God-Path of stilling the mind, the Vaiśyas of Karma-Yoga or the God-Path of dedicated action, and the Śūdras of Bhakti-Yoga or the God-Path of love and devotion.

Vishāda	Despondency (from *vi* — apart; and the verb-root *sad* — to sit).
Akarma	Inaction (from *a* — not; *karma* — action).
Śraddhā	Faith; zealous devotion to truth. (From verb-root *dhā* — to place; and *śrad* — faith.)
Niyata-Karma	Controlled action. (From *ni* — down; and verb-root *yam* — to restrain.)
Nishkāma-Karma	Desireless action; action dedicated to the Divine without any personal desire. (From *nish* — without; *kāma* — desire; and *karma* — action.)

Loka-saṁgraha — The maintenance or the holding together of the world. Krishṇa tells Arjuna that He himself acts impersonally for the keeping and leading of all beings on the path to the divine goal, and recommends that Arjuna likewise continue his activities but selflessly and in harmony with the Divine Will — thus ever helping to carry out the purpose of creation: the progressive welfare and spiritual unfoldment of all existences. (From *loka* — world, people; and the verb-root *sam-grah* — to hold together.)

Devadeva	God of gods — a title of Krishṇa.
Chelā	A disciple or spiritual servant. Originally *Cheṭa* — a servant.

Yajña — Sacrifice (from the verb-root *yaj* — to sacrifice). In early Vedic literature Yajña was an act of worship, devotion, prayer and inner surrender offered to the Gods for obtaining the fulfilment of a desire here or in the hereafter. The Bhagavad-Gītā which recommends renunciation of desire speaks of Yajña as a common divine action between gods

and men, between spirit and matter, God and nature, an offering
and an attraction from the lower to the Divine, and a descent of
the higher to help, called Divine Grace. So Yajña in the
Bhagavad-Gītā and in religious experience implies dedicated
service and unreserved self-giving to the Eternal or Brahman.

Buddhi
Higher reason, intelligence, illumined mind.
(From verb-root *budh* — to know.) In the Gītā is
'judgement and perceptive choice'.

In the metaphysical philosophy of Sānkhya the separation of
the Spirit and Nature-side of man's being must be effected by

Buddhi-Yoga
self-knowledge attained through Buddhi or the
discriminating principle. In the Gītā this uniting
with the Buddhi or higher discerning mind is called Buddhi-
Yoga and is considered one of the necessary preliminary steps in
Yoga discipline. It requires an awareness of the One-Self in all
and an action rising out of its equal serenity.

Manas
The mind, the thinking principle in general. (From the
verb-root *man* — to think.) The English word 'man' is directly
from this root. Man is fundamentally 'the thinker'
when compared to the animal.

Mānasa
Mānasa is the adjectival form of Manas. In Indian philosophy
Manas is usually the sense-mind, the sixth sense
as opposed to reason and discernment or Buddhi.

Indriya
A sense-faculty. (Said to be a power of the
Vedic God Indra.)

Prāṇa
Prāṇa (s)
The Life Breath; the life-force that works in our vital being
and nervous system. (From *pra* — forth, and the verb-root *an* —
to breathe.) The Prāṇa or breath is only one of
the five life-forces or Prāṇas spoken of in the
Upanishads. These work in various parts of the
body. Prāṇa is the chief, the dynamic energy in man, the cause
of all human life.

Prakāśa
The Light of mind. (From *pra* — forth and the
verb-root *kāś* — to shine.) Prakāśa is the light that

comes from knowledge and its assimilation.

Mṛityu	Death (from verb-root *mṛi* — to die).
Janman	Birth (from verb-root *jan* — to be born).
Śarīra	The transient form or physical body. (From verb-root *śrī* — to waste away.)
Deha	Body or (form. From verb-root *dih* — to mould, to shape.)

Man *par excellence* or 'the Thinker' as the representative man. The idea of Manu in legendary tradition is more as a symbol of
Manu   the mental demi-god than as an individual human being. (From verb-root *man* — to think.) According to *Veda* the Manus represent the first Divine law-givers who instituted sacrifices and religious ceremonies. The name Manu is especially applied to fourteen successive progenitors and sovereigns of the earth spoken of in the *Purāṇas* as reigning in the subtle worlds and guiding the conscious life of man.

A period or age of a Manu. (From *Manu* and *antara* — an interval.) A Manvantara according to the *Purāṇas* is equal to
Manvantara   12,000 years of the gods or 4,320,000 human years or 1/14 of the day of Brahmā; and each of these periods is presided over by its own special Manu. Manvantara is used generally to imply a period of manifested life.

Dissolution, death, or a period of repose or reabsorption, especially applied to the destruction of the world at the end of
Pralaya   the world-period or Manvantara. (From verb-root *lī* — to dissolve, and *pra* — away.) The verb-root reveals that dissolution means only that life leaves this plane for another plane or state, just as water dissolves into steam.

Evolution, or the unfolding or manifesting of what is within or latent. Impulsion, movement. (From *pra* — forth;
Pravṛitti   and verb-root *vṛit* — to turn; hence *pravṛit* — to flow.)

Inertia, inaction. (The prefix *a* making the word nega-

tive.) Involution, or an infolding or flowing back inwards of
what is without or already manifest. (From *ni* —
back.)

Apravṛitti
Nivṛitti

Transmigration; the passing through a succession of states;
the world of cyclic movement and change. Buddhists speak of
the wheel of Saṁsāra or the Wheel of Existence or
Rebirth. (From *sam* — together; and verb-root
sṛi — to flow; hence to flow together.)

Saṁsāra

The life-spark in all living things. In man Jīva
is the individual soul. (From the verb-root *jīv* —
to live.)

Jīva

Mukti and Moksha both mean 'Liberation', 'Spiritual Freedom', or release from the bonds of material existence. (From
verb-roots *much* and *moksh* — to liberate.) A man
who has brought his discerning and spiritual
faculties into active use, and hence has become
free from the bonds of illusion and desire can be
said to have attained Mukti or Moksha. Such an enlightened
human being who continues to live on earth freed or '*mukta*'
from ignorance and its accompanying restrictions is termed a
Jīvanmukta or 'freed while living' (from Jīvan — living).

Mukti
Moksha
Jīvanmukta

Spiritual extinction of the separate individual self. (From
nir — out; and the verb-root *vā* — to blow; hence 'blown out'.)
In Buddhism Nirvāṇa is self-extinction, a negative
Absolute. In the Gītā it is an ineffably positive
Absolute wherein the personal self is extinguished, a state of
individual at one-ness with Kṛishṇa, the Lord of all Being and
Becoming. Nirvāṇa here means extinction of all ego-limitations
but not of all possibility of manifestation, a state that can be experienced in the body.

Nirvāṇa

The 'Tree of Life' which is portrayed as rooted in God and its
branches and leaves on the earth. The tree is symbolic of cosmic
existence and is often called the 'World-Tree' or
Brahman, whose roots are above and branches
below in the world. Brahman, the Divine is a being single in

Aśvattha

essence but with two natures. The roots represent the unmanifested life in the Supreme and the trunk and branches manifested being. (From *aśva* — horse, a Vedic symbol of 'life-energy'; and the verb-root *sthā* — to stand, to exist.)

Sannyāsa   The renunciation of action based on desire. (From *sam* — complete; *ni* — down and *ās* — to throw, hence 'to throw down completely'.)

Tyāga   Abandonment (from verb-root *tyaj* — to aban-
Karmaphala-   don). The Gītā says that Tyāga is 'abandonment'
  tyāga   of all the fruits of action or *Karmaphala-tyāga*. One
Karmaphala-   who accomplishes this is called a *Karmaphalatyāgin   tyāgin*. (Phala means 'fruit'.)

Sannyāsa and Tyāga are both presented in the 18th Chapter of Gītā as a form of true inner renunciation while performing action, but Sannyāsa however, usually implies, even though wrongly, to an absolute renunciation of life and work in the world.

Achintya   Unthinkable (from *a* — not; and *chint* — to think). The Divine is described as Achintya because the mind cannot cognise It.

Anantya   Endless, infinite (from *a* — not; and *antya* — end).

Avyakta   Invisible (from *a* — not; *vi* — apart; and verb-root *añj* — to appear; hence 'not to appear apart', 'not to manifest').

The destructible (from the verb-root *kshi* — to destroy).
Kshara   Kshara is the name given to the Divine in Its ever changing and transient form as universe of matter.

Akshara   The Indestructible. The Divine in His transcendent immutable aspect is called Akshara.

Purusha   Spirit, the Witness-Soul or Conscious Spiritual Person.

Prakṛiti   'The original producer', Nature (from *pra* — forth; and verb-root *kṛi* — to make; hence to make forth, to produce).

The Supernal Spirit (*purusha* — spirit, person; *uttama* — highest). All self and nature, all being and becoming, all action Purushottama   and silence in this universe are the self-conception and self-energizing of Purushottama. He is greater than both the Immutable or Akshara and the Mutable or Kshara, and yet includes both these.

The Nature Beyond (from *para* — beyond; and *prakṛiti* — nature). Paraprakṛiti refers to the higher realms of Paraprakṛiti   Conscious Nature, the Divine Creatrix of the universe, the Mother of all things.

Aparaprakṛiti   Lower Nature; the perishable nature of manifested existence. (From *apara* — lower; and *prakṛiti* — nature.)

TRIGUṆA	Sattva	Adjectival	Sāttvika	Higher	Jyotis
	Rajas	Forms	Rājasa	Aspects	Tapas
	Tamas		Tāmasa		Śānti

The Tri-guṇas are the three modes or characteristic qualities of all Nature. (From *tri* — three; and *guṇa* — quality.) The three qualities of Prakṛiti or Nature are

Sattva — the force of equilibrium in Nature which translates itself in the qualities of good, purity, harmony, balance, happiness, sympathy, light, virtue and knowledge. Sattva implies substantial reality. (From *sat* — 'being', the present participle of *as* — to be.)

Rajas — the force of energy and motion in Nature which translates itself into the qualities of passion, action, struggle, effort and the thirst of desire. (From verb-root *raj* — to glow, to be excited.)

Tamas — the force of inertia and inconscience in Nature which translates itself also into the qualities of inaction, ignorance, incapacity, darkness, and obscurity. (From verb-root *tam* — to perish, grow sad.)

The Sāttvika-guṇa brings illumination of the mind or Prakāśa. It also leads to well-being, harmonious adaptation to life's
Sāttvika circumstances, right willing and feeling and impulse, love of beauty and right order, as well as a warmth of loving intimacy, a fineness, an enlightenment, and a poise of the whole being.

The Rājasa-guṇa encourages one in action to strive, to resist,
Rājasa and to attempt to dominate one's environment, to assert will, to fight, to create, to conquer and to aspire.

The Tāmasa-guṇa is the opposite of both the Sāttvika-guṇa and the Rājasa-guṇa. It is the opposite of Sattva whose essence is
Tāmasa enlightenment because it leads to darkness, obscure knowledge, confusion and delusion, unconsciousness, nescience and the soul's slumber. It is opposite of Rajas whose essence is movement, impulsion, energy, and creation, because it leads to sloth, torpor, life's sleep, mechanical routine, disintegration, death, and indifference to change and fresh experience.

All the guṇas, however, bind the soul, limit its full activities because they are ruled by desire and ego. *Tamas* binds a man through negligence, error and inaction, thus obscuring knowledge and encouraging the separative consciousness.

Rajas brings vanity and ambition, intense desire, and self-satisfied perversions; hence it binds the soul by its attraction of liking and longing, its desire of objects and its attachment to works, all of which are stumbling-blocks in the attainment of equilibrium.

Sattva binds also, though by a nobler desire and purer ego; it binds the man to virtue and knowledge for its own sake.

The Gītā recommends that one first strengthen the power of Sattva over Rajas and Tamas, for Sattva is the first preparatory discipline which leads to the spiritul life and is the mediator between the higher and the lower nature. It belongs, however, to the principle of mental nature whose very nature is to divide, analyse, separate, rather than unite. The infinite spiritual knowledge has its source beyond the limitations of sense and the reasoning mind. Hence the soul by its attachment to the enjoyment of the gunas and their results limits his consciousness to merely the lower and outward things of mind, life and body.

Beyond the Gunas

Krishna tells Arjuna that to be spiritually liberated and wise and perfect, one must seek beyond, behind the outer worlds, rise beyond the three gunas into a higher consciousness, free from desire and with egoistic consciousness eliminated, surrender the soul to Krishna, the Divine. This freedom from the power of the three gunas is called:

Nistraiguna or   Free from the three 'qualities of Nature'. (From
Nistraigunya   *nir* — without; *trai* — three; and *guna* — quality.)

The Gītā does not recommend a cessation of action. Krishna's injunction to Arjuna is to be a man of action but to surrender to Him the actions themselves and their fruits and to become a desireless and equal-minded instrument of His will. In this higher type of living at one with the Divine the three Gunas or qualities basic to nature or manifested life are found to take on a purer, more perfect aspect.

The Tamas quality of inaction of power and knowledge translates itself into Śānti or 'Peace' or the Spirit's eternal principle of

Śānti   calm and repose which holds all that is infinitely known and true in the Divine omnipotent Silence and yet acts and manifests in the universe at the same time. (From verb-root *śam* — to be at peace.)

The Rajas quality of ego-striving and passion translates itself into Tapas or the Self-conscious creative Will of the Divine.

Tapas   This spiritual force creates and builds the higher manifestation and its action in the aspirant is spiritual effort by means of a concentrated discipline and austerity, a burning, flaming devotion to the attaining of the spiritual goal. (From the verb-root *tap* — to burn.)

The Sattva quality of mental purity and light and balance translates itself into the expressions of God as the Fount of Harmony and Wisdom and Light or Jyotis. Jyotis is the luminous spiritual light of the Supermind or Truth-Consciousness which removes the gulf between knowledge and action and brings with it not only Sukha or mental happiness, but Ānanda or bliss and divine rapture. (Jyotis comes from the verb-root *jyut* — to be light.)

Jyotis
Sukha
Ānanda

Trigunātīta   'Gone beyond the three qualities of nature'.

Traigunātitya   'Having gone beyond the three qualities of nature'.

One expressing the three higher essential aspects of the Gunas of nature as explained above is called in the Gītā Trigunātīta of Traigunātītya. (From *tri* or *trai* — three; *guna* — quality; and *ati* — beyond; and *ita* or *itya* participle forms of verb-root *i* — to go.)

Saguna-   The Divine with qualities; hence the 'Manifested
Brahman   Divine or the Universe'. (From *sa* — with; and *guna* — quality.)

Nirguna-   The Divine without qualities; hence the Static
Brahman   Divine, the State of God's Non-Being, the Impersonal God. (From *nir* — without.)

This term is used in the Upanishads to describe the Divine as having two aspects, both 'with and without qualities'. It is a description of Purushottama or the Supreme Divine Being who is both Transcendent and Immanent and yet more. This is the Krishna of the Gītā also. (From *nir* — without; *guna* — quality; *gunī* — one possessing qualities; hence 'possessing qualities and also without qualities.)

Nirgunaguni

Māyā is of two kinds. The Māyā of Krishna is His power to

create things and give them form. (From verb-root *mā* — to
Māyā   measure, to limit, give form.) The lower Māyā
Māyāvī   is 'illusion' formed from ignorance, a limited view
                    of nature. Māyā is the inevitable result of mani-
festation because matter of any kind is a veil which hides reality.
The thicker the veil, the greater the Māyā. The closer we
unite ourselves with the Inner Essence or real Self the less
Māyāvī or less limited will be our vision of Truth which is with-
out limits, boundless.

Vibhāva   An aspect or condition, or state. (From verb-
                    root *bhū* — to become; and *vi* — apart; hence to
manifest.)

Sthiti   A state or condition. (From verb-root *sthā* —
                    to stand.)

Uttara   Higher (Uttara is the comparative form of *ut*
                    — up).

Uttama   Highest (Uttama is the superlative form of *ut*
                    — up).

Spiritual discipline, devout austerity; discipline directed by
Tapasya   the burning energy for divine attainment. (From
                    verb-root *tap* — to burn.)

Samatva   Equality, equanimity; uniform conduct towards
                    all circumstances. (From *sama* — equal, and *tva*
— a suffix meaning here 'ness'.)

Bandha   Bondage. (From verb-root *bandh* — to bind.)

The delusion of the pairs of opposites in nature, such as pain
                    and pleasure, light and darkness, etc. (From *dva*
Dvandvamoha   — pair; *moha* — delusion from verb-root *muh* —
                    to delude.)

Duḥkha   Pain, sorrow. (From *dur* — bad; and *kha* —
                    state).

Sukha   Happiness. (From *su* — good, fine; and *kha* —
                    state.)

Lābha	Gain. (From verb-root *labh* — to attain, get).
Alābha	Not-gain, loss (*a* — not).
Śubha	Good, auspicious. (From verb-root *śubh* — to shine, to be auspicious.)
Aśubha	Inauspicious.
Jaya	Victory (from verb-root *ji* — to conquer).
Ajaya	Not-victory, defeat.

Śruti
Smṛti

Inspired scripture; revealed Scripture; that which was heard directly. (From verb-root *śru* — to hear.) The Smṛitis are the remembered or traditional scriptures. (From verb-root *smṛi* — to remember.) The Śrutis are the Vedas as sacred eternal sounds heard by the Ṛishis or holy sages. They usually include the Vedic Mantras, Brāhmaṇas and Upanishads, and the Sūtras of the six great philosophical schools of India. The Smṛitis include the Vedāṅgas, the Śrauta and Gṛihya-Sūtras, the Law-books of Manu, etc., and Epics of Mahābhārata and Rāmāyaṇa, the Purāṇas, and Nitiśāstras. (See each of these in the Literature Section.)

Chitta-
vṛittinirodha

The checking of the turnings of the mind; absolute thought control. (From *chitta* — mind; *vṛitti* — turning, from verb-root *vṛit* — to turn; and *nirodha* — checking, from *ni* — down, and the verb-root *rudh* — to hold.)

Tattva-jñāna

The knowledge of the Principles of Things. *Tattva* is the 'Thatness' or essence of things. *Jñāna* is 'wisdom'. (From verb-root *jñā* — to know.)

Kshetra-jña

'Knower in the field (of nature)'; one who is spiritually conscious while in the field or realm of body-life-mind. (*Kshetra* — field.)

Dhīra	Steadfast. (From verb-root *dhṛi* — to hold.)

Spiritual self-consciousness, enlightened self-realization; the state of going entirely inside to the Spirit and often accompanied by a losing of the consciousness of the outside world —

sometimes leading to trance. In Gītā Samādhi is a calm desireless fixity of Buddhi in the Spirit, Self-poise and

Samādhi   Self-knowledge. (From verb-root with prepositional prefixes *sam-ā-dhā* — to hold together completely.)

Iśvara   Iśvara and Īś both mean 'Lord', the Personal
Īś   God, the Lord of the Universe. (From verb-root
īś — to rule.)

Maheśvara   Maheśvara is 'the Great Lord', a title given to
Krishna. (From *mahā* — great, and *īśvara* — lord.)

Parameśvara   'The Lord Transcendent' or the Highest Lord,
also a title of Krishna. (From *parama* — highest,
beyond; and *īśvara* — lord.)

Vibhūtis are manifestations of Divine might; God's power of
becoming; a great outpouring of Divine energy come down into

Vibhūti   the world. (From verb-root *vi-bhū* — to become
apart, manifest.) Vibhūtis aid the lesser transition-
al stages of evolution as the Avatāras or Divine Incarnations do
the greater stages. Vibhūtis are among those spiritual teachers,
brilliant intellectuals and scientists, artists and poets who make
a mark upon the world. Impersonally the Vibhūti is some manifestation of effective Divine power whether in Knowledge,
Love, Energy, or Strength, etc.; personally it is the animate
being in whom this power accomplishes something effective in
the world.

Yogeśvara   The Lord of Yoga or Divine Union, a title of
Krishna. (From *yoga* — union; and *Īśvara* —
lord.)

Yogaśakti   The power of Divine Union. (From *śakti* —
power, derived from the verb-root *śak* — to be
able.)

Vision of the Universal Form; the vision of Krishna's Being
given to Arjuna in the 11th chapter of the Gītā. (From *viśva*

Viśva-rūpa-   — all, universal; *rūpa* — form; and *darśana* —
darśana   vision; from verb-root *dṛiś* — to see.)

A hostile being of the mentalized-vital plane, a son of obscurity and division and a strong flowering of the Ego. An Asura is a
Asura titan in opposition to the power of Light, hence a demon or a giant of evil. The main characteristics of the Asura are the egoistic and ignorant strength and passionate struggle which refuse the higher law. (From *a* — not; and *sura* — god.)

Sura A god, a divinity. (From verb-root *sur* — to rule, possess supreme power, to shine.)

A perfected being, one who has attained the highest object of his spiritual goal, an inspired sage or holy saint here or beyond.
Siddha (From the verb-root *sidh* — to attain.) In Purāṇic literature a Siddha is a semi-divine being of great purity and power.

Undivine, titanic. All action that proceeds from violent or egoistic personal desire or from an arrogant will intent to impose
Asūrya or itself on the world or people for personal objects
Āsuric is asūrya or asuric in nature. A man who is Asūrya is a fount of evil, division and injury.

A giant of darkness, a violently egoistic human or astral being. Rākshasas may be forces represented by violent passions
Rākshasa and influences such as doubt, despair, ambition. (From verb-root *raksh* — to guard against; hence a Rākshasa is anything to be guarded against or warded off.)

Piśācha A being or demon of the lower physical-vital or astral plane. (From verb-root *piś* — to carve meat.) A name given to vampires.

Manushya A man, a human being. (From verb-root *man* — to think.)

A general name for a 'being', or 'one who has become'. (From the verb-root *bhū* — 'to become') Sometimes the word
Bhūta *bhūta* is used in reference to certain elemental forces or shades of the dead that abide in the
Bhūtāni inner planes just behind the human. Bhūtāni or

'beings' is the plural form of the word Bhūta.

Asura-Guṇas — The Undivine Qualities

Anārya Bhāva — Ignoble state, unaspiring mood, unholy condition of mind. (From *an* — not; *ārya* — holy, striving; and *bhāva* — state of becoming from verb-root *bhū* — to become).

Ahaṁkāra — Egotism, the separative ego sense. (From *aham* — I; and *kāra* — action.)

Nibandha — Bondage (from verb-root *ni-bandh* — to bind down).

Ajñāna
Avidyā — Nescience, ignorance of higher knowledge. (From *a* — not; and verb-root *jñā* — to know.) Avidyā also means Nescience. (From the verb-root *vid* — to know.)

Abhimāna — Conceit, haughtiness (from verb-root *abhi-man* — to think too much of).

Aśaucha — Impurity. (From *a* — not; and verb-root *śuch* — to be pure.)

Dvesha — Hate. (From verb-root *dvish* — to hate.)

Dambha — Deceit, hypocrisy. (From verb-root *dambh* — to deceive.)

Darpa — Pride, arrogance. (From verb-root *dṛip* — to be proud.)

Ichchhā — Desire. (From verb-root *ichchh* — to wish.)

Kāma — Desire. (From verb-root *kām* — to desire.)

Krodha — Anger. (From the verb-root *krudh* — to be angry.)

Mamatva — Possessiveness. (From *mama* — my.)

Manitva — Pride. (From *man*, the verb-root meaning to think.)

Moha   Delusion. (From verb-root *muh* — to delude.)

Daiva-Guṇas — The Godlike or Divine Qualities

Abhyāsa   Practise, repetition. (From verb-root *abhi-as* — to throw towards.)

Ārjava   Straightforwardness. (From verb-root *ṛiñj* — to make straight.)

Asakti   Unattachment. (From *a* — not; and verb-root *sañj* — to attach.)

Dāna   Charity. (From verb-root *dā* — to give.)

Dama   Control. (From verb-root *dam* — to control.)

Dayā   Compassion. (From verb-root *day* — to sympathize, to be compassionate.)

Dhṛiti   Steadfastness. (From verb-root *dhṛi* — to hold.)

Hrī   Modesty. (From verb-root *hrī* — to be modest, bashful.)

Kshamā   Patience, forgiveness. (From verb-root *ksham* — to be patient, to forgive.)

Mārdava   Gentleness, kindness. (From verb-root *mṛid* — to treat kindly, gently.)

Samachitta   Equalminded. (From *sama* — equal; and *chitta* — mind.)

Samachittatva   Equalmindedness.

Śuddhi   Purity. (From verb-root *śudh* — to purify.)

Svādhyāya   Self-study, repetition of Veda or holy scripture in low voice. (From *sva* — self; and verb-root *adhi-i* — to go over.)

Vidyā   Wisdom. (From verb-root *vid* — to know.)

Jñāna   Knowledge. (From verb-root *jñā* — to know.)

Spiritual perception; truth-consciousness; superminded activ-

Vijñāna	ity. (From verb-root *jñā* — to know; and *vi* — apart; hence to discern.)
Akāma	Desireless. (From *a* — not; and *kāma* — desire, from verb-root *kam* — to desire.)

God-surrendered Mind and Understanding. (From *arpita* — Arpitamano-surrendered from the causative form of verb-root buddhi *ŗi* — to rise upward; *manas* — mind; and *buddhi* — understanding.)

Maunin Muni	Silent (that is, like a *muni* — or a silent sage, or like one who is moved by an inward or inspired motive).
Bhaktimat	Full of devotion and loyalty. (From verb-root *bhaj* — to love.)
Sakaruṇā	Compassion. (From *sa* — with; and verb-root *kṛī* — to pour out.)
Santushṭa	Perfectly content. (From *sam* — completely; and verb-root *tush* — to be content.)

Sarva-karma-One who abandons all fruit of action. (*Sarva* — phala-tyāgin all; *karma* — action; *phala* — fruit; and *tyāgin* — one who abandons, from *tyaj* — to abandon.)

Sthiramati	Firm in intention. (From *sthira* — firm; and *mati* — intention.)
Saṭata-yukta	Always united in consciousness with Divine. (*Satata* — always; and verb-root *yuj* — to unite.)
Yaṭātman	Controlled Self. (From verb-root *yam* — to control; and *ātman* — self.)
Sarva- bhūtānām- maitra	Friend of all creatures. (*Sarva* — all; *bhūta* — being; and *maitra* — friend.)
Mārga	Path. (From verb-root *mṛij* — to pursue, search for.)
Dhyāna	Meditation. (From verb-root *dhyai* — to meditate.)

Karma-phala-   Abandonment of the fruits of action. (*Karma* —
  tyāga   action; *phala* — fruit; and *tyāga* — abandonment,
from verb-root *tyaj* — to abandon.)

Siddhi   Supernatural powers or attainments. (From
                verb-root *sidh* — to attain.)

Artha   Purpose, goal. (From verb-root *arth* — to re-
                quest.)

Absolute liberation that brings detachment from matter and
freedom from further transmigrations. (From *kevala* — alone;
Kaivalya-Mukti and the verb-root *much* — to free. This freedom
                from manifested life is the goal of Rāja-Yoga or
the Path of mental discipline.

Union with the Divine; absorption in the Divine; sustained
identity with the Divine. (From *sa* — with; and verb-root
                yuj— to unite. This is the goal of Jñāna-Yoga or
Sāyujya   the Path of Knowledge.

Resemblence to the Divine; similarity of action. (From *sa* —
with; and *driśya* — seeing.) Sādharmya is 'having like duties to
                the Divine; conscious cooperation with God in his
Sādriśya
Sādharmya   work. (From *sa* — with, like; and *dharmya* — per-
                taining to duty.) Sādṛiśya and Sādharmya are both
goals of Karma-Yoga or the Path of divine action.

Sālokya   Being on the same plane with the Divine. (From
Sāmīpya   *sa* — with; and *loka* — world.) Sāmīpya is 'nearness to'. The Sālokya and Sāmīpya are goals of Bhakti-Yoga
or the Path of Love.

Aiśvara-Yoga   The Lordly Yoga or that Divine Union spoken
                of in the Gītā by which the Divine is one with all
existences as Īśvara even though more than them. (Aiśvara is
the adjectival form of Īśvara.)

Brahma-Yoga   Union with the Infinite Divine, with the ALL
                both the unmanifest and the manifest. (From
brahma — the Infinite Divine.)

Niyata-yukta   Continuous or controlled unification with the Divine. (From *ni* — down; *yata* — controlled; and *yukta* — united.)

Ātmadāna   Giving of the self. (From *ātma* — self; and *dāna* — giving.)

Ātmasamarpaṇa   Absolute surrender of the self to the Divine. (From *ātma* — self; and *samarpaṇa*, the causative form of *sam-ṛi* — to surrender.)

Ātmaprasāda   Grace or serenity of the Divine Self. (From *ātma* — self; and the verb-root *pra-sad* — to become clear, tranquil, gracious, to favor.)

Prasāda   Prasāda is grace, favor or mediation of God; hence well-being.

Guhya — secret; Guhyatara — more secret; Guhyatama — most secret. (From verb-root *guh* — to hide.)

Rahasya — Secret. (From verb-root *rah* — to hide, to part.)

Para — beyond; Parama — supreme, highest.

Śrī — excellent, venerated, splendid; śreyas — better, more distinguished; and *śreshtha* — best, chief. (From the verb-root *śrī* — to flame, diffuse light.)

Suhṛid   Friend. (From *su* — good, kind, fine; and *hṛid* — heart.)

Maitra   Friend. (From verb-root *mith* — to unite.)

Śaraṇa   Protection, refuge. (From *śṛi* — to lean on, rest on, abide in.)

Hari   'Remover of Sin', a title of Kṛishṇa. (From verb-root *hṛi* — to take.)

OM HARI OM

LESSONS IN SANSKRIT READING AND TRANSLATION

THE SĀDHANĀ OF THE BHAGAVAD-GĪTĀ

OM TAT SAT

On the Kurukshetra where the Pāndavas and Kauravas are gathered together for Yuddha, Krishna as Gurudeva reveals to Arjuna as Nara regarding the ancient Sānkhya, Vedānta and Yoga. He explains the Svadharma and Svabhāva of the Chatur Varna: Brāhmana, Kshatriya, Vaiśya and Śūdra; and challenges Kaunteya to abandon his Anārya Bhāva of Vishāda and to arise as an Ārya. He instructs him not in Akarma but in Yajña and Śraddhā and in performing the Niyata Karma and Nishkāma-karma for Lokasamgraha. Then this Devadeva awakening his Chela's Mānasa Prakāśa teaches him of the Mrityu and Janman of all Śarīra or Deha, of Pralaya and Manvantara, of Pravritti and Nivritti, of Samsāra and Mukti, of the Aśvattha, of Sannyāsa and Tyāga, and assures the son of Kuntī that the Jīva is Achintya, Anantya, Avyakta, and Avyaya and Akshara.

With the aid of Buddhi-Yoga the son of Pāndu is taught to discern between Purusha and Prakriti, to become free from Ahankāra so that Īśvara may reign within, to rise above the Māyā of the Trigunas of Sattva, Rajas and Tamas. Then Nistraigunya. he is not bound by Aparāprakriti or Kshara and enters Akshara. This Karmayogin is further taught to ascend to Parāprakriti by transmuting the Tāmasa-guna to Śānti, the Rājasa-guna to Tapas, and the Sāttvika-guna to Jyotis. Thus Trigunātīta he is one with the Purushottama of whom Saguna Brahman and Nirguna Brahman are two inseparable Vibhāvas.

To help the Pārtha reach this Sthiti of the Uttama Brahman or Parabrahman, Bhagavan enlightens him in the Tapasya of surmounting the Dvandvamoha and attaining Samatva whether in Duhkha or Sukha, in Lābha or Alābha, in Jaya or Ajaya, and in all things Śubha or Aśubha, and in freeing himself from the

Bandha of Śrutis and Smritis and Dharmas, in conquering the Indriyas and Manas and Prāṇas and thus attaining Chittavritti-nirodha. Then as Kshetrajña the Īśa gives out the Tattvajñāna and elucidates Tad Brahman, thus aiding Bhārata to become Dhīra in Samādhi.

The Maheśvara enumerates his chief Vibhūtis and when Dhanañjaya beholds through the Yogaśakti of this Yogeśvara the Viśvarūpadarśana he sees all the various Bhūtas: Siddhas, Manus, Devas, Suras and Asuras, Manushyas, Rākshasas, and Piśāchas and knows that.

"Vāsudevah Sarvam"

Govinda describes to Pāṇḍava as Parantapa that the Daiva Guṇas: Abhyāsa, Abhaya, Ārjava, Ahimsā, Āsakti, Dāna, Dama, Dayā, Dhriti, Hrī, Kshamā, Mārdava, Satya, Samachittatva, Śuddhi, Svādhyāya, Tapas, Vidyā and Vijñāna lead to Moksha; whereas the Asura Guṇas: Ahankāra, Ajñāna or Avidyā, Abhimāna, Aśaucha, Dvesha, Dambha, Darpa, Ichchhā and Kāma, Krodha, Mamatva, Manitva and Moha lead to Nibandha. Hence one who is Akāma; Arpitamanobuddhi, Maunin, Bhaktimān, Sakaruṇā, Samachitta, Santushṭa, Sarva karmaphalatyāgin, Sthiramati, Sarvabhūtānāmmaitra, Satata Yukta and Yatātman enters Brahma-Nirvāṇa.

Parameśvara shows the son of Kuntī that the Mārgas to Mukti are many: good is Abhyāsa, better Jñāna, still better Dhyāna, but best of all Karmaphalatyāga. The Yoga of the Gītā recommends the blending of all the Siddhis and Artha of the various Yogas: the Kaivalya-mukti of Rāja-Yoga, the Sāyujya of Jñāna-Yoga, the Sālokya and Sāmīpya of Bhakti-Yoga, and the Sādriśya and Sādharmya of Karma-Yoga. This is verily the Aiśvara-Yoga or Brahma-Yoga.

The Uttara Rahasya, the Guhyādguhyatara declares that by Ātma-Dāna and Ātmasamarpaṇa one becomes Niyatayukta and receives Ātma-Prasāda. To such a Brahmavid Krishna is "Suhridam Sarvabhūtānām". For Bhagavān uvācha:

"Machchittaḥ sarvadurgāni matprasādāttarishyasi."
— XVIII, 58. 1.

and

"Īśvaraḥ sarvabhūtānām hṛiddeśe'rjuna tishṭhati."
— XVIII, 61.

Finally the Yogeśvara utters the Sarvaguhyatama or the Uttama Rahasya to Bhārataśreshṭha:

Bhagavān uvācha: "Sriṇu me paramam vachaḥ." —

"Manmanā bhava madbhakto madyājī mām namaskuru,
— IX, 34.

Māmevaishyasi satyam te pratijāne priyo'si me."
— XVIII, 65.

and

"Māmekam śaraṇam vraja!" — XVIII, 66.

The Bhagavad-Gītā ends thus:

"Hariḥ OM TAT SAT — Iti Śrīmadbhagavadgītāsūpanishatsu brahmavidyāyām yogaśāstre śrīkṛishṇārjunasamvāde samnyāsayogo nāmāshṭā daśo'dhyāyah."

OM HARIH OM

TRANSLATION OF READING LESSON

THE SPIRITUAL DISCIPLINE LEADING TO DIVINE UNION IN THE 'LORD'S SONG'

On the Field of Human Action where the Sons of Pandu and the Sons of Kuru are gathered together for Battle, Krishna as Divine Teacher reveals to Arjuna the Man regarding the ancient Philosophical School of Enumeration of the Principles, the philosophical School which reveals the Essence of the Veda, and the Spiritual Discipline that leads to Union with the Divine. He explains the Law of One's Own Being and the Own Nature of the Four Castes: the Priest-philosophers, the Warriors and

Rulers, the Merchant and Business Man, and the Laborers or servants, and challenges the Son of Kunti to abandon his Unworthy State of Despondency and to arise as a Worthy Striver. He instructs him not in Inaction but in Sacrifice and Faith and in performing the Controlled Action and the Desireless Action for the Maintenance of the World's evolution. Then this God of Gods awakening his Disciple's Mental Light teaches him of the Death and Birth of all Vanishing Forms and Bodies, of World-Manifestation and World-Dissolution, of Evolution and Involution, of the Wheel of Birth and Death and of Liberation, of the Sacred Tree of Life, of Renunciation and Abandonment, and assures the son of Kunti that the Individual Self is Unthinkable, Eternal, Invisible, Imperishable and Indestructible.

With the aid of Union with the higher Understanding the son of Pandu is taught to discern between Spirit and Substance, to become free from Egotism so that the Lord may reign within, to rise above the Illusion of the Three Qualities of Poise and Knowledge, of Passion and Action, and Inertia and Ignorance. Then Free from the Three Qualities he is not bound by the Lower Substance or the Perishable Universe and enters the Imperishable. This Divine Actor is further taught to ascend to the Substance Beyond by transmuting the Quality of Ignorance and Inertia to Peace, the Quality of Passion and Action to Illumined Force of Action, and the Quality of Poise and Knowledge to Luminous Spiritual Knowledge. Thus having transcended the Three Qualities he is one with the Highest Spirit of whom the Divine-With-Qualities and the Divine-Without-Qualities are two inseparable Aspects.

To help the son of Prithi reach this State of the Highest or the Divine Beyond the Holy Lord enlightens him in the Concentration of Spiritual Will-Force towards surmounting the Illusion of the Pairs of Opposites and attaining Equalmindedness whether in Pain or Happiness, in Gain or Loss, in Victory or Defeat, and in all things Auspicious or Inauspicious, and in freeing himself from the Bondage of the Revealed Scriptures and the Remembered Traditions and the Laws of Human Right, in conquering the Senses and Mind and Breaths and thus attaining Cessation of the Modifications of the Mind. Then as the Knower in the Body the Lord gives out the knowledge of the Principles of Being and elucidates THAT DIVINE, and thus aiding the son of Bharata to become steadfast in Spiritual Consciousness.

The Great Lord enumerates his chief Sovereign Powers of Becoming and when Arjuna as Conqueror of Enemies beholds through the Power of Divine Union of this Lord of Divine Union the Vision of the Universal Form he sees all the various Beings : the Perfected Beings, the Spiritual Fathers of Human Mind and Body, the Gods, the Divine and Undivine Beings, Humans, Hostile Beings of the Vital World, Lower Beings of the Passion plane and knows that The God of Divine Riches is ALL.

Krishna as Lord of the Cowherdsmen described to the Son of Pandu as the Conqueror of Enemies that the Divine Qualities: Practise, Fearlessness, Straightforwardness, Non-Injury, Unattachment, Charity, Self-Control, Compassion, Steadfastness, Modesty, Forgiveness, Gentleness, Truth, Equalmindedness, Purity, Study of the Holy Scriptures, Illumined Energy, Wisdom and Spiritual Perception lead to Liberation; whereas the Undivine Qualities: Egotism, Ignorance or Nescience, Self-conceit, Impurity, Hate, Hypocracy, Arrogance, Desire and Lust, Anger, Possessiveness, Pride and Delusion lead to Bondage Below. Hence one who is Without Desire, whose Understanding and Mind are Surrendered, Silent, Devoted to God, Compassionate, Equalminded, Contented, who has Abandoned all Fruits of Action, Firm in Intention, Friendly to All Creatures, Always-United and Self-controlled enters the Liberated State of the Eternal.

The Lord-Beyond shows the son of Kunti that the Paths to Liberation are many : good is Practise and Effort, better is Wisdom, still better Meditation, but best of all is Abandonment of the Fruits of Works. The Divine-Union Teaching of the 'Lord's Song' recommends the blending of the Perfections and

Goals of the various Systems of Divine Union: the Freedom from the Dualities of Life of the Divine Kingly Union: the Absorption in the Divine of the Yoga of Wisdom, the Being on the Same Plane with the Divine and the Being Near the Divine of the Yoga of Love, and the Growing into the Image of God and the Conscious Cooperation with the Divine in Action of the Yoga of Action. This verily is the Lordly Yoga or Divine-Union.

But the Higher Secret, the More Secret than the Secret declares that by Giving of Self and Surrender of Self one becomes Constantly-United and receives Grace of the Divine Self. To such a Divine-Knower Krishṇa is the "Friend of all Beings". For the Holy One said: "With Mind on Me you will pass over all difficulties by My Grace", and "The Lord, O Arjuna dwells in the Heart of all Beings."

Finally the Lord of Divine Union utters the Most Secret of All or the Highest Secret to the Best of the Sons of Bharata: The Holy One said: "List to My Supreme Word":

"Set thy mind on Me, be My devotee, sacrifice to Me, do honor unto Me, and thou shalt come unto Me. I promise thee truly, for thou art dear to Me", and "Seek refuge in Me alone!".

The Lord's Song ends thus: "God, OM THAT BOUNDLESS REALITY. Thus in the Holy Song, in the Secret Teachings, in the Divine Wisdom, in the Scripture of Divine Union, in the Colloquy of Krishṇa and Arjuna, called the Yoga of Renunciation, the Eighteenth Chapter."

VOCABULARY NO. 2

Abhaya	Ahiṁsā
Abhimāna	Aiśvara-Yoga
Abhyāsa	Ajaya
Achintya	Ajñāna
Adhyāya	Akarma
Ahaṁkāra	Akshara

Alābha

Anantya

Anārya

Aparaprakṛiti

Ārjava

Arjuna

Ārya

Asakti

Aśaucha

Aśubha

Asura

Asūrya

Asuric

Aśvattha

Ātma-Dāna

Ātma-prasāda

Ātma-samarpaṇa

Avidyā

Avyaya

Avyakta

Bandha

Bhagavan

Bhakta

Bhakti-Yoga

Bhārata

Bhārata-śreshṭha

Bhāva

Brāhmaṇa

Brahmavid

Brahma-vidyā

Brahma-Yoga

Buddhi-Yoga

Bhūta

Chatur Varṇa

Chela

Chitta

Chittavṛittinirodha

Daiva

Dama

Dambha

Dāna

Darpa

Dayā

Deha

Deva

Devadeva

Dhanañjaya

Dharma(s)

Dharmakshetra

Dhīra

Dhṛiti

Dhyāna

Dhyāna-Yoga

Duḥkha

Durga

Dvandvamoha

Dvesha

Govinda

Guhyādguhyatara

Guṇa

Gurudeva

Hrī

Hriddeśa

Ichchhā

Indriyas

Īśa

Īśvara

Janman

Jaya

Jīva

Jīvanmukta

Jñāna

Jñāna-Yoga

Jyotis

Kaivalya-mukti	Nirvāṇa
Kāma	Nishkāmakarma
Karmaphalatyāga	Nistraiguṇya
Karma-Yoga	Nivṛitti
Karma-Yogin	Niyata-Karma
Kaunteya	Niyatayukta
Kaurava(s)	Pāṇḍava
Krishṇa	Pāṇḍu
Krodha	Parama
Kshamā	Parameśvara
Kshara	Parantapa
Kshatriya	Parāprakṛiti
Kshetrajña	Pārtha
Kuntī	Piśācha
Kurukshetra	Prakāśa
Lābha	Prakṛiti
Lokasaṁgraha	Pralaya
Maheśvara	Prāṇa(s)
Mamatva	Prasāda
Manas	Pratijñā
Mānasa	Priya
Manitva	Purusha
Manu(s)	Purushottama
Manushya	Purusha-Sūkta
Manvantara	Rahasya
Mārdava	Rāja-Yoga
Mārga	Rajas
Māyā	Rājasa-guṇa
Moha	Rākshasa
Moksha	Sādharmya
Mṛityu	Sādriśya
Mukti	Sādhanā
Nāma	Saguṇa Brahman
Namaskāra	Sakaruṇā
Nara	Sālokya
Nibandha	Samachitta
Nirguṇa Brahman	Samachittatva

Samādhi
Samatva
Sāmīpya
Sannyāsa
Sannyāsa-Yoga
Saṁsāra
Saṁvāda
Sānkhya
Śānti
Santushṭa
Śaraṇa
Śarīra
Sarva
Sarvabhūtānām-maitra
Sarvaguhyatama
Sarvakarmaphala-tyāgin
Satata-Yukta
Sattva
Sāttvika-guṇa
Sāyujya
Siddha
Siddhā
Smṛiti
Śraddhā
Śruti
Sthiramati
Sthiti
Śubha
Śuddhi
Śūdra
Suhṛid
Sukha

Sura
Svabhāva
Svadharma
Svadhyāya
Tamas
Tāmasa-guṇa
Tapas
Tapasya
Tattvajñāna
Triguṇa(s)
Triguṇātīta
Traiguṇātitya
Uttama
Uttara
Vaiśya
Vāsudeva
Vibhāva
Vibhūti
Vidyā
Vijñāna
Vishāda
Viśvarūpadarśana
Yājin
Yajña
Yatātman
Yoga
Yogaśakti
Yogeśvara
Yuddha
AUM   OM
TAT   SAT

VERB-ROOTS

an — to breathe

añj — to anoint, manifest

as — to throw

bandh — to bind

bhī — to fear

bhṛi — to maintain, support

budh — to know, enlighten

dā — to give

day — to sympathize

dam — to control

dambh, dabh — to deceive, destroy

dhā — to put or place

dhyai — to meditate

dih — to mould, shape

diś — to point out

dṛip — to be proud

dvish — to hate

guh — to hide

hṛi — to take away

īś — to rule

ish — to wish

ji — to conquer

Jīv — to live

jyut — to light

kam — to desire

kāś — to shine

khyā — to name

kṛī — to pour out, scatter

krudh — to be angry

ksham — to be patient, forgive

kshi — to decay and to move

labh — to obtain

li — to dissolve

mā — to measure

mith — to unite

mṛi — to die

mṛid — to treat kindly

mṛig — to hunt

much — to free

muh — to delude

phal — to bear fruit

prī — to delight, gladden

rah — to part, separate

raj — to be excited, glow

raksh — to protect

rij, riñj — to make straight, be sincere

rudh — to check, arrest

rūp — to form

śak — to be able

sañj — to attach

śās — to teach

smṛi — to remember

śradh — to be faithful

sthā — to stand, be

sṛi — to go, to flow

śṛī — to waste away

śri — to lean on, to serve

śrī — to flame

śru — to hear

śubh — to beautify

śuch — to be pure, glow

śudh — to purify

sur — to rule, shine

tam — to perish, be sad

tap — to be hot, practise austerity

tush — to rejoice, be glad

tyaj — to abandon

vā — to blow

vad — to speak

varṇ — to paint, depict

vṛit — to turn

yaj — to sacrifice

yam — to control and to give

yudh — to fight

PREFIXES

a — 'not' before a vowel

an — 'not' before consonants

abhi — toward, into

ati — beyond

adhi — above, besides, over

apara — below

dur, duḥ, dus,
  dush — bad, hard

nir, niḥ, nis,
  nish — without, out

pra — before

sva — self

sam — equal

su — good, well, auspicious

vi — apart

uttara — higher

uttama — highest

SUFFIXES

anta — end   antara — between   vid — knowing

TITLES OF THE CHAPTERS OF
THE BHAGAVAD GĪTĀ

1. Arjuna-Vishāda-Yoga — Union by means of the Despondency of Arjuna.

2. Sānkhya-Yoga — Union by means of the philosophy of the ancient Sage, Kapila.

3. Karma-Yoga — Union by means of Action.

4. Karmabrahmārpaṇa-Yoga — Union by means of Entrusting Action to Brahman, the Omnipresent Divine.

5. Sannyāsa-Yoga — Union by means of Renunciation.

6. Dhyāna-Yoga — Union by means of Meditation.

7. Vijñāna-Yoga — Union by means of Spiritual Discernment.

8. Akshara-Brahma-Yoga — Union of the Imperishable, Omnipresent Spirit.

9. Rājavidyā-Rājaguhya-Yoga — Union by means of Royal Wisdom and Royal Mystery.

10. Vibhūti-Yoga — Union by means of Divine glories.

11. Viśvarūpa-Darśana-Yoga — Union by means of the Vision of the Universal Form.

12. Bhakti-Yoga — Union by means of Devotion.

13. Kshetra-Kshetrajña-Vibhāga-Yoga — Union by means of Discrimination between the body and the Knower-in-the body.
14. Guṇatraya-Vibhāga-Yoga — Union by means of Discrimination between the Three Qualities of Nature.
15. Purushottama-Yoga — Union by means of the Supreme Spirit.
16. Daivāsura-Sampad-Vibhāga-Yoga — Union by means of Discrimination between Divine and Demoniacal Natures.
17. Śraddhātraya-Vibhāga-Yoga — Union by means of Discrimination as regards the Three kinds of Faith.
18. Moksha-Yoga — Union by means of Liberation.

NAMES AND TITLES GIVEN TO KṚISHṆA IN THE BHAGAVAD GĪTĀ

1. Achyuta — The Unchanging One; the Unfallen One.
2. Ādideva — The Primeval God.
3. Ādya — The Primeval, the First.
4. Anantarūpa — One having infinite forms.
5. Aprameya — The Immeasurable One.
6. Apratimaprabhāva — One of power incomparable.
7. Bhagavān — The Holy, Glorious, or Divine One.
8. Bhūtabhāvana — One causing the welfare of living beings.
9. Bhūteśa — Lord of beings.
10. Deva — God, the Divine One, the Shining One.
11. Devadeva — The God of Gods.
12. Devavara — The Best of Gods.
13. Deveśa — Lord of Gods.
14. Govinda — Knower of the earth, Knower of the senses, Protector or Procuror of cows.
15. Hari — Remover of sin.
16. Hrishīkeśa — Lord of the senses.
17. Īśa — Lord.
18. Janārdana — The Mover or Stirer of man; Giver of all that men ask.

19. Jagannivāsa — Abode of the World.
20. Jagat-pati — Lord of the World.
21. Kamalapatrāksha — One whose eyes are like the lotus-
    leaf.
22. Keśava — Having fine hair.
23. Keśinisūdana — The Slayer of the demon Keśin.
24. Krishṇa — The Black One; the Dark Mystery of Truth;
    the Pure One.
25. Mādhava — Descendant of Madhu.
26. Madhusūdana — Slayer of the demon Madhu.
27. Mahābāhu — The great-armed One.
28. Mahātman — The Great Self.
29. Mahāyogeśvara — The Lord of great Yoga or the Great
    Yoga-Lord.
30. Nidhāna — The Refuge.
31. Para — The Beyond.
32. Parameśvara — The Lord of the Beyond, the Supreme
    Lord.
33. Prabhu — The Lord.
34. Purāṇa — The Ancient One.
35. Purushottama — The Best of Men.
36. Sakhā — The Friend.
37. Sarva — The All.
38. Sahasrabāhu — The thousand-armed One.
39. Śrībhagavān — The Very Holy One; the Honourable
    Lord.
40. Vāsudeva — The God of Wealth.
41. Vishṇu — The Pervading One.
42. Viśvarūpa — The Universal Form.
43. Viśveśvara — The Lord of All.
44. Vārshṇeya — Descendant of Vrishṇi.
45. Viśvamūrti — The Universal Form.
46. Vattā — The Knower.
47. Yādava — Descendant of Yadu.
48. Yogeśvara — Lord of Yoga or Yogins.
49. Yogin — The One who has become united with the Divin-
    ity within.

NAMES AND TITLES GIVEN TO ARJUNA IN THE BHAGAVAD GĪTĀ

1. Arjuna — The Pure, the White.
2. Anagha — The Sinless One.
3. Bhārata — Son of Bharata (from root *bhṛi* — support).
4. Bhāratarshabha — Bull of the Bhāratas.
5. Bhārataśreshtha — Best of the Bhāratas.
6. Bhāratasattama — The most virtuous and true of the Bhāratas.
7. Dhanañjaya — Conqueror of riches, human and divine.
8. Dehabhṛitāṁvara — Best of the embodied.
9. Guḍākeśa — "Thick-haired" or Conqueror of sleep.
10. Kapidhvaja — Monkey-ensigned One, Buddhi-awakened one.
11. Kuruṇandana — Gladdener of the Kurus.
12. Kaunteya — Son of Kuntī.
13. Kurupravīra — Great Hero of the Kurus.
14. Kuruśreshtha — Best of the Kurus.
15. Mahābāhu — Great-armed one.
16. Pāṇḍava — Son of Pāṇḍu.
17. Parantapa — Destroyer of foes.
18. Pārtha — Son of *Prithā* or *Kuntī*.
19. Purushottama — Best of men.
20. Purushavyāghra — Tiger among men.
21. Savyasāchin — Drawing bow with left hand (hence ambidexterous).

In the *Mahābhārata* Arjuna says:

"They called me Dhanañjaya because I lived in the midst of wealth, having subjugated all the countries and having taken away their treasures. They called me Vijaya (Victory) because when I go out to battle with invincible kings I never return from the field without vanquishing them. I am called Śvetavāhana (White vehicle) because when battling with the foe white horses decked in golden armor are always yoked unto my car. They call me Phālguna because I was born on the breast of the Himavat on a day when the constellation Uttara Phālguna (the spring season) was resplendent like the sun. I am known as Bibhatsu (Detestable) among gods and men for my never having committed a detestable deed on the battle-field. And since both of my hands are capable of drawing the Gāndiva I am known as Savyasāchin among gods and men. They call me Arjuna because my complexion is very rare within the four boundaries of the earth and because also my acts are always stainless. I am known among human beings and celestials by the name of Jishnu (Triumphant), because I am unapproachable, incapable of being kept down, a tamer of adversaries and son of the slayer of Pāka. And Krishna, my tenth appellation, was given to me by my father, out of affection towards a black-skinned boy of great purity."

THE BHAGAVAD GĪTĀ — THE HOLY SONG

Mystical Interpretations of the Sanskrit Names Found in Chapter I. According to P. D. Goswami's Śrīmad Bhāgavad-Gītā of 1891 (Arranged and compiled by Judith Tyberg).

Each name is followed by a suggested esoteric meaning as well as the word's literal meaning in parentheses.

For further explanation of Sanskrit philosophical terms used as definitions of characters, study the exposition of these in other chapters of this book.

1. *Dhritarāshtra* — Father of matter side of nature, illusion, the physical body (the firm kingdom).

2. *Kurus* or *Kauravas* — The blind father of the material aspects of nature, the dark forces of the universe or the evil and undeveloped propensities expressed by the lower man.

3. *Sañjaya* — Reflection, turning within for guidance (the completely victorious).

4. *Pāndu* — Conscience, intuition of divinity (the pale, the pure).

5. *Pāṇḍus* or *Pāṇḍavas* — The father of the spiritual aspects of nature, the light side of the universe or the virtues expressed by the higher man.

6. *Kurukshetra* — The plane of human consciousness and mental activity (plain of Kuru, an ancient ancestor).

7. *Duryodhana* — Passion, lower desire. Eldest son of Dhritarāshtra (hard to fight).

8. *Droṇa* — (his preceptor) — Revolution through material spheres, experience, *Saṁsāra*, obstinacy (vessel).

9. *Drupada* — Keen penetration, concentration, pure love (swift-footed).

10. *Dhrishṭadyumna* — Drupada's clever son, Self-control, leader of the spiritual forces (intense light or splendor).

11. *Bhīma* — Dauntlessness, control of breath, that is, control of the forces of nature, endless strength (the formidable).

12. *Arjuna* — The purity of mind and heart, the aspiring human, renunciation, (the white).

13. *Yuyudhāna* — Kṛishṇa's charioteer — Truth, faith, sometimes called *Sātyaki* (wishing to fight).

14. *Virāṭa* — Equanimity (without attachment).

15. *Dhrishṭaketu* — Restraint, *Yama*, *Ahiṁsā*, first step in Yoga (intense flame).

16. *Chekitāna* — Higher intelligence, a Seer through *Māyā* (intensely shining).

17. *King of Kāśī* — Divine pleasure, enthusiasm, a sun-quality (the shining).

18. *Purujit* — Control of mind and senses, Pratyāhāra (many conquering).

19. *Kuntibhoja* — Peace and pleasure derived from the destruction of evil, *Āsana* (sin-destruction-enjoyment).

20. *Śaivya* — Blessedness, the enlightenment that brings liberation, *Niyama* (blessedness, from *śiv* — to bless).

21. *Yudhamānyu* — Dispassionateness, *Prāṇāyāma* (restraining passion).

22. *Uttamaujas* — Highest valor, *Vīrya* (highest strength).

23. *Saubhadrā* — One of Arjuna's wives, auspiciousness, happiness due to kindness (beautiful, fortunate).

24. *Abhimanyu* — Highmindedness, Dhyāna (above passion).

25. *Draupadī* — Wife of the five *Pāṇḍavas* and daughter of *Drupada*. Loyalty, the child of keen perception. Draupadi's five sons are the control of the five senses:
    Śrutasoma — renowned for spiritual knowledge.
    Śrutakīrti — renowned for glory.
    Śatānika — the hundred-formed one.
    Śrutasena — renowned army.
    Prativindhya — like the Vindhya mountains.

26. *Bhīshma* — Ātman considered separate from Brahma, Ahaṁkāra, individual consciousness, first cause of separateness (the terrible).

27. *Karṇa* — Selfishness, bigotry, evil desire which has become an opposition, hence a stimulus on the higher path, the Dweller on the Threshold (a helm).

28. *Kṛipa* — Kindliness and pity without discrimination, emotion (kindness).

29. *Aśvatthāman* — Worldliness, superficiality, love of transient things (that which does not stand or last till the morrow or dawn).

30. *Vikarṇa* — Heresy of hatred, repulsion, dislike (a strong helm).

31. *Somadatta* — Inconstancy (gift of the moon).

32. *Bhūriśravas* — Irreverence, lack of devotion (frequent motion). *To blow shells* is to display energy or activity.

33. *Krishna* — The Divinity in man, the Universal Self, the Christ or Buddha within every man (dark, blackness to our senses).

34. *Pañchajanya* —That power of Krishna which extends over the five races, the five elements, and the five senses.

35. *Devadatta* — Devotion, the power to abide in the divine (the gift of God).

36. *Paundra* — That courage and valor that shatters all opposition beneath its power (that which shatters).

37. *Yudhishthira* — Righteousness, *Dharma* (firm in battle).

38. *Kuntī* or *Prithā* — *Pāndu's* first wife, mother of three older *Pāndava* brothers, spiritual intellect which is sin-destroying (sin-killer).

39. *Mādrī* — *Pāndu's* second wife, mother of the *Pāndava* twins, the spiritual intellect which is compassionate (compassion).

40. *Ananta-vijaya* — That power that conquers eternally: spiritual qualities (endlessly conquering).

41. *Nakula* — One of the *Pāndava* twins, (the stillness of the mind, night). The inseparable twin of:

42. *Sahadeva:* — The other *Pāndava* twin: spiritual awareness, devotion (always shining, day).

43. *Sughosha* — The power of harmony (a pleasing sound).

44. *Manipushpaka* — The power of an Initiate in the Occult Mysteries (a jewelled serpent or wise man).

45. *Prince of Kāśī* — Spiritual splendor (light).

46. *Śikhandin* — Illumination, halo of spirituality (bearing a crest).

47. *Sātyaki* — Truth, Krishna's charioteer (truth).

48. *Hanumān* — Spiritual light, the *Buddhi* principle, the monkey ally of *Rāma* (big jaw, a monkey).

49. *Gāṇḍīva* — A bow or bridge direct from divinity, a present given to Arjuna from *Agni*, the Divine Fire.

(For Dhrishtadyumna, Virāta, Drupada, Krishna and previously mentioned names see above).

(*Varṇa saṅkara* means mixed caste.)

Harih-Om Tat Sat   *Vishṇu, That Boundless Truth*

Iti Śrīmadbhagavadgītāsūpanishatsu brahmavidyāyām yogaśāstre śrīkrishṇārjunasaṁvāde'rjunavishādayogo'nāma. — Prathamo'dhyāyaḥ.

Thus in the *Upanishads*, called the holy Bhagavad-Gītā, in the science of the Supreme Spirit, in the book of devotion, in the colloquy between the holy Krishna and Arjuna, stands the First Chapter, by name —

THE DESPONDENCY OF ARJUNA

A BRIEF EXPLANATION OF SOME OF THE PRINCIPLE CHARACTERS IN THE GENEALOGY OF THE PĀṆḌUS AND KURUS OF THE *MAHĀBHĀRATA*

1. *Śāntanu* — Divinity of the Universe, *Brahman* (abode of peace).

2. *Gaṅgā* — Māyā, illusion (swift-goer).

3. *Satyavatī* — Nature, the manifested universe (resembling truth).

4. *Parāśara* — The Light-Bringer, the Hindu Hermes (the crusher).

5. *Vyāsa* — The Passer on of Light, Intuition (the divine arranger).

   Krishṇa Dvaipāyana — The unseen light within (the dark boy born on an island).

6. *Chitrāṅgadā* — Matter (beautifully ornamental, of varied form).

7. *Vichitravīrya* — Life, vitality (powerful, manifold strength).

8. *Ambā* (*Ambikā, Ambālikā*) — Harvest, fruits of nature (a good woman, a mother).

9. *Gāndhārī* — Separateness (smell, lead).

10. *Śūra* — Divine Splendor (the warrior, the mighty).

11. *Sūrya* — The Sun-god, the Buddhi principle.

12. *Dharma* — God or principle of harmony, law, and right (divine law).

13. *Vāyu* — The god of the wind and air, Universal *Kāma*, vital (air).

14. *Indra* — God of the sky, Universal Mind or *Mahat* (the heavens).

15. *Nāsatya* — One of the *Aśvins*, the horsemen of the Sun. The bringer of night, involution of matter (disappearance).

16. *Dasra* — One of the two *Aśvins*, the bringer of day, evolution of spirit (the shining one).

CHAPTER IV

THE DIVINE AND HIS MANIFESTATIONS

Tat   A pronoun meaning 'that'. The Vedic Sages often used *Tat* as a noun to express the Unutterable Principle, the Inexpressible Mystery of the Infinite Divine or God. They would ask of their disciples: *"Kas tvam asi?"* — "Who art thou" and then instructed them in the essence of Vedānta Truth: *"Tat tvam asi"*. — *"That* thou art". Thus revealing to them their Oneness with the Divine and their infinite possibilities of spiritual unfoldment.

Idam   A pronoun meaning 'this'. The Vedic sages often used *Idam* as a noun to express the manifested Universe or the Revealed God in contradistinction to *Tat* or 'That' which implied the Inexpressible Underlying and Omnipresent Reality within and above all things.

Brahman
Brahma
Brahmavid   The Infinite Divine (*bṛih* — to expand); the Absolute; the One; God; the Divine Spirit which pervades all and is All. Brahma-knowing or 'God-knowing' which is goal of spiritual seekers (*vid* — to know).

Brahmavidyā   Wisdom of Brahma or 'Divine Wisdom'.

Brahmatej   'The fire of the Divine' or the burning glow of God.

Brahma-Yoga   Divine Union or Union with God (*yuj* — to unite).

Brahma-Loka   The Divine World (*lok* — to see).

Brāhmī-sthiti   Firm-standing in the Divine (*sthā* — to stand).

Śabda-Brahman   The Divine as the primal sound-energy (*śabd* — to sound). In the *Ṛig-Veda*, the oldest of Sanskrit writings, Brahman was the word for 'Divine Prayer'. In the Vedānta Śabda-Brahman is used for the 'Written Veda'.

In the Purāṇas Śabda-Brahman is the sound-power inherent in Parabrahman or the 'Supreme Spirit' or the Transcendent.

The Brahman Beyond (*para* — beyond). The Divine as Transcendent; the Supracosmic Divine who supports with his timeless and spaceless existence all this cosmic manifestation of his own being and nature in Space and Time.

Parabrahman

The Supernal Person (*purusha* — spirit, person; *uttama* — highest). All self and nature, all being and becoming, all action and silence in this universe are the self-conception and self-energising of Purushottama. He is greater than both the Immutable or *Akshara* and the Mutable or *Kshara*, and yet includes both these opposites.

Purushottama
or
Para Purusha

The Being which is beyond the Universal Person or Cosmic Person; the Transcendent, Infinite, who is at once the infinite and finite, the illimitable and self-limiting, the one and the many, and informs with His Being not only the Gods above, but all beings and things below, (*parāt* — than the Supreme *para* — beyond, higher; hence 'the Spirit that is beyond the Supreme'.

Parātpara
Purusha

The Most Excellent Lord (*parama* — highest; *Īśvara* — lord); the Divine as the Ineffable Lord of all existence who by his spiritual control of his own manifested Power in nature unrolls the cycles of the world and the natural evolution of creatures in those cycles. He is the origin, father and mother, and foundation and eternal abode of Self and cosmos and master of all existences.

Parameśvara

Paramānanda   The Most Ineffable Bliss: a description of the Divine as utmost felicity (*parama* — highest; *ānanda* — bliss).

The Divine Being of the Bhagavad Gītā who gives advice of a spiritual nature to Arjuna. Historically Kṛishṇa was an Avatāra of Vishṇu, or a manifestation of the All-Pervading God, and died 3102 B.C.

Kṛishṇa

Vasudeva or   'The Shining God' or 'The God of Wealth'; an
Vāsudeva   epithet given to Kṛishṇa or Vishṇu as 'the God of
All that is'.

'The Godhead in humanity', 'The Incarnate Divinity' (*nara* —
man; *ayana* — path or going, from *i* — to go). Nārāyaṇa always
implies the Divinity that becomes manifest in man.
Nārāyaṇa   Also an epithet of Vishṇu, who as the God in man,
lives constantly associated in a dual unity with *Nara*, the human
being. *Sādhus* or holy men in India address each other as
"Nārāyaṇa!". Their greeting is "*Namo Nārāyaṇāya*" — "Honor
to the God in man!"

The human-soul and the divine Soul in companionship and
communion. This figure of God as Nārāyaṇa symbolizes the
truth that reassures and brings God close, and
Nara-Nārāyaṇa   in a gracious mediating form which is living
and inspiring.

Chaitanya   The All-Conscious Being that is source and Lord
Purusha   of the Universe (*chaitanya* — consciousness; from
Chaitanya   *chit* — to think).

Virāṭ-Purusha   The Universal Spirit (*vi-rāj* — to rule everywhere).

The Divine Element in the becoming (*adhi* — above; *daivata*
— divine; from *div* — to shine); the Purusha or Soul in Nature,
Adhidaivata   the Subjective Being who observes and enjoys all
Adhidaiva   this mutable becoming. The divine powers of
mind, will and sense are all Its powers.

Trimūrti   The Hindu Trinity of Brahmā, Vishṇu and Śiva
(*tri* — three; *mūrti* — aspects or faces). The Īśvara
or Lord in three phases:

The Evolver, Creator or Emanator (from *bṛih* — to expand).
The Preserver and Sustainer (*viś* — to enter, pervade). The
Brahmā   Destroyer and Regenerator. *Śiva* means 'kindly',
Vishṇu   'auspicious'; thus Śiva is often called 'the Propi-
Śiva   tious One', because he destroys the old and worn

out and degenerate and lower, and awakens something higher and more spiritual.

This is Śiva's terrible aspect of destruction (*rud* — to weep). Śiva's beneficent aspect has been preserved more in the South

Rudra-Śiva   of India and his destructive or Rudra-aspect has been accentuated in the North.

Maheśvara   'The Great Lord', an epithet of Śiva (*mahā* — great; *Īśvara* — lord). Śiva is also called:

Mahāyogin   'The Great Yogin' or that great uniter of man's soul to God, so-called because he destroys all obstacles in the way of the Divine Consciousness (*yuj* — to unite).

The Lord, the Ruler; God (*īś* — to rule). The Divine (Brahman) as Creator and Lord of the Universe or Lord of Nature. The Personal God in the Yoga system of

Īśvara or Īśa   philosophy as expounded by Patañjali.

Brahmāṇḍa   'The Egg of Brahmā' or the Universe or Cosmos (*aṇḍa* — egg).

The Lordly Yoga or that Divine Union spoken of in the Bhagavad Gītā by which the Transcendent is one with all existences even though more than them as becomings

Aiśvara-Yoga   of His own Nature (adjectival form of Īśvara).

Purusha-Yajña   'Self-sacrifice' (*yaj* — to sacrifice). That great sacrifice in which the Soul gives itself to the Divine.

Ātman   The true Self in man, pure indivisible Being (*at* — to breathe). Its existence is light, self-concentrated force and self-delight.

Ātma-dāna   Gift of Self to the Divine (*dā* — to give).

Ātma-   Self-surrender to the Divine (*sam-ṛi* — to deliver over completely).
samarpaṇa

Ātma-prasāda   The Grace of the Divine Self (*pra-sād* — to be bright, to propitiate).

Ātma-jñāna   Self-knowledge (*jñā* — to know).

Ātma-vidyā   Self-knowledge (*vid* — to know).

Ātmarati   The peaceful joy of the Divine Self within (*rati* — joy).

'The Self Beyond': Brahman or the Divine as the Supreme Spirit that ensouls the forms and movements of the Universe in contradistinction to the *Ātman* that ensouls the human being (*parama* — beyond, supreme).

Paramātman

Akshara   'The Immutable' or the Indestructible Self (*a* — not; *kshi* — to destroy, to perish).

Kshara   'The Mutable' or the changing universe or nature.

'The Immutable Self'; the Self standing back from the changes and movements of Nature, calm, pure, above them as on a summit not immersed in them, but watching them in an impartial state. The spirit unsubjected to *Prakriti* or Nature.

Akshara-
  Purusha

'The Mutable Self'; the Soul immersed in and reflecting the changes and movements of Nature; the Soul subjected to *Prakriti* or Nature; hence the Personal Self.

Kshara-Purusha

'The One on the Summit', descriptive of Akshara-Purusha or the Immutable Self which stands above the changes and perturbations of the natural being (*kuta* — summit; *sthā* — to stand).

Kuṭastha

Virāj (Virāṭ)   The Ruling spirit of the material and external nature (*virāj* — to shine forth; to rule everywhere).

The ancient Hindu scriptures tell in their poetic manner that the Universe was sung into being by the inspiration rising in the divine mind of Brahmā, the Father of the Universe. This Divine Thought in Brahmā's mind

Vāch

was carried by *Vāch*, the Divine Voice or Mystic Sound, often called the Mother of the Universe, and gave rise to *Virāj*, the Divine World or the manifested Universe of harmony.

The Life-Spark; the Divine as the individual spiritual presence in every living thing. Jīva is Īśvara, but only
Jīva
in his partial manifestation (*jīv* — to live).

Purusha   'The Spirit' or the Spiritual Person, the Witness
Soul or Conscious Being supporting the action of
Nature or *Prakriti*.

'The original producer', Nature (*pra-kri* — to produce). Prakriti is that producing element out of which springs the universe
with all its various spheres and bodies. In the Sāṅ-
Prakriti
khya philosophy Prakriti is executive Nature as opposed to Purusha, which is portrayed as the Soul governing,
taking cognizance of and enjoying the works of Prakriti. In Sri
Aurobindo's higher interpretation of the Bhagavad-Gītā he
points out that Prakriti is the will and executive power of the
Purusha, his activity of being, the Purusha in power. Sāṅkhya's
Prakriti stops with Buddhi, the discriminating principle, the
higher intelligence, and so made an unbridgeable division between soul and nature and made them two distinct primary en-
tities and hence cosmic existence came to be understood as just
a result of the illusion or *Māyā* of the three qualities of Nature,
the qualities of poise, action, and inertia, or *Sattva*, *Rajas* and
Tamas (q.v.). But in the higher interpretation Prakriti has two
aspects:

Parāprakriti   The Nature Beyond; the higher Divine Nature
which is the true creatrix of the universe, the Vir-
gin Mother of all things (*para* — beyond).

The lower Nature; the perishable and external and apparent
Nature which manifests all the minds, lives and bodies of beings
in this world (*a* — not, *para* — beyond; hence low-
Aparāprakriti
(same as   er). Only a dark shadow of Parāprakriti. Parāprakriti
Sāṅkhya's   is the will and executive power of Purushottama.
Prakriti)   In Sāṅkhya the Akshara Purusha is the highest

expression of Spirit, that is the Purusha or Spirit uninvolved in Prakriti or Nature. But the Gītā refers to a higher Purusha, the Purushottama beyond it and which is both in Prakriti and beyond it. It embraces both and is the reality of experience and joy. Thus Purushottama and Mūlaprakriti are the Transcendent Divine and His Divine Nature which are inseparable.

Higher reason, intelligence (*budh* — to know); judgment, perceptive choice. In Sāṅkhya metaphysics the separation of Purusha from Prakriti must be effected by self-knowledge through the discriminating principle in man, Buddhi. The Gītā also accepts this as a necessary step in its Yoga discipline.

Buddhi

In the Vedas Pradhāna is 'the Originator', the primary germ, the original source of the visible or material universe, the Prakriti of Sāṅkhya philosophy (*pra-dhā* — to place before, send out).

Pradhāna

'Root-Nature' (*mūla* — root; *prakriti* — nature); the original root or germ out of which matter or all forms are evolved; the primary cause or originant. The first faint vibrations of Universal Life are caused by the interaction of Parabrahman and Mūlaprakriti, its Divine Essence Beyond and its first divine vesture. Mūlaprakriti is the source of Prakriti or of all forms ranging from the finest to the grossest.

Mūlaprakriti

The Divine Power (*śak* — to be able); the Conscious Force of the Divine; the 'Mother' of Hindu religion. This divine energy is personified as the wife of Deity or the Goddess, called *Devī* in the *Purāṇas* and *Tantras*, and is worshipped under various names according to her mild or more fierce aspects. The chief of these are Maheśvarī, Lakshmī, Sarasvatī, Umā, and Gaurī; and Kālī and Durgā.

Śakti
Devī

The 'Mother' of the *Tantras*; the female energy or power of Īśvara (q.v.). The same as Śakti.

Īśvarī

The Divine 'Mother' in regard to Purushottama, the Supreme Divine consciousness above the worlds. Ādyā Śakti carries the

Ādyā Śakti   Supreme in herself and manifests the Divine in the
               worlds through Akshara and Kshara (q.v.) (*ādyā* —
above).

Parā Śakti   The Divine 'Mother' in regard to Akshara-
               Purusha. She holds Purusha immobile in herself
and is also herself immobile in him at the back of all creation.

Aditi   Boundless Space; 'Mother Infinite' (*a* — not;
diti — limit).

The most beloved life of Krishna, the Avatāra or manifestation of Vishnu. As Krishna has become the name for the
               Divine, so Rādhā is the personification of absolute
Rādhā   self-giving and total consecration of all the being.

'Illusion'; temporary limitation (*māyā* — that which is measured from *mā* — to measure). Its derivative philosophical
               meaning is an imperfect understanding of Reality.
Māyā   Māyā generally implies that which limits and hence
prevents us from cognizing perfect Truth which is boundless,
beyond limits. Māyā is the inevitable result of manifestation
because matter of any kind is a veil which hides the God within.
Anything that is impermanent and subject to change is subject
to Māyā.

There are two kinds of Māyā: the divine and the undivine,
the formations of Truth and the formations of falsehood. Daivī
Daivī Māyā   (divine) Māyā or Para Māyā are the Divine or
or   Higher Māyā or the Universe in measured Time
Para Māyā   and space, the world-creation, the boundless finite
or Brahman in His becoming or world-existence. The lower
Māyā is a temporary wrong self-experience. The true freedom
from Māyā is not an external escape from things of the world,
but is the freedom of Brahman which is in no way limited by the
circumstances through which He expresses Himself.

Māyāvī   The closer one unites oneself to the Divine the
              less māyāvī or illusive will be our vision of Truth.

The doctrine in Advaita Vedānta that teaches that the world

Māyāvāda — is unreal and that it is created by the power of illusion.

'The Cosmic Play'; the idea that creation is a play of the Divine Consciousness existing for no other reason than for the mere joy of it. Śrī Aurobindo says "What then was the commencement of the whole matter? Existence that multiplied itself for sheer delight of being and plunged into numberless trillions of forms so that it might find itself innumerably."

Lilā

A god, a divinity, a Power of Light, a 'Shining One' (from verb-root *div* — to shine). Deva is a very general and inclusive term for all grades of spiritual beings ranging from the unevolved divine sparks up to the highest of the Gods who are fuller divine manifestations and self-conscious Divinities.

Deva

Devadeva — God of Gods, a title of Krishna, the divine manifestation in human form.

The Great God, a title of Śiva, the God of Śaivism. The chosen deity (from verb-root *ish* — to wish, seek; and *devatā* — a divinity). From the many names and forms of God in Hinduism the worshipper or aspirant to divine realization chooses one which answers to his spiritual longing and makes that the object of his adoration and love.

Mahādeva
Ishṭadevatā

Divine (the adjectival form of *deva* — god). The *daiva* — or *daivika* — nature is godlike, hence universal in feeling and expression.

Daiva
Daivika

Lord of creatures; a supreme God above spoken of in Vedas; Lord of the Becoming. (From *prajā* — creature; and *pati* — lord.)

Prajāpati

Being; absolute, eternal, immutable and undivided Existence; the Divine Brahman or God. Sat is the divine counterpart of physical substance. (Sat is present participle of *as* — to be.)

Sat

Non-being; non-existence; often used for the inconscient, the basis of the material world. (From *a* — not; and *sat* — being.)

Asat
Śūnya
Asat is also used for the Silent Unknowable beyond Sat, that Something which is inconceivable to the mind, speech or defining experience; the featureless Absolute of Advaita Vedāntins and similar to the Śūnya or Void of the nihilistic Buddhists; the Tao as the omnipresent and transcendental Nihil of the Chinese; and the indefinable omnipresent ineffable Permanent of the Mahāyāna school of Buddhism.

Bhāva
Becoming; a state of flux; a state of mind or consciousness; a play of emotion or sense-reaction. (From verb-root *bhū* — to become).

Mad-Bhāva
'My State', a phrase used in the Gītā to represent the Divine's transcendent activity or play.

Chit
Consciousness; a self-aware force of existence. (From verb-root *chit* — to think, to be aware); the divine counterpart of lower mind.

Chit-Śakti
Consciousness-force; the Divine's Power of active consciousness and formative activity. (From verb-root *śak* — to be able.)

Ānanda
Cosmic Bliss, Divine Joy, Delight of Existence. Ānanda is the secret source and support of all existence; it is ecstacy and beatitude. (From the verb-root *nand* — to rejoice.)

Sachchidānanda
(Sat-chit-ānanda)
'Being-Consciousness-Bliss', the Supreme Reality's very being. In the manifested life of Sat-Chit-Ānanda, Sat translates itself into Person or substance; Chit with Śakti into Conceptive Knowledge and Executive Force, and Ānanda into Love. Sat-Chit-Ānanda is the nature of Parāprakṛiti or Higher Nature or the pure state of Ātman or Brahman, or the Divine in man and universe, and is also the fountain-source of all the lower manifested life.

Sachchidānan-
damayīśakti
(Sat-chit-
ānanda-mayī-
śakti)

The Power composed of Pure Being, Consciousness and Bliss; the Divine Mother-Force
of Śrī Aurobindo's philosophy.

TABLE OF THE DIVINE AND ITS MANIFESTATIONS

Masculine	*Feminine*	*Religion and Scripture*
Prajāpati	Aditi	Veda
Tat	Idam	Upanishad
Parabrahman Parampurusha	Mūlaprakṛiti	Upanishad
Purushottama	Parāprakṛiti	Bhagavad-Gītā
Akshara	Kshara	Bhagavad-Gītā
Brahman	Pradhāna or Māyā	Advaita Vedānta
Purusha	Prakṛiti	Sāṅkhya
Virāj (Virāṭ)	Vāch or Śata-rūpa	Purāṇa and Epics
Kṛishṇa or Bhagavān	Rādhā	Vaishṇavism & Bhāgavata Purāṇa
Rāma	Sītā	Vaishṇavism & Rāmāyaṇa
Īśvara	Īśvarī or Śakti	Tantra
Mahādeva	Devī	Tantra
Śiva	Śakti	Śaivism and Tantra
Para Purusha	Ādya-Śakti	Śrī Aurobindo
Parātpara Purusha Parameśvara	Para-Māyā	
Akshara-Purusha	Daivī-Māyā	Śrī Aurobindo
Kshara-Purusha	Śakti Aparā-Prakṛiti Aparā-Māyā	Śrī Aurobindo

TRIPLICITIES

Bhagavad-Gītā	*Advaita-Vedānta*	*Purāṇa*
Purushottama	Brahma	Brahma
Akshara, Kshara	Īśvara, Māyā	Virāj, Vāch

Tantra		*Śrī Aurobindo*
Maheśvara		Pūrṇa Brahma
Īśvara-Īśvarī	Sat-Chit-Ānanda	Sat-Chit-Ānanda-Mayī-Śakti
Śiva-Śakti	Sachchidānanda	Sachchidānandamayī-śakti

THE TEN AVATĀRAS OF VISHṆU

The ten *Avatāras* of *Vishṇu* are: 1. *Matsya* or Fish, the water animal, symbol of the beginning of physical man and the saving of the fine seeds of man-to-be. Also Conqueror of *Hayagrīva*. (Similar to the Bible story of Noah's Ark). 2. *Kūrma* or Tortoise, the amphibian, symbol of the vital physical man with all his keenest desires being churned out of the ocean of Infinity. Also Conqueror of the *Asuras*, the Titans. 3. *Varāha* or Boar, the mammal, symbol of animal man struggling to master earth. Also Conqueror of *Hiraṇyāksha*. 4. *Narasiṁha* or Man-Lion, bridging man and animal, symbol of the turning towards conscious power. Also Conqueror of *Hiraṇyakaśipu*. 5. *Vāmana* or Dwarf, the small undeveloped Godman taking possession of existence. Also Conqueror of *Bali*. 6. *Paraśurāma* or *Rāma* with the Axe, the vital *Rājasic* man who brings ethics into social life by repeatedly destroying the pure physical forces of the *Kshatriyas*. 7. *Rāma*, hero of the *Rāmāyaṇa*, the *Sāttvic* mental man, the ideal human. Also Conqueror of *Rāvaṇa*. 8. *Kṛishṇa*, the overmental spiritual man, bringer of *Ānanda* into life. Also Conqueror of *Kaṁsa*.

9. *Buddha*, who led to *Nirvāṇa*, a negative supreme liberation which reveals the oneness of all beings and hence led to his compassionate abandonment of *Nirvāṇa* to raise mankind. Also Conqueror of *Māra*. 10. *Kalki* or White Horse, the Divine man, called 'white horse' to symbolize strength and power of all colors, hence 'power of full plenitude'. Also Conqueror of *Yama*, Death, of all duality, all opposition and all darkness. The Divine Man on Earth, One with the Infinite Divine.

The stories of these Avatāras and their conquests of the demons are told in the *Purāṇas*, the legendary histories of India.

VOCABULARY

Adaivī-māyā
Adhidaiva
Adhidaivata
Aditi
Ādyā Śakti
Akshara
Akshara-Purusha
Ānanda
Aṇḍa
Aparāprakṛiti
Asat
Ātma-dāna
Ātma-jñāna
Ātman
Ātma-prasāda
Ātmarati
Ātmaśakti
Ātmasamarpaṇa
Ātmavidyā
Bhāva
Brahma
Brahman
Brahmā

Brahmaloka
Brahmāṇḍa
Brahmatej
Brahmavid
Brahmavidyā
Brahmayoga
Brāhmī-sthiti
Chaitanya
Chaitanya Purusha
Chit
Chitśakti
Daiva
Daivika
Daivīmāyā
Daivīprakṛiti
Deva
Devadeva
Devī
Idam
Īś
Īśa
Ishṭadevatā
Īśvara

Īśvarī
Jīva
Kālī
Kas tvam asi ?
Krishṇa
Kshara
Kshara-Purusha
Kuṭastha
Lakshmī
Līlā
Madbhāva
Mahādeva
Mahākāla
Mahat
Mahāyogin
Maheśvara
Māyā
Māyāvī
Māyāvāda
Mūlaprakṛiti
Namo Nārāyaṇāya
Nara
Nara-Nārāyaṇa
Nārāyaṇa
Nitya-Vāch
Para
Parabrahman
Paramānanda
Paramātman
Paramāyā
Parameśvara

Parāprakṛiti
Parapurusha
Parāśakti
Parātpara Purusha
Pradhāna
Prajāpati
Prakṛiti
Purusha
Purushayajña
Purushottama
Rādhā
Rati
Rudra-Śiva
Śabdabrahma
Sachchidānanda
Sachchidānandamayīśakti
Śakti
Sarasvati
Sat
Śiva
Śūnya
Tat
Tat tvam asi
Trimūrti
Umā
Vāch
Vāsudeva
Virāj or Virāṭ
Virāṭ-Purusha
Vishṇu

NEW VERB-ROOTS

sthā — to stand
tij — to sharpen, excite
rādh — to succeed

rud — to weep
vad — to speak

"Whatever beautiful and glorious creature thou seest in the world, whatever being is mighty and forceful (among men and above man and below him), know to be a very splendour, light, and energy of Me and born of a potent portion and intense power of my existence."

From the Bhagavad-Gītā, X-41.
(From Śrī Aurobindo's translation)

CHAPTER V

INDIAN RELIGIONS

Hinduism is a name given in the West to the religious and social institutions of the Hindus. In India this 'league of religions' is called the Sanātana Dharma or the 'Eternal Religion'. It is a complex system of religious beliefs and culture based on the Vedas, Upanishads, Purāṇas, Tantras and Bhagavad-Gītā. Though very diversified it is still a unified mass of spiritual thought, aspiration, and realization. It is a broad-based religion for it takes into its fold all aspects of truth through the ages. It is not the religion of one prophet but the 'Law or *Dharma* of Life' as revealed by many sages and prophets through the ages. It comprises within its fold Brāhmanism, Vaishṇavism, Śaivism, Śaktism and many of the modern movements of the last hundred years. Influences of Buddhism, Jainism, Parsiism, Sufism and Christianity have played a great part in the historic and religious development of the Sanātana Dharma. This is in accord with the character of Indian religion which expands as new truth is unveiled. The Veda-passage exemplifying this principale is "Truth is One ; sages speak of it in various ways" — "*Ekam sad viprā bahudhā vadanti*". Hence Hinduism is also Vaidika-Dharma.

[Marginal note: Hinduism Sanātana Dharma Vaidika-Dharma]

A system of religious institutions originated and elaborated by the Brāhmaṇas or 'priest-caste' in India, and based on the Mantras, Brāhmaṇas and Upanishads of the Vedas. The three divisions of the Veda are the fountain-source of the three main aspects of Brāhmanism or Vedic Religion. They are:

[Marginal note: Brāhmanism Vedic-religion]

1. Karma-kāṇḍa — the 'Action-portion' dealing with rituals led to the sacrificial ceremonies or *Yajña* (*yaj* — to sacrifice).

2. Upāsanā-kāṇḍa — 'Worship-portion' (*upa-ās* — to sit

near) dealing with worship, prayer and meditation led to *Bhakti* or devotional service and loving worship of God or Īśvara.

3. Jñāna-kāṇḍa — 'Knowledge-portion' dealing with wisdom led to the *Vedānta* system of thought and culture.

The religious worship that regards Vishṇu as the Supreme. It is a religion of love and beauty wherein the figures of human feeling and love and devotion are transfigured into those of divine soul-experience. Śrī Chaitanya was the fine flower of this type of *Bhakti* or devotion to God as Vishṇu or of Vishṇu in one of his manifested forms. The goal of Vaishṇavism is an eternal nearness to the Divine, not union with Him. Some of the main divisions of this religious system are:

    Vaishṇavism

1. The Rāmānujas — Worshippers of Īśvara as the Supreme Being.

2. The Nimbārkas — Worshippers of Kṛishṇa and Rādhā.

3. The Mādhvas — Worshippers of Vishṇu as the Supreme Being.

4. The Rāmānandas — Worshippers of Rāma and Sītā (Kabir their great disciple) and Tulsidas (their great Hindi poet who wrote the Rāmāyaṇa in Hindi).

5. The Vallabhāchāryas — Worshippers of Kṛishṇa and Rādhā.

6. The Chaitanyas — Worshippers of Kṛishṇa. This is the Bengal School of Vaishṇavism.

7. The Viṭṭhal Cult — Worshippers of Viṭṭhal or Viṭhoba (a corrupt form of word Vishṇu).

The religious worship that regards Śiva as the Supreme. Śiva is the source and essence of the universe as well as its disintegrator and destroyer. The temples dedicated to him in his reproducing and all-powerful character as denoted by the *Linga* or phallus are scattered all over

    Śaivism

India. This religion is considered to be of Dravidian origins. The main classes of Śaivas are:

Pāśupata System   The Worshippers of Śiva as Paśupati, Lord of Souls. They sprinkle their bodies with ashes and resort to the Yoga of Śiva.

Kāpāla and Kālāmukha Sects   The worshippers of Bhairava or Śiva as 'The Terrible'. Kashmir Śaivism has 2 branches with beliefs similar to Advaita Vedānta in regard to soul and God or Śiva.

1. Spandaśāstra School.

2. Pratyabhijñaśāstra School.

Vīraśaiva or Lingāyat Sect   Worshippers of Śiva as the *Linga* as the sign of omnipotence. The Śaiva Siddhānta is the great book.

Śaktism or Tāntrism   The religious worship of Śakti or the Divine Energy under its female personification as wife of Śiva or as the 'Divine Mother'. This is a philosophical and religious system which sought to raise the whole man into the divine perfection as envisaged in the Veda. It regarded life as '*līlā*' or the 'Cosmic Play' of the Divine. It considers that man, alone of all creations, has the unique possibility of awakening to the power of the macrocosm which is latent within him. When this power called Kuṇḍalinī-śakti is roused from its sleeping state at the base of the spine it proceeds upward through centres or *Chakras* of man's being rendering them dynamic with power. When this Śakti reaches the highest and most holy centre through spiritual training it becomes one with Śiva and man becomes possessed of the loftiest spiritual consciousness and bliss. The secrets of physical, vital, mental and soul-transformation are contained in its disipline. Hence it is a system fraught with danger for the unspiritual man and has developed some spurious sects indulging in undesirable practices. The tenets of this school are found in the Tantra texts. Two schools are known to exist: the *Vāma-*

chāra or the 'Left-Hand Practice' of an impure ritual; and the *Dakshiṇāchāra* or the 'Right-Hand Practice' of a pure ritual.

The spiritual discipline demands an absolute self-surrender to the Will of *Mahāmāyā* or *Śakti*, the 'Divine Mother' in her many forms.

The teachings of the *Jinas* or 'Conquering Ones', the title given to the 24 teachers or *Tīrthankaras* through whom their faith is said to have come down the ages. The last of these teachers, Mahāvīra was born in 569 B.C.

Jainism

He with his eleven chief disciples were the first open seceders from Brāhmanism. Buddhism along with Jainism are called the two schisms or unorthodox religions of India. Neither of these religions believe in God, in Brāhmanical sacrifices or the authority of the Veda. Jainism teaches that all men may become perfect by their own efforts inspired by the example of their great saints. They encouraged asceticism for at least 12 years of a man's life. They teach that all life is sacred so the highest law of duty is *Ahiṁsā* or 'Non-Injury' to any living creature, and that there is no divine power higher than man.

The religion based on the teachings of Gautama (best on earth), the Buddha (enlightened), called also Prince Siddhārtha (attained purpose) or Śākyamuni (sage of the Śākya clan). Buddha was born in the 6th century B.C.

Buddhism

At age of 29 years Siddhārtha abandoned his wife, Yaśodharā (holder of glory), to devote himself entirely to spiritual pursuits and Yoga practice. Finally under the Bodhi (wisdom) tree he attained enlightenment during deep meditation, and entered into the state of Nirvāṇa, the divine state of liberation from all worldly bondage. Choosing to return to the world-state out of compassion for his fellow beings he then travelled all over India as a Teacher and Savior of humanity preaching to all without exception his new and fresh approach to the fundamental truths of the Sanātana Dharma as taught in the sacred scriptures of India.

Buddha was a great reformer, who broke away from the

tyranny and ritualism and caste system practised by many Brāhmins of the time. His teachings were fundamentally the same as Brāhmanism, but were given a new turn and emphasis. Ceremonial was given up, severe asceticism was discouraged. Ethics was the aspect stressed by him among the populace and he preserved his deeper wisdom for his circle of devoted disciples.

Buddhism spread rapidly and by 300 B.C. had become one of the principle religions of north India. In the early centuries of the Christian era Brāhmanism which came to be known in its altered form as Hinduism began to assert itself once more but greatly altered and influenced both by Buddhism and Śaivism. By the 12th century after the destructive results of the Moslem invasion Buddhism practically disappeared from India, but wherever Hinduism travelled the teachings of Buddha also took root. So Buddhism has been flowering and spreading in Ceylon, Burma, Siam, Tibet, China, Japan and other neighbouring countries, and still remains the principle religion, though varied in form, in all these countries.

Buddha's principal teachings are of a non-theistic and anti-monastic nature. He taught: All things are impermanent, transitory. There is no abiding unchanging Self or Ātman, no unchanging Absolute or Brahman; All is in a constant flux, in a state of becoming. To free oneself from the wheel of Saṁsāra or continuous embodied existence one must free oneself from Karma, the causes and effects of action. One must abandon desire through an understanding of the four cardinal truths regarding suffering. One must follow the *Dharma* or moral and spiritual law by treading the noble eightfold path to Liberation, i.e., right views, right speech, right resolve, right conduct, right livelihood, right effort, right recollection and right contemplation. Buddha taught a way of life, avoiding the two extremes of self-indulgence and self-mortification and prescribed the 'Middle Way' which would lead to Liberation or the Nirvāṇa of full enlightenment. The followers of Buddha gradually divided into different schools. (Regarding further details see under section devoted entirely to Buddhism.)

The religion of the Parsis or followers in India (mostly in Bombay) of Zarathustra or Zoroaster. The Parsis are the direct

Parsiism
descendants of the ancient Persians who emigrated to India at the time of the conquest of Persia by the Arabs in the 8th century. Their religion recommends benevolence and charity and their ideal is good thoughts, good words, and good deeds. The Parsis are revered for their sagacity, activity and commercial enterprise and are a valuable part of any community in which they live.

The religious mysticism of the Sufis, or Islamic mysticism. Sūfi is an Arabic word applied to men or women who adopted

Sufism of Islam
an ascetic way of life (from sūf — wool, referring to the garment worn by them). Sufism stresses the all-pervading presence and intimate relation of Allah to all creatures in contrast to the belief of most Mohammedans in a God of arbitrary power and unapproachable supremacy. The aspiration of the Sufi is to die to self and live in God. To hide their religious zeal from Arab tyranny they developed a vocabulary of human love and wine as the symbolic expressions of their mystical love and ecstasy and oneness with God. The monastic strain which Mohammed had prohibited in the practice of Islam gradually developed in Sufism and was very likely brought about by the influences of Christianity and Buddhism. The wide popularity of Sufism in India in the middle ages became one of those synthesizing forces between the religions of the Hindus and Moslems and in time paved the way for great mystics like Kabir and Guru Nānak.

The religious teachings of Mohammed, the Prophet of Arabia. Islam means 'peace', 'surrender' to the will of Allah, the

Islam
One God. Its doctrines and practices are based on the Koran and on the sayings and life of Mohammed as contained in the traditions. The five cardinal teachings of Islam are: 1. The Oneness of God and the revelation of His will through a series of prophets, the last of which was

Mohammed. Hence their saying "There is no God but Allah and Mohammed is His Messenger". 2. Prayer. 3. Fasting. 4. Charity. 5. Pilgrimage to Mecca, the birth-place of Mohammed, the holy city of the Moslems.

The religion of the Sikhs (sikha — disciple) founded by Guru Nānak in Lahore during the medieval times. The constant conflict between the cultures of the Hindus and the Mohammedan invaders from the Northwest brought about a gradual synthesis of the two religious faiths. Guru Nānak (1469-1539), recognized as gifted with divine wisdom and experience originated a practical common-sense philosophy-religion which reconciled Hindus and Mohammedans and taught them that both Allah and Brahma could be equally pleased by loving service to man, their creation. True living and loving sacrifice, not empty ritual are the essence of Sikhism. Its God is immanent and transcendent, just and true, called by different names among different peoples. It is without caste or priestcraft and gives equality to all its members, male and female. It maintains that idolatry is superstition, and renunciation of the world a cowardly escape. It is democratic and accepts the principle of evolution, abides by the law of Karma (cause and effect) and believes in reincarnation. Salvation or complete unity with God can be obtained only through one's own effort. The common Sikh greetings is "Sat Siri Akal" or "God is true. Truth is eternal."

Sikhism emphasizes selfless service or *seva*, company of wise or *sat-sang*, meditation or *bani*, that is, meditation on the attributes of God, self-sacrifice or *kurbani*, and the conquests of anger, lust, fear, hate, greed and ego. The Sikhs live a simple peasant life, are puritans, rarely drink and never smoke. The Sikhs recruited many of their followers from the Scythian tribes who pushed their way into the Punjab. They are proud and sturdy, great horsemen and swordsmen and their spartan life and love of adventure make them excellent soldiers.

The Sikhs became a militant order under Guru Gobind

Singh (1666-1708) in order to fight against Mogul oppression. Then the brotherhood of the Khalsa Panth or "The Pure Way" was instituted. Personal courage became the highest of all virtues and cowardice the basest of all crimes. Every Sikh, after baptism, must use *Singh* (the lion) as his second name.

To be distinctive as members of the Khalsa they were to have five symbols, each beginning with K: *Keś* — long hair, *kenga* — comb, *kachh* — short trouser, *kara* — iron bangle, and *kirpan* — sword. They were to be ever ready to go thru any ordeal for their faith, to make any sacrifice for the emancipation of their fellow men. Their great religious book is the *Granth Sahib*.

These above religions are the main traditionary movements. The modern religious developments will be treated under Movements of the Hindu Renaissance.

The following is a recent statement of the proportions of the different religions in India and Pakistan:

Hindus (Brahmanism, Vaishṇavism, Śaivism, Śaktism, Vedāntism) 67.76%; Sikhs 1.23%; Jains 0.35%; Buddhists 3.62%; Parsis 0.03%; Mohammedans 22%; Christians 1.78%; and Animistic religions of hill tribes etc. 2.21%.

"The whole root of difference between Indian and European culture springs from the spiritual aim of Indian civilisation. It is the turn which this aim imposes on all the rich and luxuriant variety of its forms and rhythms that gives to it its unique character. For even what it has in common with other cultures gets from that turn a stamp of striking originality and solitary greatness. A spiritual aspiration was the governing force of this culture, its core of thought, its ruling passion. Not only did it make spirituality the highest aim of life, but it even tried, as far as that could be done in the past conditions of the human race, to turn the whole of life towards spirituality. But since religion is in the human mind the first native, if imperfect form of the spiritual impulse, the predominance of the spiritual idea, thought and action into the religious mould and a persistent filling of every circumstance of life with the religious sense; it demanded a pervading religio-philosophic culture. The highest spirituality indeed moves in a free and wide air far above that lower stage of seeking which is governed by religious form and dogma; it does not easily bear their limitations and, even when it admits, it transcends them; it lives in an experience which to the formal religious mind is unintelligible. But man does not arrive immediately at that highest inner elevation and, if it were demanded from him at once, he would never arrive there. At first he needs lower supports and stages of ascent; he asks for some scaffolding of dogma, worship, image, sign, form, symbol, some indulgence and permission of mixed half-natural motive on which he can stand while he builds up in him the temple of the spirit. Only when the temple is completed, can the supports be removed, the scaffolding disappear. The religious culture which now goes by the name of Hinduism not only fulfilled this purpose, but, unlike certain other credal religions, it knew its purpose. It gave itself no name, because it set itself no sectarian limits; it claimed no universal adhesion, asserted no sole infallible dogma, set up no single narrow path or gate of salvation; it was less a creed or cult than a continuously enlarging tradition of the Godward endeavour of the human spirit. An immense many-sided and many-staged provision for a spiritual self-building and self-finding, it had some right to speak of itself by the only name it knew, the eternal religion, *sanātana dharma*." Śrī Aurobindo in "Foundations of Indian Culture."

VOCABULARY

Ahiṁsā

Allah

Āryan

Bhagavad-Gītā

Bhairava

Bhakti

Bodhi-tree

Brahma

Brāhmanism

Brāhmaṇa

Buddha

Buddhism

Chaitanya

Chakra

Dakshiṇāchāra
Dharma
Dravidian
Ekam sad viprā bahudhā
  vadanti
Granth Sahib
Guru Govind Singh
Guru Nānak
Hinduism
Islam
Īśvara
Jainism
Jina
Jñānakāṇḍa
Kabir
Kālāmukha
Kāpāla
Karma
Karmakāṇḍa
Kashmir Śaivism
Kṛishṇa
Kuṇḍalinī-śakti
Līlā
Linga
Liṅgāyāt
Madhva
Mahāmāyā
Mahāvīra
Mantra
Nimbārka
Nirvāṇa
Parsiism
Pāśupata
Paśupati
Pratyabhijñaśāstra
Purāṇa
Rādhā

Rāma
Rāmānanda
Rāmānuja
Rāmāyaṇa
Śaiva Siddhānta
Śaivism
Śakti
Śaktism
Śākyamuni
Sanātana Dharma
Saṁsāra
Siddhārtha
Sikh
Sikhism
Singh
Sītā
Śiva
Spandaśāstra
Sufism
Tantra
Tantraism
Tīrthaṅkara
Tulsidās
Upanishad
Upāsanā
Upāsanākāṇḍa
Vaidika-Dharma
Vaishṇavism
Vallabhāchārya
Vāmachāra
Veda
Vedānta
Vīraśaiva
Vishṇu
Viṭhoba
Viṭṭhal
Yajña

Yaśodharā   Zarathustra
Yoga   Zoroaster

SIKH TERMS

Bani   Kshalsa Panth
Kachh   Kurbani
Kara   Sat-sang
Kenga   Sat-Siri Akal
Keś   Seva
Kirpan   Singh

"The fundamental idea of all Indian religion is one common to the highest human thinking everywhere. The supreme truth of all that is a Being or an existence beyond the mental and physical appearances we contact here. Beyond mind, life and body there is a Spirit and Self containing all that is finite and infinite, surpassing all that is relative, a supreme Absolute, originating and supporting all that is transient, a one Eternal. A one transcendent, universal, original and sempiternal Divinity or divine Essence, Consciousness, Force and Bliss is the fount and continent and inhabitant of things. Soul, nature, life are only a manifestation or partial phenomenon of this self-aware Eternity and this conscious Eternal." Śrī Aurobindo in "Foundations of Indian Culture".

CHAPTER VI

SANSKRIT LITERATURE — VEDIC

The 'Collections of Wisdom-Scriptures' (*sam-hita* — placed together; *veda* — wisdom). They are: The most celebrated of

Veda-Saṁhitās
Ṛig-Veda
Sāma-Veda
Yajur-Veda
Atharva-Veda

Vedas: a Scripture of Illuminating Hymns of Wisdom called Sūktas or Mantras composed of Ṛiks (*rich, ṛik* or *ṛig* — verse) addressed to the Devas or Gods of the Elements and the Pheno- mena of Nature, but also symbolic of aspiring prayers to the subtler and higher powers in man. Scripture of Harmonious Joyful Chants or Sāmans to be sung to certain melodies. A recast of the Ṛig-Veda broken up into parts and arranged anew for purposes of being chanted at the Soma sacrifice: Scripture of Sacrificial Rites or Yajus (*yajur*) or the right ordaining of action. It consists principally of prayers and invocations applicable to the consecration of the utensils and materials of sacrificial worship, but also symbolic of the means by which man attains divinity. This Veda is divi- ded into two parts, 'The White' and 'The Black'. Scripture of the ancient Atharvans composed chiefly of formulas intended to counteract disease and evil.

Vyāsa   The composer or 'Arranger' of the Vedas.

Each of these Vedas consists of the following divisions:

Sūktas or
Mantras

Poetic hymns of praise (*su-ukta* — beautifully said). Words of Vibrant Power (*man* — to think).

Brāhmaṇas*

Works in prose dealing with Vedic ritual along with myths and traditional matter (*brahman* — divine prayer).

Āraṇyakas

Philosophical prose treatises attached to the Brāhmaṇas for ascetics of the forest (*araṇya* — forest).

* See next page for detailed lists.

Upanishads*   Treatises in poetry and prose on spiritual and philosophical subjects (*upa-ni-shad* — sit down near).

Sūtras   Aphoristic rules on all subjects expressed in terse and technical language so that they might easily be committed to memory and meditated upon (*sūtra* — thread).

Vedāngas*   Limbs (anga) of the Veda dealing with various scientific subjects usually written in Sūtra form.

Bhāshyas   Commentaries on the various divisions of the Veda (*bhāsh* — to discuss).

Upa-Vedas   The Minor Scriptures of Wisdom. They are:

Āyur-Veda   Scripture dealing with medicine (*āyus*).

Dhanur Veda   Scripture dealing with archery (*dhanus* — bow).

Śastra-Śāstra   Scripture dealing with arms (*śastra* — weapon).

Gandharva-Veda   Scripture of music (*gandharva* — celestial musician).

Sthāpatya-Veda   Scripture of architecture (*sthāpatya*).

Śilpa-Śāstra   Scripture of fine arts (*śilpa*).

Detailed lists of Brāhmaṇas, Upanishads, and Vedāngas.

BRĀHMAṆAS

of Ṛig-Veda — Aitareya-B, and Kaushitaki-B.

of Sāma-Veda — Pāñcha-viṁśa-B, and Shaḍ-viṁśa-B.

of Yajur-Veda — Śatapatha-B, and Taittirīya-B.

of Atharva-Veda — Gopatha-B.

* See next page for detailed lists.

UPANISHADS

The traditional sequence of the ten principal Upanishads upon which Śankara wrote his commentaries is that given in the following useful *versus memorialis:*

Īśa-Kena-Katha-Praśna-Munda-Māndūkya-Tittiri
Aitareyam-cha Chhāndogyam Brihadāranyakam tathā.

Among the 100 or more Upanishads the following are the most well-known as grouped according to their Vedic origin:

of Rig-Veda — Aitareya-U, and Kaushitaki-U.

of Sāma-Veda — Chhāndogya-U, and Kena-U.

of Yajur-Veda — Īśa-U, Taittirīya-U (or Tittiri), Śvetāśvatara, and Brihadāranyaka-U.

of Atharva-Veda — Katha-U, Praśna-U, Mundaka-U, Māndūkya-U.

(In Sanskrit *a* plus *u* makes *o* so we find the compounds of Īśopanishad, Kathopanishad, etc.).

VEDĀNGAS

The six Vedāngas or 'Limbs of the Vedas' are:

Śikshā	— Phonetics	Nirukta*	— Etymology
Chhandas	— Prosody	Jyotisha	— Astronomy
Vyāvakarana*	— Grammar	Kalpa*	— Ceremonial

*Pānini, the most eminent of all native Sanskrit Grammarians was the author of:

Ashtādhyāyī, Dhātu-pātha, Gana-pātha, Lingānuśāsana and Śikshā.

*Yāskas is well-known for his 'Nirukta', a commentary on Vedic words.

*KALPA or Ceremonial is of two kinds:

1. Śrauta-Sūtra based on the Vedas or Śruti and Kalpa-Sūtra — Rules for Vedic ceremonial.

2. Smārta-Sūtra based on Smṛiti or 'Remembered Tradition'.
    Gṛihya-Sūtras — Rules for domestic ceremonial.
    Dharma-Sūtras — Rules for conventional and religious customs and laws.

The Ancient (purāṇa, from verb-root *pur* — to precede) Legendary Histories of India full of the spirit of Bhakti or the

Purāṇas

God-loving movements of Vaishṇavism and Śaivism. They have been very influential among the populace. The outward nature basis of the early Vedic religion which appealed to the physical mind of the general masses was replaced by the great Trinity of Brahmā, Vishṇu and Śiva, the Emanator, Preserver, and Destroyer and Benefactor respectively. This new pantheon with its outward symbolic figures appealed to the inner mind of the populace and gave examples for his religious aspirations and were easier to understand than the spiritually veiled nature-symbolism of the Vedas. The idea of the Divine in man was popularized by the worship of the Avatāras.

The 18 Purāṇas are classified into three categories according to the aspect of God they give worship. They are:

Those in which Vishṇu is honored:

| Vaishṇava-Purāṇas | Vishṇu | Bhāgavata | Padma |
| | Nāradīya | Garuda | Varāha |

Those in which Śiva is honored:

| Śaiva-Purāṇas | Matsya | Linga | Skanda |
| | Kurma | Śiva | Agni |

Those in which Brahmā is honored:

| Brāhmaṇa-Purāṇas | Brahmā | Brahma-vaivarta | Vāmana |
| | Brahmāṇḍa | Mārkaṇḍeya | Bhavishya |

Besides these there is the *Vāyu-Purāṇa* which seems to be the oldest of them all and is sometimes substituted for the Agni or Śiva Purāṇas. But of all the Purāṇas the *Vishṇu* and *Bhāga-*

vata are the most famous and popular. The **Bhāgavata** which treats of the story of Kṛishṇa has powerfully influenced the religious beliefs in India.

These mythological works are truly the repository of the modern popular religious creed of the Hindus. They are an amplification of the traditions found in the Epics of India. Every Purāṇa is supposed to have 5 *lakshaṇa* or characteristics, that is, they should deal with (1) Creation, (2) Destruction and Renovation of the World, (3) Genealogy of Gods and Heroes, (4) Reign of the Manus or the original law-givers at different stages of the social development of the Human Race, (5) the lives and works of their descendants. However all the Purāṇas do not meet this qualification. These works are all written in verse, and their invariable form is that of a dialogue between a highly enlightened master and a disciple, interspersed with the dialogues and observations of other individuals.

Besides the above works there are certain works subordinate to them known as the 18 Upa-Purāṇas. Then there are also the Sthala-Purāṇas or chronicles recounting the history and merits of some holy 'place' or shrine (sthala), where their recitation usually forms an important part of the daily service to God.

Upa-Purāṇas
Sthala-Purāṇas

Religious treatises which are generally in the form of a dialogue between Śiva, the Divine Lord, and Śakti, the Divine Energy. They teach of mystical formulae or rituals (tantra) for the worship of the Divine Mother or the Superconscient Divine Energy and for the attainment of superhuman powers. The Tantras sought to raise the whole man into divine perfection. They teach that the divne play or Līlā can be fulfilled in man who is of all creations a microcosm of the macrocosm. Man can therefore awaken in him cosmic power. This potential power is called Kuṇḍalinī-Śakti (serpent-power) and when awakened according to specific rites and meditations proceeds upward through the six *chakras* or

Tantras
Śakti
Līlā
Kuṇḍalinī-
Śakti
Chakras
Śāktas

'wheels' or mystic centres of man's being and makes them dynamic with various powers. When the seventh and highest chakra or centre is reached at the top of the head the Śakti or Female Energy becomes one with Śiva or God, thus making the mystic union which brings a divine state of consciousness, wisdom, power and bliss. Followers of the Tantras are called Śāktas.

These Tantras are very numerous and their authority in many parts of India, especially in Kashmir and Bengal seems to have superceded the Veda. Each Tantra is said to treat of five subjects: (1) Creation, (2) Destruction of the World, (3) Worship of the Gods and Goddesses, (4) the attainment of the six superhuman faculties, and (5) the four modes of the union with the Supreme by meditation. The discipline of the Tantras combines all the old systems of Yoga, those of divine works, knowledge and love plus the physical and vital development, hence it is very powerful though dangerous system of spiritual growth.

The Tāntrika and Paurāṇa ideas, names, forms and symbols are only the more modern concrete representations of the combined monism, unitarianism and universalism and synthetism of the Vedas.

Some of the important Tantras are:

Mahānirvāṇa-T	Prapañchasāra-T	Brahma Yamalā-T
Kulāṇava-T	Tantrarāja-T	Vishṇu Yamalā-T
Kulasāra-T	Rudra Yamalā-T	Toḍala-T

Manuals of worship (*ā-gam* — to come near): a general name for a class of popular scriptures dealing with the worship of a
Āgamas   particular aspect of God and prescribing detailed courses of discipline for the worshipper. The Āgamas are divided into three main branches according to the deity that is worshipped.

Pāñcharātra   The Vaishṇava Āgamas wherein Vishṇu is
     Āgamas   worshipped. Some of the most important are:

Īśvara Paushkara	Bṛihad Brahma-Saṁhitā
Paramā	Jñānāmṛitasāra-Saṁhitā
Sattvatā	

Śaiva-Āgamas — These worship and glorify Śiva. Its chief work is the Kāmikam-Āgama.

Śakta-Āgamas — Another name for the Tantras wherein Śakti or Devī (Female Energy of God) is worshipped.

DHARMAŚĀSTRA — LAW BOOKS

Mānava-dharma-śāstra (Manusmṛiti or Laws of Manu) — The traditional and most revered Law book of ancient India. It is composed of 12 books. They deal with creation, transmigration, liberation, and give detailed instructions to all classes of men concerning their duties in life.

Yājñavalkya's Dharma-śāstra or smṛiti — This Law book is next in importance and is based on the 'Laws of Manu' but represents a more advanced stage in the definition and theory of its laws. This work deals with rules of conduct in regard to society and caste, with civil and criminal law and with penance.

Parāśara / Nārada — Two other famous law-givers and authors of Dharma-smṛitis or Law-books.

BHAKTIŚĀSTRAS — Scriptures of Religious Devotion.

Itihāsa — The two great epic-poems of India. (Itihāsa — iti+ha+āsa — so it was, i.e., history.)

Rāmāyaṇa by Vālmīki / **Rāma** / **Sītā** / **Hanumān** / **Rāvaṇa** — The great epic which narrates the adventures of Rāma, an Avatāra or incarnation of Vishṇu. It is composed of 48,000 lines of sixteen syllables, divided into seven books. The famed characters of this epic are Sītā, Rāma's wife, Hanumān, the great Monkey King who aids Rāma in his battle against Rāvaṇa, the Demon-King of Laṅkā, who stole Sītā. The poem is often called the 'Illiad of the East', because of its rich poetic beauty and ethical idealism. Because of its spirit of large and tender humanity it has an absolute and all-commanding sway and influence in India. It is said to be permeated with a "vision and faculty divine".

The great epic of the Bhāratas of 220,000 lines divided into 12 books. It is a great collection of poetry consisting of legen-

Mahābhārata by Vyāsa Kurus, Pāṇḍavas dary philosophical material worked into and around a central heroic narrative which portrays the struggles between the two Bhārata families: evil-minded Kurus and the virtuous Pāṇḍavas.

The glorious purpose of this epic is to unite one with Truth and hence it is said to be "sin-clearing and virtue-increasing".

Bhagavad-Gītā A small portion of this epic is: The 'Lord's or Holy Song'. It is the immortal scripture containing in 18 chapters the spiritual law of action as revealed by Kṛishṇa, an Avatāra or incarnation of Vishṇu, to Arjuna, the best of Bhāratas. It has been called the 'universal spiritual song of humanity'.

Nala and Damayantī One of the well-known stories of the Mahā-bhārata from the Vana-parvan or 'forest book'.

Sāvitrī An epic gem of high poetic value from the third book of the Mahābhārata. It is the story of how Love conquers Death.

Yoga-Vāsishṭha by Vālmīki A poem of 32,000 ślokas of deep practical mysticism and lofty philosophical thought and literary beauty. It has been called the 'crest-jewel' of Vedānta works. It is the inner Spiritual Story of Rāma.

The Great Poems. In Kālidāsa poetry and drama attained its highest peak of perfection. He was one of the nine literary

Mahākāvyas Kālidāsa (c. 400 A.D.) 'gems' at the court of Vikramāditya. His two finest contributions are *Raghu-vaṁśa*, 'the Race of Raghu', which celebrates the ancestry and deeds of Rāma and consists of some 19 cantos; and *Kumāra-sambhava*, 'the Birth of the War-God' in 17 cantos. Other well-known poems of his are *Meghadūta*, the 'Cloud-messenger' and *Ritu-samhāra*, the 'Collection of Seasons'.

Famous poems from other writers are *Kirātārjunīya*, 'Combat between Arjuna and Kirāta 'in 18 cantos and *Naishadhīya*, 'the Life of Nala, king of Naishadha' by Śrī Harsha (c. 1200 A.D.) and *Gītagovinda* by Jayadeva which is a religious drama concerning Kṛishṇa, and the beautiful *Subhāshita-ratna-Bhandagara* by Bhartṛihari.

Nāṭakas   Dramas. The celebrated dramas of Kālidāsa were *Śakuntalā*, a mythological pastoral play in 7 acts; and *Vikramorvaśī*, the 'Valor-won Urvaśī' in 6 acts.

Other famous dramas are *Mṛichchhakaṭikā*, 'the Little Clay Cart' by Śudraka, *Mahāvīracharita*, 'Life of a Great Hero' and *Uttara-rāma-charita*, 'the Later Life of Rāma' by Bhavabhūti (c. 700 A.D.) and *Ratnāvalī*, 'the Pearl-necklace' and *Nāgānanda* or 'Joy of Serpents' by Śrī Harshadeva.

Some of the best prose Kāvyas are Bhaṭṭabāna's *Kādambarī* and *Harshacharita*.

BOOKS ON SOCIAL SCIENCES

Kāma-Sūtra by Vātsyāyana — A book on the science of Eugenics and Erotics.

Artha-śāstra by Kauṭilya — A book on the science of Polity, treating of economical life and politics.

Bṛihatsaṁhitā by Varāhamihira — A book of scientific information.

Ethical Scripture: that literature which deals with wise and moral behavior, with political wisdom, moral philosophy and **Nīti-Śāstra** precepts (*nī* — to lead, guide). The popular method of teaching in India has for ages been by means of allegory, fairy-tale, fable or legend.

Jātaka-Mālā 'Garland of Birth-Stories' being the stories of Buddha in his many lives on earth.

Pañcha-Tantra   'Five Books' of stories written for the training of young princes in discreet behavior.

Hitopadeśa   'Book of Good Counsel': a collection of animal tales giving good advice to princes (*hita-upadeśa* — good advice). Aesop derived many of his fables from this work. Other collections are *Vetālapañcaviṁśati*, 'A Demon's 25 Stories' and *Brihat-kathā-mañjarī* by Kshemendra or *Kathā-sarit-sāgara*, the 'Ocean of Rivers of Stories' by Somadeva.

VOCABULARY

SANSKRIT LITERATURE

Āgama

Aitareya-Upanishad

Āraṇyaka

Artha-śāstra
  by Kauṭilya

Ashtādhyāyī
  by Pāṇini

Atharva-Veda

Āyur-Veda

Bhagavad-Gītā

Bhāgavata-Purāṇa

Bhakti-Śāstra

Bhāshya

Brāhmaṇa

Brāhmaṇa-Purāṇas

Brihadāraṇyaka-Upanishad

Brihat-kathā-mañjarī
  by Kshemendra

Brihat-samhitā
  by Varāhamihira

Chhandas

Chhāndogya-Upanishad

Dhanur-Veda

Dharmaśāstra

Dharma-smriti

Dharma-sūtra

Gandharva-Veda

Gītagovinda
  by Jayadeva

Grihya-sūtra

Harshacharita
  by Bhaṭṭabāna

Hitopadeśa

Īśa-Upanishad

Itihāsa

Jātaka-Mālā

Jyotisha

Kādambarī
  by Bhaṭṭabāna

Kalpa-sūtra

Kāma-sūtra
  by Vātsyāyana

Kathā-sarit-sāgara
  by Somadeva

Kaṭha-Upanishad

Kaushitaki-Upanishad

Kāvya

Kenopanishad

Kirātārjunīya
 by Śrī Harsha
Kumāra-Sambhava
 by Kālidāsa
Lakshaṇa
Mahābhārata by Vyāsa
Mahākāvya
Mahāvīracharita
 by Bhavabhūti
Mānava-dharma-śāstra
Māṇḍukya-Upanishad
Mantra
Meghadūta
 by Kālidāsa
Mṛichchhakaṭikā
 by Śūdraka
Muṇḍaka-Upanishad
Nāgānanda
 by Śrī Harshadeva
Naishadhīya
 by Śrī Harsha
Nāṭaka
Nirukta
Nīti-Śāstra
Pāñcharātra Āgama
Pañcha-Tantra
Praśna-Upanishad
Purāṇa
Raghu-vaṃśa
 by Kālidāsa
Rāmāyaṇa by Vālmīki
Ratnāvalī
 by Śrī Harshadeva
Ṛig-veda
Rich (Ṛik, Ṛig)
Ṛitu-saṃhāra
 by Kālidāsa

Śaiva-Āgama
Śaiva-Purāṇa
Śākta-āgama
Śakuntalā
 by Kālidāsa
Sāma-Veda
Śastra-Śāstra
Śatapatha-Brāhmaṇa
Sāvitrī
Śikshā
Śilpa-Śāstra
Smārta-Sūtra
Smṛiti
Śrauta-Sūtra
Śruti
Sthala-Purāṇa
Sthāpatya-Veda
Subhāshita-ratna bhandagara
 by Bhartṛihari
Sūkta
Sūtra
Śvetāśvatara-Upanishad
Taittirīya-Upanishad
Tantra
Tāntrika
Upa-Purāṇa
Upanishad
Upa-Veda
Uttara-Rāma-charita
 by Bhavabhūti
Vaishṇava Āgama
Vaishṇava-Purāṇa
Vedāṅga
Veda-Saṃhitā
Vetālpañchaviṃśati
 by Kshemendra

Vikramorvaśī
 by Kālidāsa
Vishṇu-Purāṇa

Vyāvakaraṇa
Yajur-Veda
Yoga-Vāsishṭha (Vālmīki)

FAMOUS NAMES & AUTHORS

Brahmā
Bhaṭṭabāna
Bhartṛihari
Bhavabhūti
Damayantī
Hanumān
Harshadeva (Śrī Harsha)
Jayadeva
Kālidāsa
Kshemendra
Kauṭilya
Kṛishṇa
Kuru
Manu
Nala

Nārada
Pāṇḍava
Pāṇini
Parāśara
Rāma
Rāvaṇa
Śaṅkara
Sītā
Śiva
Śūdraka
Vālmīki
Vishṇu
Vyāsa
Yājñavalkya
Yāska

CHAPTER VII

UPANISHADS — PHILOSOPHICAL AND RELIGIOUS TERMS

Tat A neuter pronoun meaning 'that'. The Upanishadic sages often used *Tat* to express the Infinite, Indescribable, Transcendent Divine, the Unutterable Boundless Principle from which all in the Cosmos sprang. They felt that no adjectives could truly describe It.

Idam A neuter pronoun meaning 'this'. *Idam* was used to express God as this manifested Universe in contradistinction to *Tat* as the Super-Spirit.

Sah
Īśa
Īśvara
Purusha
Aham Sah
So'ham
So'ham asmi
Hamsa

A masculine pronoun meaning 'that' or 'he'. Sages use *Sah* (So) to express the Universal Person or Spirit, the Cosmic Lord known as *Īśa*, *Īśvara* or *Purusha*. One of the well-known mantras of the Īśa Upanishad is "Aham Sah", "So'ham" or "So'ham asmi" meaning "He I am", thus implying that the Self of man and the Self of the Universe are one. *Hamsa* is the 'swan'. The swan is used as a symbol of the Universal and the Individual Spirit. *Hamsa* is derived from the saying "Aham Sah", "I am He", the Universal Person. (Here in *Hamsa*, the first and the last letters of the mantra have been omitted.) Thus in this word is hidden the oneness of God and man, also the purity and whiteness of the Spirit as well as its migratory nature as it embodies form after form in order to express more and more of its divine potentialities.

Ekatva Oneness, one-pointedness. (*Eka* — one; *tva* — ness) *Ekatva* is a quality which makes one see the Self or the Divine in all existences in the Self and all as the Self.

Immortality (*a* — not; *mṛi* — to die). In the Upanishads im-

Amṛita — mortality does not only imply soul-survival, but that condition of Self-consciousness which is free from all limits and bondage, free from all pairs of opposites, such as knowledge and ignorance, life and death. It is a state of Absolute Being, of Consciousness-Power-Bliss, a continuity of Self-Consciousness of Soul-life from one life to another. A human can attain *amṛita* when living in a superconsciousness above relativities, liberated while existing in a physical instrument or body made perfect.

Prabhu — 'Lord' of the Universe, the Cosmic Person (*pra* — forth; *bhū* — to become; hence, to appear, to rule).

Manu — The mental being in a terrestrial body. The four eternal *Manus* are fathers of man's mental being (*man* — to think).

Kavi — A poet; a seer or hearer of the Truth, one gifted with insight, who reveals some highest light in forms of ideas and words (*kū* — to sound).

Yati — A striver after truth; an ascetic (*yat* — to strive).

Dhātṛi or Dhātā — A Creator, establisher, a divine being who personifies creative or ordaining functions (*dhā* — to create, execute).

Dīkshā — Initiation, dedication, consecration for some religious purpose (*dīksh* — to consecrate; *dīksh* is the desiderative or wishing form of the verb *daksh* — to grow, to increase).

Tīrtha — A place of pilgrimage; usually a holy place on some river-bank or mountain where some sage has lived or died. The Ganges (*Gaṅgā*) is such a *tīrtha* (*tṛī* — to cross over, fulfil).

Anushṭhāna — Religious exercise (*sthā* — to stand and prefix; *anu* — after; hence to follow out).

Āvṛitti	Repetition (*ā* — toward, back to; *vṛit* — to turn hence to repeat).
Jñāna	Wisdom; inspired and direct knowledge which comes from spiritual insight. It is more than the intellectual knowledge or reasoned philosophy (*jñā* — to know).
Jñānin or Jñānī	A knower of Divine Truth.
Ajñāna	Nescience, lack of the understanding of the spiritual laws and wisdom.

Neti, Neti   "Not thus, not thus" (*na* — not; *iti* — thus). This phrase covers the Vedāntic teaching that the Transcendent Divine or God cannot be described in human terms but only explained somewhat by the negatives of various descriptive words. No conceived knowledge can explain It.

Madgu	The Water-bird, symbol of Life or Prāṇa, the Life-giving principle (*majj* — to sink in water).
Manīshin	The Thinker; Man in the mental state (*man* — to think).
Antaryāmin	The Inner Guide, the Divine Person within each man who is moulding him into the Divine Image (*antar* — within; *yāmin* — guide).

Jivātman   The Spirit or individual Self in living creatures (*jīva* — life; *ātman* — self). The *Jīvātman* is a portion of the Divine supporting individual existence in Nature. It does not evolve, but presides over manifested existence. It is Sri Aurobindo's 'Central Being'. In other words it represents the 'multiple divine' in manifestation.

Antarātman   The Inner Self, the Soul, the God-spark, which is a conscious form or projection of the *Jīvātman* (*antar* — within; *ātman* — self). It is that which is evolving in expression in human life, which gathers the essence of all experience and develops soul-perception and brings about in time God-realisation. *Antarātman* is the *Jīvātman* entering birth. It is the 'Psychic Being of Man' according to Sri Aurobindo.

Another name for Soul, Nature in evolution, or the Psychic Being considered as the 'Person of Divine Consciousness in Man' which aspires and opens the nature to Divine Truth (*chaitya* — consciousness; from *chit* — to think; and *purusha* — person). The *Chaitya-Purusha* unifies embodied existence.

Chaitya-Purusha

The subtle inner instrument of man's being, the inner mind, life and voice or power of expression; the conscience (*antar* — within; *karana* — acting).

Antaḥkaraṇa or Antaskaraṇa

In the Kaṭha Upanishad there are two paths open to the disciples: the *preyas* or dearer and pleasanter, and the *śreyas* or better and more blessed (*preyas* — comparative form of *priya* — dear; *śreyas* — comparative form of *śrī* — blessed).

Preyas
Śreyas

The 'taste' or essential delight-giving quality of all experience; also the juice or sap; the essence of things that gives enjoyable response. The expression of *ānanda* or the bliss of higher consciousness (*ras* — to feel, be sensible of).

Rasa

Truth in action; universal truth proceeding directly and un-reformed out of the infinite. *Ṛita* is the working out of the *Satya* or Reality or 'that which IS' *Ṛita* is also the *Dharma* of the later language of religion, hence the 'Right or Divine Law', or 'sacred action' (*ṛi* — to rise, tend upward).

Ṛita
Satya

The five life-breaths or forces that work in our vital and nervous being. The five *Prāṇas* are *Prāṇa, Vyāna, Samāna, Apāna,* and *Udāna.* The *Prāṇa* is the supreme breath, the pure life-force itself. It controls our breathing, and enables us to draw in the universal Life-forces

Prāṇas
(Aśva)

into our physical being and cast out through the breath certain gases which are destructive to the body (*pra* — forth; *an* — to breathe). The Vedas portrayed this breath as a 'Horse', *Aśva*, whose various energies are depicted as the chariots of the Gods.

The life-breath which governs the circulations in the body, and hence is that which separates and disintegrates, and resists

Vyāna the destructive elements that are ever at work, and keeps the body in shape (*vi* — apart; *ā* — towards; *an* — to breathe).

The life-breath which controls digestion and assimilation, and hence is that which carries on the chemical processes and

Samāna keeps the equilibrium in the body (*sama* — equal; *an* — to breathe).

Apāna The life-breath which casts out of the human system all that is waste material, the death-force of the lower part of the body (*apa* — away; *an* — to breathe).

The life-breath which directs the vital currents of the body upward to their sources, to the higher centers of their being, the

Udāna breath of death in the upper part of the body, the vital current or upbreath which aids in spiritual development, the channel of communication between the physical and spiritual parts of one's being (*ud* — up; *ā* — toward; *an* — to breathe).

Kośa is a sheath, a vessel (*kush* — to enfold). The Upanishads divide man into *Ātman*, the Divine Self and its five *Puru-*

Kośa

Annamayakośa

Annamaya-purusha

Prāṇamayakośa

Prāṇamaya-purusha

Manomayakośa

Manomaya-purusha

shas or spirits and their five *Kośas*. The *Ātman* or Divine Self envelops itself in the physical body or *Annamayakośa*, 'sheath built of food' (*anna* — food, matter; *maya* — formed) and becomes the *Annamayapurusha*, the material consciousness or the physical Person. The *Ātman* envelops itself in the vital and nervous part of man's being or *Prāṇamayakośa*, 'the sheath built of life-force' (*prāṇa* — breath; *maya* — formed) and becomes the vital and nervous con-

Vijñānamaya-
kośa
Vijñānamaya-
Purusha or
Mahadātman
Ānandamaya-
kośa
Ānandamaya-
purusha
Ānanda

sciousness or Person or the *Prāṇamayapurusha*. The *Ātman* embodies itself in the mental part of man or the *Manomayakosa*, 'the sheath built of mind' (*manas* or *mano* — mind; *maya* — formed) and becomes the mental consciousness or mental Person, the *Manomayapurusha*. The *Ātman* embodies itself in the supra-intellectual or the truth-conscious part of man or the *Vijñānamayakosa* or 'sheath built of discrimination or Wisdom' (*vijñāna* — supermind, truth-consciousness; *maya* — formed) and becomes the Supermental or Truth-conscious Person the *Vijñānamayapurusha* or *Mahadātman* (*mahat* — vast; *ātman* — self). The *Ātman* envelops itself in that part of a human being enjoying the state of infinite beatitude or the *Ānandamayakosa* (*ānanda* — bliss; *maya* — formed) and becomes the *Ānandamayapurusha* or the Blissful Person.

Above these five sheaths and their consciousnesses are:

The *Ātman* in a state of infinite divine self-awareness is in the sheath built of *Chit* or divine consciousness, the *Chidmayakosa* and becomes the *Chaitanya Purusha* or the Person of Absolute Consciousness. *Chit-Tapas* (*tap* — to burn) is divine

Chidmayakosa
Chaitanya
Purusha
Chit-Tapas
Sat
Sadmayakosa
Sat Purusha
Sachchidānanda

self-awareness and infinite all-effective Will, the sheath of *Chaitanya Purusha*. The *Ātman* in its pure divine state exists in the sheath built of Reality or *Sat*, the *Sadmayakosa*, and becomes the *Sat Purusha* or the Pure Divine Person. Hence the Divine is described as *Sachchidānanda* (*sat-chit-ānanda*).

Thus in the Upanishads is portrayed the sevenfold ladder of the evolutionary growth of the soul as it rises in spiritual attainment towards the infinite expression of its innate divine qualities. The Supreme Being or Brahman becomes in manifestation *anna-prāṇa-mano-vijñāna-ānanda-chit-sat* or the physical-vital-mental-truth-consciousness-blissful-conscious-force Reality.

The *Ātman* or Divine Self within man expresses itself in the Ānandamayakośa or Bliss-sheath, also considered as the *Kāraṇa Śarīra* or Causal body (*kāraṇa* — cause; *śarīra* — body). The Vijñānamayakośa, Mano-mayakośa, and the Prāṇamayakośa are often given the general name of *Sūkshma Śarīra* or Subtle Body (*sūkshma* — subtle, fine) or *Linga Śarīra* or Astral Body (*linga* — sign, model). The Annamayakośa or Physical Body is called the *Sthūla Śarīra* or the Gross Body. These three bodies are also spoken of in the Tāraka Rāja Yoga schools as *Upādhis* or bases and called *Kāraṇopādhi*, *Sūkshmopādhi*, and *Sthūlopādhi*, the causal, subtle, and physical bases of Ātman or Self.

Kāraṇa Śarīra
Sūkshma Śarīra
Linga Śarīra
Sthūla Śarīra
Upādhi
Kāraṇopādhi
Sūkshmopādhi
Sthūlopādhi

Avasthā is a state of consciousness (*ava* — down; *sthā* — stand). There are four *Avasthās*: Jāgrat, Svapna, Sushupti and Turīya. *Jāgrat* is the waking state or that condition of consciousness in which man normally acts when awake (*jāgṛi* — to be awake). It is the consciousness of the outer intelligence which enjoys external things, a state in which the senses and mind are turned without. *Svapna* is the sleeping-dreaming state or that condition of consciousness which the inner intelligence experiences during sleep, after death or in reverie, a state wherein things subtle are perceived (*svap* — to sleep or dream). *Sushupti* is the deep-sleeping state, a state of utter self-oblivion and utter unconsciousness for the human ego, but a conscious state for the soul and higher intelligence. The reaches of this state are so spiritual and vast that the limited brain-mind cannot hold or record the experiences (*sushup* is the intensive form of the verb *svap* — to sleep). *Turīya* is the fourth state of consciousness, the pure divine-spiritual conscious at-one-with God (*chatur* — four). It is a self-conscious state which may be experienced by one either in trance or in deep spiritual meditation, sometimes called *Samādhi*. *Samādhi* is a spiritual self-aware consciousness at-

Avasthā
Jāgrat
Svapna
Sushupti
Turīya
Samādhi

one-with Spirit (*sam* — together; *ādhā* — to direct to, here implying 'uniting'). These four states correspond to the physical, mental, causal and divine worlds.

Kośa	*Upādhi*	*Śarīra*	*Avasthā*
Annamayakośa	Sthūlopādhi	Sthūla Śarīra	Jāgrat
Prāṇamayakośa Manomayakośa	Sūkshmopādhi	Sūkshma Śarīra	Svapna
Vijñānamayakośa Ānandamayakośa	Kāraṇopādhi	Kāraṇa Śarīra	Sushupti
Chidmayakośa Sadmayakośa	Ātman	Ātma	Turīya (Samādhi)

There are various divisions of man given in the different philosophical schools and in the Upanishad. Below are some:

Paramātman — The Self Beyond, God, the Divine, Brahman (*parama* — beyond; *ātman* — self).

Ātman — The highest Self, one with Brahman and all other selves (*at* — to breathe).

Jīvātman — The Spiritual Self which presides over the evolution of the soul. "Jīvātman is one the Divine Many and dependent on the One; the Ātman is the One supporting the Many" (Sri Aurobindo). (*Jīva* — life; *ātman* — self.)

Bhūtātman — The Remembering Self, the Self that has been (*bhūta* — has been; *ātman* — self).

Prāṇātman — Personal Self, the Self of Vitality (*prāṇa* — life, breath; *ātman* — self).

Sthūlātman — The Gross Self, the Self of the Body (*sthūla* — gross; *ātman* — self).

Sūtrātman — The Thread-Self, the mystic golden thread of consciousness that binds all the Selves in the human being with Brahman, the Divine (*sūtra* — string; *ātman* — self).

Bahirātman   The outer Self (*bahir* — outside; *ātman* — self).

Planes	*Ātman*
Physical	Sthūlātman (Gross Self, the physical body)
Subtle and Mental	Prāṇātman (Personal Self, Self of Vitality)
Causative	Bhūtātman (the Self that has been)
Spiritual	Jīvātman (Spiritual Self)
Divine	Ātman (Divine Self)
Plane Beyond Human	Paramātman (Brahman)

CHAKRAS

The seven Chakras (*chakra* — wheel, nodus, plexus, center) are the seven psychological centers in the subtle body. Various faculties and divinities are said to be present in these centers. The seven Chakras are:

1. Sahasradala or Sahasrāra-chakra or padma: the thousand-petalled lotus on top of the head; the higher consciousness center, that which centralizes spiritual mind, higher mind, intuitive mind and acts as a receiving station for the intuition proper and overmind. This center links the brain with greater mind-planes above.

2. Ājñā-chakra or padma: the center of will, inner mind, occult vision, dynamic thought in the middle of the forehead.

3. Anāhata-chakra or Hṛitpadma: the heart-center, the emotional center. The psychic or soul is behind it.

4. Viśuddhi-chakra: the throat center, center of expressive externalizing mind or outward-going mind.

5. Maṇipura-chakra or padma or Nābhipadma-chakra: the psychological center at the navel; the main seat of the

dynamic vital consciousness whose range is from heart level to the center below the navel; the center of the higher vital commanding the larger life-forces, passions and desire-movements.

6. Svādhishṭhāna-chakra: the center in the abdomen below the navel; the center of the lower vital commanding the smaller vital movements of greed, lust and sense.

7. Mūlādhāra-chakra: the center at the bottom of the spine, the physical center, the sex-center, and subconscient center.

LOKAS

A Loka is a state of light and a soul's expansion; a heaven. The Godhead has built this universe in a complex system of worlds which we find both within us and without, subjectively cognized and objectively sensed. It is a rising tier of earths and heavens; it is a stream of diverse waters; it is a Light of seven rays, or of eight or nine or of ten; it is a Hill of many plateaus. The seers often image it in a series of trios; there are three earths and three heavens. More, there is a triple world below, Heaven, Earth, and the intervening Mid-region; a triple world between, the shining heavens of the Sun, a triple world above, the supreme and rapturous abodes of the Godhead.

Bhūrloka The material world; the body and material living are man's earth-world (*bhū* — earth).

The world of various becoming; the vitalistic existence of emotion, passions, affections, of which desire is the pivot; it forms the mid-world of man. The vital or nervous
Bhuvarloka plane is just above our material earth; through it the gods come to commune with man, but it is a confused wideness and its paths are many but intricate and tangled (*bhū* — to become).

Svarloka The world of light; pure thought and feeling and pure psychic state are man's sky, his heaven.

Steadfast purity and clarity of high mental existence (*svar* — heaven).

The world of vastness; the home of the Gods is an absolute Truth which lives in solar glories beyond mind. Man ascending
Maharloka
thither strives no longer as the thinker but is victoriously the seer. His will, life, thought, emotion, sense, acts are all transformed into values of (*mahas* — vastness) an all-puissant Truth and remain no longer an embarrassed or a helpless tangle of mixed truth. He moves in the ranges of the unobstructed Vast; feeds no longer on broken fragments, but is suckled by the tears of Infinity.

Janaloka
Janarloka
The world of creative delight of existence, the world of great gods (*jan* — to be born, hence Spiritual birth).

Taparloka
Tapoloka
The world of infinite Will or conscious Force (*tapas* — spiritual force).

Satyaloka
The world of the highest truth of being (*satya* — truth).

The aspiring material creature becomes the straining vital man; he in turn transmutes himself into the subtle mental and psychical being; this subtle thinker grows into the wide, multiple and cosmic man open on all sides of him to all the multitudinous inflowings of the Truth; the cosmic soul rising in attainment strives as the spiritual man for a higher peace, joy and harmony; from then in the Bliss towards infinite Consciousness of Absolute Being, to the transcendental harmony of them all. In Vedāntic and Purāṇic systems the seven *Lokas* correspond to the seven psychological principles or forms of existence:

anna — bhūr	ānanda — janar
prāṇa — bhuvar	chit — tapas
manas — svar	sat — satya
vijñāna — mahar	

TALAS

A *Tala* is a state of darkness, self-obscuration and self-distortion. The seven *Talas* are the nether poles of the *Lokas*. They are the seven inferior states, sometimes called hells:

The nether pole of Satyaloka. Atala is of such ethereal matter that it is said to be *a* (-not) *tala* (-material world), to suggest
Atala   that it can scarcely be considered a material place, or state of spiritual annihilation.

The nether pole of Taparloka, meaning a change (*vi*) toward a *tala* or material state; hence Vitala is more of material or dark stuff. Vitala is a state in which the spiritual is
Vitala   darkened by the giving up of self-conscious effort or *tapas*.

The nether pole of Janarloka. Sutala is a *su* (-good) *tala* (-material place). Each lower *tala* becomes more substantial in its dark or material aspect and becomes a state
Sutala   where one becomes a slave of desire and passion.

The nether pole of Maharloka. It is a *rasa* (-sense) enjoyment *tala* (-place), the objective World of sense-enjoy-
Rasātala   ment.

The nether pole of Svarloka. *Tala-atala* implies a place not a place; hence not fully a material state, but almost, hence a sphere of almost wholly sense and outer objectives
Talātala   and indulgence.

                    The nether pole of Bhuvarloka. Mahātala is the
Mahātala   *mahā* (-great) *tala* (-place) or material or shadowy sphere or state of darkness where ego and selfishness rule.

The nether pole of Bhūrloka, our earth. It is the *pāta* (-sunken, fallen) *tala* (-place); a name for the subconscient; the beings there have 'no heads', that is to say, there
Pātāla   is no mental consciousness; men have, all of them, such a subconscient plane in their own being, and from there rise all sorts of irrational and ignorant (headless) instincts, im-

pulsions, memories, etc., which have an effect upon their acts and feelings without their detecting the real source. At night many incoherent dreams come from this world or plane.

Pṛithivī — Bhūrloka, physical earth.

Dyaus — Svarloka, the triple lower world of the Pure Mind, with its three heavens; the blue expanse of the heavens.

Dyāvāpṛithivī — Heaven and Earth deities (*dyaus* plus *pṛithivī*).

Rodasī — The two earths, Dyaus and Pṛithivī, the pure mental and physical consciousness; the two firmaments.

Tridhātu — The triple principle; heaven.

Antariksha — Bhuvarloka, the mid-region of life-force; the intermediate or connecting level of the vital and nervous consciousness.

Uttama
Madhyama — Higher, middle, and lower regions.
Adhama

Trishu
Tanushu — In the three levels or bodies (body, life, and mind), (*tri* — three, *tanu* — body).

TATTVA

Tattva is a true principle. *Tat* or *tad* meaning 'that' implies the essential being of anything; hence *tattva* is a 'that-ness', or the real being of anything. Each philosophy of India names a certain number of principles or *tattvas* as fundamentals to its system of thought.

In Vedānta *tattva* is regarded as a compound of *tad* and *tvam* 'that and you', and implying "That, the eternal Brahman or Divine (art) thou." In the Sāṅkhya philosophy there are 25 Tattvas, or fundamental principles: Avyakta, Buddhi, Ahaṁkāra, the five Tanmātras, the five Mahābhūtas, the five

Buddhīndriyas, the five Karmendriyas, Manas and Purusha.

Avyakta Mūlaprakṛiti The Unmanifest (*a* — not; *vi-añj* — to appear). The Unevloved (Evolver of all things); the primordial element whence all the phenomena of the material world are developed. Also called *Mūlaprakṛiti* or Root-Nature.

Buddhi The intellectual faculty (*budh* — to know). Perceptive choice.

Ahaṅkāra The conception of individuality, of ego, of self (*aham* — I; *kāra* — action).

Tanmātra The *Tanmātras* are the rudimentary or subtle elements (*tad* — that; *mā* — to measure). The five *Tanmātras* are:

The five Tanmātras: from which are derived the five Mahābhūtas or Pāñchabhautikas:

Śabda — Sound	Ākāśa — Ether
Sparśa — Touch	Vāyu — Air
Rūpa — Sight	Tejas — Fire
Rasa — Taste	Apas — Water
Gandha — Smell	Pṛithivī — Earth

The five *Jñānendriyāṇi* (or *Buddhīndriyāṇi*) are the five organs of perception or sense. An *indriya* is a force or power of *Indra*

Jñānendriya Buddhindriya (the god of the higher mind), hence any exhibition of power: a faculty of sense or an organ of sense (*jñāna* — knowledge; *indriya* — sense, organ of sense; *buddhi* — intellectual perception).

The five sense-organs are: Niyantṛi, ruler (*ni* — down; *yam* — control):

Śrotra — Ear	Diśaḥ — the Quarters of Space
Tvak — Skin	Vāyu — the Wind-God
Chakshus ⎫ Akshu ⎭ Eye	Āditya — the Sun-God

Jihvā — Tongue   Varuṇa — God of the Expanse
Ghrāṇa — Nose   Aśvins — Horsemen of the Sun

Karmendriya   The Karmendriyāṇi are organs of action
                  (*karma* — action; *indriya* — sense, organ).

The five organs of action are: Niyantṛi, ruler:

Vāch — Voice or larynx   Agni — the God of Fire,
                                    Divine Will

Pāṇi — Hand   Indra — the God of the
                                    Firmament, Mind

Pādas — Foot   Vishṇu — the All-Pervader
Pāyus — Anus, organ of   Mitra — the God of Harmony
        excretion
Upastha — Organ of   Prajāpati — the Lord of
          generation   Creation

Manas   The Mind.

Purusha   The Spirit, the Divine Person.

Bahirindriya   An external organ (*bahis* — external); a name
                 given to the organs of sense and the organs of
action generally.

Antarindriya   An internal organ (*antar* — internal, within); a
                 name given to the four *Antarindriyāṇi* which are:

Manas — The mind, or organ of thought (*man* — to think).

Buddhi — The intelligence, discrimination (*budh* — to know).

Ahaṁkāra — Egoism, consciousness of self (*aham* — I; *kāra*
— action).

Chitta — The storehouse of memory (*chit* — to think, cogi-
tate).

Antaḥkaraṇa   The internal organ of thought, feeling, and
Antaskaraṇa conscience (*antaḥ* — within; *karaṇa* — acting).

The function of the mind is to receive images of things translated into the five senses and then translated again into thought-

sensations. It also receives impressions from direct grasping of images.

Kalpa   A cycle of time (*kalp* — to be in order).

Kalā   A small part; 1/16 part (*kal* — to count).

YUGA — Age or Cycle

"God's *Līlā* in man moves always in a circle, from *Satyayuga* to *Kali* and through *Kali* to the *Satya*, from the Age of Gold to the Age of Iron and back again through the Iron to the Gold. In modern language the *Satyayuga* is a period of the world in which a harmony, stable and sufficient, is created and man realizes for a time, under certain conditions and limitations, the perfection of his being. The harmony exists in his nature by the force of a settled purity; but afterwards it begins to break down and man upholds it, in the *Tretā*, by force of will, individual and collective; it breaks down further and he attempts to uphold it in the *Dvāpara* by intellectual regulation and common consent and rule; then in the *Kali* it finally collapses and is destroyed. But the *Kali* is not merely evil; in it the necessary conditions are progressively built up for a new *Satya*, another harmony, a more advanced perfection. In the period of the *Kali* which has passed, still endures in its effects, but is now at an end, there has been a general destruction of the ancient knowledge and culture. Only a few fragments remain to us in the Vedas, Upanishads and other sacred works and in the world's confused tradition. But the time is at hand for a first movement upward, the first attempt to build up a new harmony and perfection. That is the reason why so many ideas are abroad for the perfection of human society, knowledge, religion and morals. But the true harmony has not yet been found."

— Sri Aurobindo

Satyayuga   The age of innocence, of innate goodness, the
Kṛitayuga   age when Dharma or Truth prevails (*satya* —
                   truth; *yuj* — to unite). Also called *Kṛitayuga* (*kṛita*

— perfect, well-done, past participle of *kri* — to do).

Tretāyuga   The age of only three-fourths of the truth. The material forces then begin to exert their opposing influence (*tretā* — three).

Dvāparayuga   The age of two parts or one-half of the truth. Material darkness increases and brings about a decline of spiritual powers (*dvāpara* — twofold).

The Dark-Age, the *Yuga* in which only one part of the truth prevails, because materiality and ignorance with their evil relations of selfishness and anger and indifference hold sway over men's hearts. We are now in the
Kaliyuga
Kaliyuga; this dark age commenced at the death of Krishna at midnight between February 17th and 18th in the year 3102 B.C. (*kal* — to incite, to impel).

Yugasandhyā   Age of the "evening or morning twilight".

Yugadharma   The true law of the age.

CHATUR ĀŚRAMA — THE FOUR STAGES OF LIFE

Āśrama	*Follower*	*Purushārtha*
Brahmacharya	Brahmachārin or Brahmachārī	Artha
Gārhasthya	Grihasthin or Grihasthī	Kāma
Vānaprastha	Vānaprasthin or Vānaprasthī	Dharma
Sannyāsa	Sannyāsin or Sannyāsī	Moksha

The four *āśramas* or "stages of life" were a graded order to aid in the working out of a complete life leading to spiri-
Āśrama
tual freedom. These four states of Life were:
Brahmacharya (1) *Brahmacharya* (*brahma* — divine; *charya* —
Gārhasthya going), the stage of the student, wherein all out-
Vānaprastha ward-going energies, sense enjoyments and emo-
Sannyāsa
tional reactions must be controlled so as to give
full power to the development and training of the inner and outer man; (2) *Gārhasthya* (*griha* — house; *sthā* — exist), the

stage of the householder or married man; (3) Vānaprastha (*vana* — wood; *pra-sthā* — go forth), the stage of the philosophical recluse and ascetic; (4) *Sannyāsa* (*sam* — wholly: *ni* — down; *as* — to throw), the state of the renunciation of worldly possessions. Each stage represented an increasing spirituality.

In the first stage the *Brahmachārin* devoted himself entirely to study and training not only in necessary arts, sciences, and branches of knowledge but in ethics and a grounding of the spiritual life as taught in the Vedas. This period prepared the student for the right working out of the four objects of life or *Purushārtha* (*purusha* — human; *artha* — object); *Artha* — wealth, *Kāma* — desire, *Dharma* — fulfilling the divine law, and *Moksha* — spiritual liberation.

Purushārtha
Artha
Kāma
Dharma
Moksha

In the second stage, a *Gṛihasthin* or one following the household life, lived out his acquired knowledge and served the three first objects of life: wealth, desire and the following of divine right and law. He married, had children and faithfully discharged his duties to family, community and society.

In the third stage, the *Vānaprasthin* or one following the retired life in the forest became free from attachment to social bonds in order that he might meditate on the higher things of the spirit and pass on the wisdom attained to those seeking guidance.

In the fourth and last stage, the *Sannyāsin*, or one who became a renunciate, freed himself of all his last remaining ties and wandered over the world in a spiritual detachment from all forms of social life and existed with the barest necessities, and deep within himself communed with the Universal Spirit, preparing for *Moksha* or Liberation and Unity with God. The *Sannyāsin* represented the crown of human life in Hindu religion. In later times the physical renunciation of outward ties of life became the sign of spirituality, rather than the inner freedom of non-attachment to whatever the circumstances of life might be. All these four stages were not obligatory on all.

Most people never went beyond the first two, some passed on into the third stage, and only a few took up the last ideal stage.

Tanu — Body, person.

Akshi — Thin, small.

Linga — A mark, sign, guise; also the male organ or phallus worshipped in the form of a stone or marble column and placed in temples dedicated to Śiva.

Vāha — Vehicle, carriage (*vah* — to carry).

Śarīra — One's body (*śri* — to waste away).

Mūrti — Substantial form or body (*murch* — to become solid).

Amūrta — Bodiless, immaterial (*a* — not; *murch* — to become solid, to congeal).

Pratishṭhā Ādhāra — Gross matter; earth; the south pole of being (*prati* — down, upon; *sthā* — to stand; to rest upon, to be established). Receptacle, support; the three basic principles of man, body, life, and mind, taken as a whole as a vehicle for the human soul (*ā-dhṛi* — to support).

Viś — A house, also a tribe or people (*viś* — to enter).

Vināśa — Destruction, annihilation (*vi-naś* — to perish, destroy).

Sṛishṭi — Creation or self-production (*sṛij* — to let go, to release, emit).

Sambhūti — Birth, origin, production (*sam-bhū* — to come together, be produced).

Bhāva — Existence, state of being or becoming (*bhū* — to be, become).

Sambhāva — Birth.

Asambhāva — Non-birth (*sambhū* — to be produced).

Āyus — Life, vital power (*i* — to go).

Aṇḍaja   Egg-born.

Jāraja   Womb-born.

Svedaja   Sweat-born.

Udbhijja   Sprout-born.

Bīja   Seed, origin.

Vikāra   Change of form (*vi* — apart; *kri* — to make).

Āropa   Superimposition, causing to rise (*ā* — to, toward; causative form of *ruḥ* — to rise up).

The mystic utterances preceding the Gāyatrī verse from the Ṛig-Veda: bhūr, bhuvaḥ, svaḥ — earth, mid-world (vital world), heaven-world (world of mind) (*vi-ā-hṛi* — to utter, speak).

Vyāhṛiti

The up-singing, the circling upwards of the voice or Soul in Song; to chant the Sāma-Veda; one's aspiration upwards. Also a name for the sacred syllable Om or *a-u-m*, the expressed aspiration of the soul rising to the Gods and to Brahman, the Divine (*ud-gai* — to sing, chant).

Udgītā

Jyoti   Spiritual Light (*jyut* — to light). The light of Supermind.

Prakāśa   Light of mind (*kās+pra* — to shine forth).

Jyotiṁshi   Stars.

Akshara   The Undying, a name for the syllable Om, which is symbolic of Brahman, the unchanging Reality, where sound is in its pure, undifferentiated state.

Praṇava   The mystical or sacred syllable Om (*pra-ṇu* — to reverberate).

Om   The sound aspect or living symbol of Brahman, the Divine.

Nādabrahman   The Sound of Brahman (*nad* — to sound).

"The principle of *Adhyātma-Yoga* (*adhi* — supreme; *ātman*
— self) is, in knowledge, the realization of all things that we see
Adhyātma-   or do not see but are aware of — men, things, our-
Yoga   selves, events, gods, titans, angels — as one divine
Parātpara   Brahman, and in action and attitude, an absolute
self-surrender to the *Parātpara*, the transcendent, infinite and
universal personality who is at once personal and impersonal,
finite and infinite, self-limiting and illimitable, one and many,
and informs with His being not only the Gods above, but man
and the worm and the clod below".   (Sri Aurobindo)

Paramārtha   The highest purpose or goal; the essential truth
              (*parama* — highest; *artha* — purpose).

Vyavahāra   Common life or practice; the usual, the real or
              practical or illusory, as opposed to the ideal or
paramārtha (*vi* — apart; *ava* — down; *hri* — to take).

Sacrifice performed at the coronation of a king. Its religious
symbolism implied the fulfilling of the royal and religious ideals
Rājasūya   of one who is the leader and protector of his people
              (*rāja* — king; *sū* — to create, bestow, authorize).

Aśvamedha   Horse-sacrifice, the offering of the horse, sym-
              bolic of the vital and energic nature of man (*aśva*
— horse; *medha* — sacrifice).

That portion of one's past action which is found to fructify
in the present life and cannot be averted (*pra* — before; *rabh*
              — begin). It is ripe for reaping. It cannot be
Prārabdha   avoided or changed. Grace of Guru is when to-
Karma   gether with His instructions the Guru bestows the
gether with His instructions the Guru bestows the
capacity to translate them into action, this is His Grace. But it
cannot enter because the receptacle is turned upside down.
When one becomes receptive one is able to receive Grace.

Sañchita   Accumulated works (*sam* — together; *chit* —
Karma   thought, conscience).

Kriyamāna   That action which is now being made for fruition
Karma   in the future (present participle of *kri* — to act, do).

Ādeśa   Command (*ā* — toward; *diś* — to show; hence, to command).

Jugupsā   "The shrinking of the limited being from that which is not himself and not sympathetic or in harmony with himself, its impulse of self-defence against 'others' " — Sri Aurobindo (from wishing form of root *gup* — to hide).

Siddhi   An occult faculty (*sidh* — to attain).

Āgamī Karma   Coming action (*gam*+*ā* — to come).

Vartamāna Karma   Turning, unfolding action (*vṛit* — to turn).

Ārādhanā   Worship of the Divine, love, self-surrender, aspiration for the Divine, a calling of the Name of God, prayer to God, adoration (*ā* — toward; *rādh* — to propitiate, worship).

Sādhanā
Tapasya
Dhyāna   "*Sādhanā* is practice of yoga. *Tapasya* is the concentration of the will to get the results of *sādhanā* and to conquer the lower nature. *Ārādhanā* is worship of the Divine, love, self-surrender, aspiration to the Divine, calling the name, prayer. *Dhyāna* is inner concentration, meditation, going inside in Samādhi. *Dhyāna*, Tapasya and Ārādhanā are all parts of *sādhanā*" (Sri Aurobindo).

Granthi   Knot. In metaphysics the *Granthis* are the entanglements of subtle nerve force in the psycho-physical nature of man that block the free flow of the spiritual forces in man's being. These knots formed by our ties to the lower separative elements of our nature, resulting in desire, passion, selfishness, etc., can only be loosened by various spiritual disciplines (*grath* — to string together).

Kha   Sky, space; also any aperture in the body (*khan* — to dig, excavate).

Ukti   Word, speech (*vach* — to speak).

Sanskritokti   The Sanskrit language (*samskrita-ukti*).

Dhī   Thought, especially religious thought, reflection, memory, creative intellectual force (*dhī* — to reflect, think).

Chetas   Consciousness, intelligence, thinking soul (causative of *chit* — to think; to cause to think, to be conscious of, understand, reflect).

Chintā   Thought, care, anxiety (*chit* — to think).

Medhā   Mental Vigor, grasping power of mind; wisdom (*midh* — to understand, unite).

Mati   Opinion, notion, belief. In earlier Vedic time *mati* implied devotion, prayer, and worship (*man* — to think, believe).

Kratu   Will, the effective power behind action, the energy of consciousness directed through mind. *Kratu* may be said to be 'mental will' plus Agni or 'divine will' (*kri* — to do).

Tarka   Reasoning, conjecture, speculation, inquiry; a philosophical system of thought (*tark* — to reason, conjecture).

Kāraṇa   Cause. In metaphysics, the Spirit or Brahman, the 'northpole of being' (causative form of *kri* — to make; to cause to make).

Brahmopāsanā
Upāsana
Upāsaka
Upāsikā   Brahma-upāsanā or Worship of Brahma or the Divine. *Upāsana* is worship or adoration or homage to God or one of his aspects or manifestations. One who so worships is an Upāsaka (masculine) or *Upāsikā* (feminine) (*upa-sad* — to sit near, to honor).

Dakshiṇa   Right; southern (as being on right side of person facing east); the right-hand or higher doctrine. Also a sacrificial gift (*daksh* — to be strong, able).

Sannyāsa-Yoga   The Yoga of renunciation; or that union with God that is brought about by renunciation (*sam-ni-as* — throw down or aside completely).

Sāmya   Identity.

Kevala   Absolute, only, alone, uncompounded. *Kevala* is descriptive of the Vedāntic doctrine of Śaṅkara which believes God as absolutely One with no Second.

Kevalatva   Absolute unity.

Kṛitātman   A perfected soul (*kṛita* — perfect, done; *ātman* — self).

Dharmakārya   The work of Dharma, or Truth in action (*dharma* — truth, right; *kārya* — action).

Ātma-śakti   The power of Ātman or the Divine in Man (*Ātman* — divine self; *śakti* — power).

Ātmarati   The *Rati* or peaceful joy of Ātman or the Divine in Man (*ram* — to delight in).

Dhātu-prasāda   The peace and grace that comes from within or as a result of purification of the root of one's being, that is of one's mind and other inner instruments (*dhātu* — root; *prasad* — to give blessing, grace).

Prajñā   Wisdom, foreknowledge, universal intelligence (*prajñā* — to foreknow, to be wise).

Satyakāma   Desire for Truth (*satya* — truth; *kām* — to desire).

Satyadharma   The law of Truth (*satya* — truth; *dharma* — law, right).

Sattva-Śuddhi   Purification of the essence or inner instruments of one's being (*sattva* — essence; *śudh* — to purify).

Smṛiti-Śuddhi   Purity of remembrance which is an immediate awareness of what one is seeking or meditating on (*smṛi* — to remember).

Śāstrī A teacher, also a punisher (*śās* — to teach, to punish).

Pravrajya A mendicant, wandering ascetic (*pra* — forth; *vraj* — to go).

Paramahaṁsa An ascetic of the highest order who has subdued all his senses by abstract meditation (*haṁsa* — swan; *parama* — beyond).

Satsaṅga The company of the good (*sat* — the good; *saṅga* — company, meeting).

Dṛishṭi Inner sight, vision, truth ideation (*dṛiś* — to perceive, see).

Karuṇā Compassion (*kṛī* — to pour out, scatter).

Śraddhavan Having faith (*śrat* — faith).

Dama Self-control (*dam* — to subdue, conquer).

Svasti / Svastu Well-being, success. Svastu, a term of salutation, such as "Hail!", "Health!", "May it be well with thee!" (*su* — well; *astu* — may be).

Viveka Right judgement, discrimination, the power of separating Spiritual and material values, truth from untruth, reality from illusion (*vi-vich* — to distinguish, divide asunder).

Smara Memory (*smṛi* — to remember).

Āśā Hope (*ā-śaṁs* — to hope, wish).

Bala Strength, force, vigor (*bal* — to breathe, live).

Śama Tranquility (*śam* — to be quiet).

Samarpaṇa Surrender to God (causative form of *ṛi* plus *sam* — to join together, to deliver).

Yaśas Glory, beautiful appearance.

Vidhi Law, rule, injunction (*vi-dhā* — to arrange, put in order).

Puṇya — Meritorious, virtuous (*puṇ* — to act piously).

Śānta — Peaceful, quiet (*śam* — to be quiet, peaceful).

Divya — Divine (*div* — to shine).

Saṁkalpa — Determination, intention, conception (*sam* — completely, implying perfection; *klṛip* — to be in order, come into existence; therefore, to determine).

Svātantrya — Following one's will, freedom of will, independence (*sva* — own; *tantra* — rule).

Ātmavīrya — The strength of the Self.

Svārājya — Self-rule, independent rule (*sva* — self; *rāj* — rule).

Nirvṛitatva — Peacefulness (*nir* — without; *vṛit* — to turn).

Anīś — Not a Lord; Man who is not free, but subject to ignorance (*a* — not; *īś* — to rule).

Enas — Evil.

Pāpa — Sin, evil.

Pāpman — Evil, misfortune.

Maraṇa — Dying (*mṛi* — to die).

Śoka — Sorrow (*śuch* — to bewail, lament).

Moha — Delusion (*muh* — to deceive, delude).

Rāga — Passion (*raj* — to burn).

Vīta-rāga — Passion-free (*vi-i* — to go away; *rāga* — passion).

Śukra — Clearness, brightness; the essence or seed of anything; semen, sperm (*śuch* — to shine).

Lakshya — A mark; that which is to be characterized; observable (*laksh* — to observe).

Pratikṛiti — An image, anything made after an original (*prati* — back; *kṛi* — to make).

Asura
: The controlled and intellectualized but unregenerated Ego (*a* — not; *sura* — god).

Rākshasa
: The violent kinetic Ego; a name given to Rāvana, the Demon-King of Lankā, the opponent of Rāma. Also a name applied to the demon-like people of Lankā of the epic poem, the Rāmāyana. These people of the earlier times had received the name Protectors (*raksh* — to protect) because of some service rendered to the God Brahmā.

Samskāra
: The *Samskāras* are old associations stored in the memory of the race and the individual; formed habits; mental impressions and recollections (*sams-kri* — to put together).

Vidyut
: Lightning (*vi-dyut* — to flash forth, lighten).

Adhibhūta
: The spiritual or fine substrata of material elements.

Ādhibhautika
: Adjectival form (*adhi* — above, over; *bhū* — to become).

Adhideva
: A presiding deity or divine agent operating in the material elements (*adhi* — above, over; *deva* — god).

Ādhidaiva or Ādhidaivika
: Adjectival form of *Adhideva*.

Adhyātman
: The Supreme Self (ātman) or spiritual state of being.

Ādhyātmika
: Adjectival form of *Adhyātman*.

Āhāra
: Food, "what is brought near"; also, sense-objective (*ā-hri* — to bring near).

Āhāra-śuddhi
: Purity of sense-contacts or purity of food (*śudh* — to purify).

Chitta-śuddhi
: Purification of mental and moral habits, of memories stored within (*chitta* — memory, recollections; *śudh* — to purify).

Nāḍī-śuddhi — Nerve purification (*nāḍī* — nerve).

Nāḍī — A tubular or reed-like organ, such as a vein, artery or nerve; a pipe.

Sarvāṇī bhūtāni — All Beings; the plural form of sarva-bhūta, every being.

Medhā — Mental vigor, grasping power of mind, wisdom (*midh* — to understand).

There are four necessary functions of the mind which are basic in all conscious action. *Vijñāna* is the comprehensive spiritual perception which holds an image of things in its essence and totality; supramental perception (*vi-jñā* — to discern). *Prajñāna* is the outgoing apprehensive consciousness which perceives the proper relation of things to each other (*prajñā* — to be wise). *Saṃjñāna* is the essential sense-faculty of the mind which makes the contact with an image; the inbringing apprehensive consciousness which brings about the feeling of the object (*sam-jñā* — to know with, be in harmony with). *Ājñāna* is the mental operation by which the consciousness dwells on an image in order to govern and possess it in power (*ā-jñā* — to command, assure). First the sensing of an object, *Saṃjñāna*; second the apprehending of it in knowledge, *Ājñāna*; third comprehension which leads to possession of it in power, *Prajñāna*; last *Vijñāna*, which gives the complete and essential view, the spiritual perception of the supermind.

(Vijñāna, Prajñāna, Saṃjñāna, Ājñāna)

Parārdha — The higher half of universal experience; the spiritual and divine half of existence (*para* — beyond; *ardha* — half).

Aparārdha — The lower half of universal existence; the material, vital and mental parts of existence (*apara* — lower).

The various Vidyās, Upāsanās or Sādhanās of Upanishad are:

Brahma-vidyā — Wisdom of Brahma or the Divine.

Karmāṅga The ritualistic worship, said to bring about
Vidyā   worldly benefits (*karma* — action; *aṅga* — portion;
          vidyā — knowledge).

The wisdom of the living breath, the life-force; the Puissance of the Creative Consciousness. It leads one to carry out success-
Prāṇa-vidyā fully in the individual life the functions of the Universal Life, having no divided Will but acting one with the Will of the Lord; hence the wisdom which leads to union with the creative and dynamic Energy of Īśvara, the Universal Lord, and makes one a dynamic channel of Universal Life.

The Wisdom that reveals the Delight or "secret honey" (*madhu*) of the creative Spirit or the Absolute, that brings
Madhu-Vidyā unification and balance and harmony to all the variations of the Divine Play.

The wisdom which leads the awakening of the heart to the realization of the Cosmic Self active in all beings; the oneness
Vaiśvānara of each with the Universal Spirit (*vaiśvānara* —
Vidyā   universal being).

The wisdom enjoined by the sage Śāṇḍilya; the discipline which envisages the Spirit (Purusha) as the soul in relation to
Śāṇḍilya- its material, vital and mental vehicles as well as
Vidyā   to its higher spiritual sources, light and powers; hence a comprehensive vision of the soul in its various aspects.

The wisdom and discipline that brings about the realization of the Vast Self (*bhūmā*), the Infinite Self which includes the
Bhūmā-vidyā All, the Immortal which dispels all darkness and sorrow, sickness and death.

Bhārgavi   The realization that Matter is Brahman and
Varuṇi Vidyā also Life, Mind, Supermind, and on to bliss or Ānanda are Brahman. Bhārgavi Varuṇi was the disciple of this wisdom.

Dahara Vidyā
Brahmapura

The realization of the Ātman in the "little space", the subtle inner region within the heart, the *Brahmapura*, city of Brahma (*dahara* — little space).

Samvarga-vidyā

The wisdom that leads to absorption into the Divine (*sam* — together; *vṛij* — to sweep; to sweep together).

Pratīka-
upāsanā-
vidyā

Worship of a limb or part of the main worship; worship of a symbolic form. A *pratīka* could be the Sun as symbol of God.

Tad-vanam

The transcendent Delight, Ānanda, Divine bliss, the fountain source of all as well as the beatic state of self-fulfilment in the universe.

Uttama
Brahman

The Highest Divinity, Purushottama (q.v.).

Paribhū

The Lord who pervades the universal activity (*pari* — around; *bhū* — to become).

Devayāna is "the path of the gods" (*deva* — god; *yāna* — path); the path of higher consciousness, beyond mind; the path of wisdom; also called *Uttarāyaṇa*, the more northern or superior path (*uttara* — higher; *āyana* — going) and *Parārdha*,

Devayāna
Uttarāyaṇa
Parārdha
Aparārdha
Pitṛiyāṇa
Dakshiṇāyana
Aparārdha

the higher half (*para* — beyond; *ardha* — half). Those who reach this realm of Light, this supreme Liberation from bondage are freed from the cycle of rebirth, but may choose to return to earth as an agent of the Divine in order to lighten and elevate the lower and as yet unevolved beings.

Aparārdha is the lower half. The *Pitṛiyāṇa* is "the path of the fathers" (*pitṛi* — father; *yāna* — path); the path of works, of Karma; the path that mental man follows during his progressive evolution on earth; also called *Dakshiṇāyana*, the more southern or inferior path (*dakshiṇa* — southern, inferior) and *Aparārdha*, the lower half (*apara* — lower; *ardha* — half). Those who are still bound to the limitations of mind, life and body consciousness must return again and again along this pathway until they reach to the light and immortal Life of the Path of the Gods, the Higher Path of consciousness.

Retas   The fundamental physical unit, the force in the seed of sex-center; the semen virile, the sperm, seed (*ri* — to flow).

Ojas   Strength, vigor, the primal energy of aether, the most refined form of matter (*vaj* or *uj* — to be strong).

Virya   Spiritual force (*vir* — to be powerful).

Brahma-charya   In the Indian practice of *Brahmacharya* or chastity the *Retas* is said to be changed into *Ojas* which becomes creative of spiritual force or *Virya*.

Prajāpati   Lord of creation, a title applied to various gods of the Vedas and Purāṇas (*prajā* — creation; *pati* — lord).

Rudra   "The Roarer", a god of the Ṛig Veda who rules over the Tempests. Symbolically the "Mighty One" of the heavens who leads in the upward evolution. He smites all that opposes the Power of God, battles against all evil and is very intolerant of the slightest defect. Because he clears the way for the beneficent forces of God he is also "the Merciful". *Rudra* is the Śiva of the Vedas (*rud* — to roar; and to drive away evil).

Sanatkumāra   The Eternal Divine Child or Youth. The name of the Divine Being who leads purified men to the realization of Truth (*sanat* — eternal, always; *kumāra* — youth).

Hiraṇya-para-kośa   The golden highest sheath, the body of Brahman, the Divine (*hiraṇya* — golden; *para* — beyond; *kośa* — sheath).

Hiraṇya-garbha   "The golden foetus"; a name of Brahmā, so called as born from a golden egg formed out of the seed deposited in the waters when they were produced as the first creation of the Self-Existent or Brahma (*hiraṇya* — golden; *garbha* — foetus, womb).

Yājñavalkya   The name of an ancient sage of Brihadāraṇyaka-Upanishad; also a celebrated author of some law-books.

Skanda   The Warrior God who gives battle to the Asuric or demon-like beings and forces for the spiritual uplift of man so that they might be transmuted for divine use.

Śambhu   The beneficent, a name of Śiva (*śam* — auspicious; *bhū* — to become).

Viśvasṛij   All creating, a name of Brahmā, the Creative aspect of the Trinity (*viśva* — all; *sṛij* — to create).

Vidhātṛi   Distributor, Creator, a name of *Brahmā* (*vi* — apart; *dhā* — to place; hence to distribute).

Samrāj   A Supreme ruler, a name of various gods (*sam* — completely; *rāj* — to rule).

Viśvarūpa   All forms, a name applied to various gods (*viśva* — all; *rūpa* — body).

Gandharva   The *Gandharvas* are the musicians of the Gods in Hindu mythology. Symbolically they represent the powers of the vital world that preside over artistic activities.

Agni   The Fire God, symbolic of the Cosmic Divine on the physical plane or in the body, the flame or power of the Will in consciousness, or the Divine Will in the World.

Agni Jātavedas   The fire or heat of conscious force which is the "knower of all births" (*jāta* — born; *vid* — to know).

Vāyu   The Wind God, symbolic of the Cosmic Divine on the vital plane, or in the vital nature of man. The Life Force or the Life Breath.

Vāyu
Mātariśvan   The great Life-Principle which moves and expands infinitely in the Mother Element or the Infinite Expanse or the many forms of existence (*mātari* — in the mother; *śva* — breathe or move).

Indra   The God of the Sky or Firmament, symbolic of the Cosmic Divine on the mental plane or the illumined mind of man.

Maghavan   The Liberal, the Bountiful, a title of Indra.

Umā   Daughter of Haimavat and wife of Śiva, symbolic of the Supreme Nature, the universal matrix, or the wisdom-power of the Divinity in man; the Grace of God.

Umā
Haimavatī   Umā, the daughter of Haimavat, the Snowy Height, symbolic of the Supreme Nature of the Pure Summit of Being; the highest Power of the One; Brahman's Power or the Divine in its highest manifestation.

Vana   The Vedic word for "delight", the Ānanda or "bliss" of the later Upanishads; ecstatic bliss of the Divine. In later Sanskrit *vana* also means "woods".

Sūrya   The Sun, symbolic of Truth, Divine Light (*sū* — to press out).

Agni
Vaiśvānara   *Vaiśvānara* is the Universal Person, hence *Agni Vaiśvānara* is the Universal Divine Power which contains all the gods and all the worlds (*viśva* — all; *nara* — man).

Pūshan   A name for the Sun as Fosterer and Increaser, hence symbolic of that Power of Truth that brings about an expansion of consciousness and of Self-perception.

Yama   Originally a name of the Sun as Ordainer; symbolically *Yama* is the Guardian of Dharma or Cosmic Law, the Law of the Truth which is the condition of Immortality. Also called the God of Death, since he dispenses death to those not fit for immortality (*yam* — to restrain).

Yama Vaivasvata   Yama as son of Vivasvan (shining forth), a name for the Sun; hence symbolic of the Son of Truth from which the law is born.

In the Upanishads, a living supernatural being, spiritual apparition, a Daemon, the "genius" of Greek Philosophy, God **Yaksha** as guardian angel (*yaksh* — to move quickly, towards, or flash upon). In later Purāṇic literature the *Yakshas* are lower Godheads, attendants of Kubera, Keepers of Wealth.

In the Kaṭha Upanishad, the father of Nachiketas, who offers his son as sacrifice to Death; also called *Āruṇi*, *Gautama*, and **Vājaśravas** *Auddālaki*. All these names are symbolic of the **Āruṇi** outer physical man open to inspiration even though **Gautama** in the midst of material plenty (*vaja* — wealth; **Auddālaki** *śravas* — fame) (*gau-tama* — best on earth) (*āruṇi* — son of *Aruṇa*, meaning ruddy, or dawn) (*auddālaka* — descendent of Uddālaka, a word meaning a kind of honey taken by bees from the earth).

In Kaṭha Upanishad, the boy Nachiketas is offered to Death by his father. This is symbolic of the Flame of the Soul released **Nachiketas** from the bonds of physical being, still unconscious of the spiritual life ahead, hence a Kumāra or Youth (*na* — not; *chiketas* — conscious). The triple Nachiketas fire is the Fire or the Divine Spirit hidden within the Universal Being of Matter, Life and Mind; also called the Vaiśvānara flame (*viśva* — all; *nara* — man), the Universal Divine Will. Nachiketas, awakened as the Flame of the aspiring Soul rises from the earth-life to the abode of Yama, the Dispenser of Death, the Guardian of the Law, the Son of Truth.

Gārhaspatya Agni   The householder fire; the God-spark in physical man or in the earth. The householder frees the Fire of Earth, the fire in the wood. The first of the three sacred fires (*griha* — house; *pati* — lord) used at sacrifices.

Āhavānīa Agni   The sacrificial Fire; electricity or lightning, symbolic of the Divine Fire of the mid-world and of the life-energies in man; the Eastern Fire. The second of the three sacrificial fires.

The third of the three sacrificial fires, the Southern Fire or Fire of Discernment, symbolic of the God of mind or intuition, **Dakshiṇa Agni** fire in the sky or heaven as portrayed in the moon and sun and stars.

Gathered from Sri Aurobindo's writing on the Upanishads:

The Upanishads are epic hymns of self-knowledge and world-knowledge and God-knowledge. The great formulations of philosophic truth with which they abound are not abstract intellectual generalisations, things that may shine and enlighten the mind, do not only live and move the soul to ascension, but are ardours as well as lights of an intuitive and revelatory illumination, reaching as well as seeing of the one Existence, the transcendent Godhead, the divine and universal Self. They are discoveries of the Divine's relation with things and creatures in this great cosmic manifestation.

The Upanishads are chants of inspired knowledge. They breathe like all hymns the tone of religious aspiration and ecstasy. Though the Upanishads are mainly concerned with an inner vision and not directly with outward human action, all the highest ethics of Buddhism and later Hinduism are still emergences of the very life and significance of the truths to which they give expressive form and force. Further there is something greater than any ethical precept and mental rule of virtue, — the supreme ideal of a spiritual action founded on oneness with God and all living beings.

"I am He that moves the Tree of the Universe and my glory is like the shoulders of a high mountain. I am lofty and pure like sweet nectar in the strong, I am the shining riches of the world, I am the deep thinker, the deathless One who decays not from the beginning."

This is Trishanku's voicing of Veda and the hymn of his self-knowledge (from the Taittirīya Upanishad).

SANSKRIT VOCABULARY — UPANISHADS

Ādeśa

Adhama

Ādhāra

Ādhibhautika

Adhibhūta

Adhidaiva

Ādhidaivata

Ādhidaivika

Adhideva

Adhyātman

Adhyātma-Yoga

Ādhyātmika

Āditya

Āgāmī Karma

Agni

Agni-Jātavedas

Ahaṁkāra or Ahaṅkāra

Aham Saḥ

Āhāra

Āhāra-Śuddhi

Āhavānīya

Ājñā-chakra or padma

Ājñāna

Ākāśa

Akshara

Akshara Purusha

Akshi

Akshu

Amrita

Amūrtta

Anāhata-chakra or Hṛitpadma

Ānandamaya-kośa

Ānandamaya-puruśa

Aṇḍa-ja

Anīś

Annamaya-kośa

Annamaya-purusha

Anna, prāṇa, manas, vijñāna-
 ānanda, chit, sat

Antaḥkaraṇa or Antaskaraṇa

Antarātman

Antariksha

Antarindriya(āṇi)

Antaryāmin

Anushṭhāna

Apāna

Aparārdha

Aparāvidyā

Apas or Āpas

Ārādhanā

Āropa

Artha

Āruṇi

Āśā

Asambhāva

Āśrama

Asura

Aśva

Aśvamedha

Aśvin

Atala

Ātmarati

Ātmaśakti

Ātmavīrya

Auddālaki

Avasthā

Avidyā

Āvṛitti

Avyakta

Āyus

Bahir-ātman
Bahirindriya
Bala
Bhārgavi Varuṇi Vidyā
Bhāva
Bhūmā-Vidyā
Bhūrloka
Bhūtātman
Bhuvarloka
Bīja
Brahmachārin
Brahmacharya
Brahma-vidyā
Brahmopāsana
Buddhi
Buddhīndriya(āṇi)
Chaitanya Purusha
Chaitya Purusha or
   Antarātman
Chakra(s)
Chakshus
Chatur Āśrama
Chetas
Chidmayakośa
Chitta
Chit-Tapas
Chitta-śuddhi
Dahara-Vidyā
Dakshiṇa
Dakshiṇāgni
Dakshiṇāyana
Dama
Devayāna
Dharma
Dharmakārya
Dhātṛi, Dhātā
Dhātu-prasāda

Dīkshā
Diśaḥ
Divya
Dṛishṭi
Dvāpara-Yuga
Dyaus
Dyāvāpṛithivī
Ekatva
Enas
Gandha
Gandharva
Gārhapatya
Ghrāṇa
Granthi
Gṛihastha
Gṛihasthin
Haṁsa
Hiraṇyagarbha
Hiraṇya-para-kośa
Idam
Indra
Īśa
Īśvara
Jāgrat
Janarloka
Jāra-ja
Jātevedas
Jihvā
Jīva or Jīvātman
Jñāna
Jñānendriya(āṇi)
Jñānin
Jugupsā
Jyotīṁshi
Jyotis
Kalā
Kali-yuga

Kalpa
Kāma
Kāraṇa
Kāraṇa-Śarīra
Kāraṇopādhi
Karmāṅga Vidyā
Karmendriya(āṇi)
Karuṇā
Kavi
Kevala
Kevalatva
Kha
Kośa
Kratu
Kṛitātman
Kṛita-Yuga
Kriyamāṇa Karma
Lakshya
Linga
Linga Śarīra
Loka
Magdu
Madhu-Vidyā
Madhyama
Maghavan
Mahābhūta
Maharloka
Mahātala
Mahat Ātman or Mahadātman
Manas
Maṇipura-chakra or padma or
  Nābhi-padma-chakra
Manīshin
Manomaya-kośa
Manomaya-purusha
Manu
Maraṇa

Mati
Medhā
Mitra
Moha
Moksha
Mūlādhāra-chakra
Mūlaprakṛiti
Mūrti
Nābhipadma-chakra
Nachiketas
Nādabrahman
Nāḍī
Nāḍī-śuddhi
Nāsika
Neti, neti
Nirvṛitatva
Niyantṛi
Ojas
Om
Pāda
Pāñchabhautika
Pāṇi
Pāpa
Pāpman
Paramahaṁsa
Paramārtha
Paramātman
Parārdha
Parā-vidyā
Paribhū
Pātāla
Pāyus
Pitṛiyāna
Prabhu
Prachetas
Prajāpati
Prajñā

Prajñāna
Prakāśa
Prāṇa(s)
Prāṇamaya-kośa
Prāṇamaya-purusha
Prāṇātman
Praṇava
Prāṇa-Vidyā
Prārabdha Karma
Pratikṛiti
Pratīka-Upāsanā
Pratishṭhā
Pravrajya
Preyas
Pṛithivī
Puṇya
Purusha
Purushārtha
Pūshan
Rāga
Rājasūya
Rākshasa
Rasa
Rasātala
Retas
Ṛita
Rodasī
Rudra
Rūpa
Śabda
Sādhanā
Sadmayakośa
Saḥ
Sahasradala-chakra or padma
Sahasrāra
Śama
Samādhi

Samāna
Samarpaṇa
Sambhāva
Śambhu
Śambhūti
Saṅkalpa
Saṁnyāsa (Sannyāsa)
Samrāj
Saṁskāra
Samvarga-vidyā
Sāmya
Sanatkumāra
Sañchita Karma
Śāṇḍilya-Vidyā
Saṁjñāna
Sannyāsin
Saṁskṛitokti
Śānta
Śarīra
Sarvāṇi bhūtāni
Śāstrī
Sat Purusha
Satsaṅga
Sattva Śuddhi
Satya
Satyadharma
Satyakāma
Satyaloka
Satyamayī
Satya-Yuga
Siddhi
Śiśna
Skanda
Smara
Smṛiti Śuddhi
So'ham
So'ham asmi

Śoka
Śreyas
Sparśa
Śraddhayam
Sṛishṭi
Śrotra
Sthūla-śarīra
Sthūlātman
Sthūlopādhi
Śukra
Sūkshma-Śarīra
Sūkshmopādhi
Sūrya
Sushupti
Sutala
Sutrātman
Svādhishṭhāna-chakra
Svapna
Svarājya
Svarloka
Svasti
Svātantrya
Sveda-ja
Tad-vanam
Tala
Talātala
Tanmātra
Tanu
Taparloka or Tapoloka
Tarka
Tat
Tattva
Tejas
Tīrtha
Tretā-Yuga
Tridhātu
Trishu Tanushu

Turīya
Tvak
Udāna
Udbhij-ja
Udgītha
Ukti
Umā
Umā Haimavatī
Upādhi
Upāsaka
Upāsikā
Upāsana
Upastha
Uttama
Uttama Brahman
Uttarāyaṇa
Vāch
Vāha
Vaiśvānara
Vaiśvānara-Vidyā
Vajaśravas
Vana
Vānaprastha
Vānaprasthin
Vartamāna Karma
Varuṇa
Vāyu
Vāyu Mātariśvan
Vidhātṛi
Vidhi
Vidyā
Vidyut
Vitala
Vijñāna
Vijñānamaya-kośa
Vijñānamaya-purusha
Vikāra

Vināśa
Vīrya
Viś
Vishṇu
Viśuddha-chakra
Viśva Purusha
Viśvasṛij
Viśvarūpa
Vītarāga
Viveka
Vyāhṛiti

Vyāna
Vyavahāra
Yājñavalkya
Yaksha
Yama Vaivasvata
Yaśas
Yati
Yuga
Yugadharma
Yuga-sandhyā

MACROCOSM

BRAHMAN   — God   — Divine
PARAMĀTMAN — The SELF Beyond — Divine

MICROCOSM

REALITY
  Sat-Purusha
  Sad-maya-kośa

**CONSCIOUSNESS-
POWER**
  Chit-Purusha
  Chid-maya-kośa

BLISS
  Ānanda-Purusha
  Ānanda-maya-kośa

SUPERMIND
  Truth-Consciousness

Vijñāna-Purusha
Vijñānamaya-kośa

SPIRIT
  Self in All, Central
  Being, Ātman, Jīvātman
  (Jīva), Kāraṇa-Purusha

SOUL — PSYCHE
  God-spark, Antarātman
  Son of God with Infinite
  Potential, True Indivi-
  dual Purusha behind
  Heart

<table>
<tr><td>

SOUL-NATURE IN EVOLUTION
Psychic-Being
Chaitya-Purusha

</td><td>

VITAL FORCE
Life Energy
Prāna-Purusha
Prānamaya-kośa

</td></tr>
<tr><td>

EGO
Personal Outer Self
Formed by Nature
to individualize outer
consciousness, Ahaṅkāra

</td><td>

MIND
Manaḥ-Purusha
Manomaya-kośa

</td></tr>
<tr><td>

PHYSICAL
Anna-Purusha
Anna-maya-kośa

</td><td>

STEPS TO SUPERMIND
Higher Mind
Illumined Mind
Intuitive Mind
Overmind

</td></tr>
</table>

Sat-Chit-Ānanda make up the Divine Consciousness.

Supermind reveals Divine Will, Power and Knowledge.

The inner mind, life and body are called the Sūkshma states which flow from the Cosmos, and reveal knowledge beyond the objective world. (The Psychic of the Western Metaphysics)

The above diagram is a representation of Sri Aurobindo's interpretation of the divisions of man for the understanding of his Yoga of Integral Divine Manifestation:

His revelation of the Veda and the Upanishads.

LOKAS and TALAS

The Universe is divided into seven great planes or worlds of beings, each of which is bi-polarized into Lokas and Talas. These pairs of Lokas and Talas are as inseparable as two sides of a coin. The Lokas represent the heavens, the vast places of light and becoming. The Talas represent the nether poles, the inferior dark places that lead to separateness and annihilation of being.

MACROCOSM

PARA-PURUSHA — Absolute — God — Divine
(of the Veda)

LOKA(S)	TALA(S)
SATYA-LOKA World of true existence	**ATALA** No place, extinction of the soul's being
TAPAR-LOKA World of self-conscious energy	**VITALA** A change toward matter, spiritual darkness
JANAR-LOKA World of creative delight	**SUTALA** A good matter state, desire and passion rule
MAHAR-LOKA World of large consciousness	**RASĀTALA** State of sense enjoyment
SVAR-LOKA World of luminous mentality	**TALĀTALA** State of purely outward passion and sense indulgence
BHUVAR-LOKA World of vital becoming	**MAHĀTALA** The great state of darkness where ego rules
BHŪR-LOKA World of material becoming	**PĀTĀLA** The fallen state where dark ignorance rules

Chapter VIII

THE SYSTEMS OF YOGA

Haṭha Yoga

The chief processes of a Haṭha Yogin are Āsana and Prāṇāyāma. Some of the most important Āsanas are Sūrya Namaskāra, Padmāsana, Siddhāsana, Śīrshāsana, Sarvāṅgāsana, Matsyāsana, Halāsana, Paśchimottānāsana, Bhujaṅgāsana, Śalabhāsana, Dhanurāsana, Matsyendrāsana, Mayūrāsana, Padahastāsana, Trikoṇāsana, Chakrāsana, and Śavāsana. He also practises the Kriyās: Neti, Dhauti, Nauli, Basti and Trāṭaka, as well as the Bandhas and Mudrās.

Prāṇāyāma is the control of Prāṇa through Kumbhaka, Pūrvaka, and Rechaka. The chief aim of Prāṇāyāma is to unite the HA, or the Sun-breath, known as Prāṇa, with the THA, or Moon-breath, known as the Apāna. Thus a Haṭha Yogin gets Siddhis and the Kuṇḍalinī power rises through the six Chakras to the Sahasrāra.

Yoga of the Body and Life-breath

The chief processes of one seeking the Purification of his body and breath are the Physical Postures and Breath Control. Some of the most important postures are: Greeting the Sun, the Lotus pose, the Adept pose, the Head pose, the Shoulder stand, the Fish pose, the Plough pose, the Forward-double pose, the Cobra pose, the Locust pose, the Bow pose, the Spinal twist pose, the Peacock pose, the Feet-hand pose, the Triangle pose, the Wheel pose, and the Dead body or relaxation pose. He also practices the Purifying Exercises: Nostril cleaning, Inner and outer purification, Abdominal contractions, Intestinal purification, Steady gazing, as well as the Methods of physical control and Body positions.

Breath-control is the control of the Life-force through Retention of breath, Breathing in and Breathing out. The chief aim of Breath-control is to unite the HA, or the Sun-breath, known as the Breath that controls our breathing, with the THA, or Moon-breath, known as the Life-current which casts wastes out of the body. Thus the one seeking Purification of body and breath gets Powers and the Spiritual Mother-energy rises through the six Holy Centers of the body to the Thousand-petalled Lotus at the top of the head.

Karma Yoga

The Sādhaka of Karma Yoga must practice Īsvarārpaṇa and perform Nishkāma Karma as a Pūjā of Nārāyaṇa. Through inner Sannyāsa, Karmaphalatyāga, and Yajña, he rises above the Dvandvamoha : Duḥkha and Sukha, Lābha and Alābha, Jaya and Ajaya, Śubha and Aśubha, Rāga and Dvesha, and attains Samatva.

"Samatvam yoga uchyate."

The Sādhaka also serves others with Ātma-Bhāva, Prema, and Bhakti. He frees himself of Saṃskāras and Vāsanās and cultivates Vairāgya, Śama, and Sadāchāra. Finally, he attains Sādriśya and Sādharmyamukti.

"Yogaḥ karmasu kauśalam."

The Path of Selfless Dedicated Action

The Disciple of the Yoga of Selfless Dedicated Action must practice Surrender to the Lord and perform Desireless Action as a Worship of the God in Man. Through inner Renunciaton of All Material Bondage, Abandonment of the Fruits, and Performance of Sacrifice, he rises above the Illusion of Dualities: Pain and Happiness, Gain and Loss, Victory and Defeat, Blessedness and Misery, Love and Hate, and attains Equality.

"Equal-mindedness is called Union with God."

The Devotee of Yoga also serves others with Consciousness One with the Spirit, Divine Love, and Devotion to God. He frees himself of Past Attachments and Past Impressions and cultivates Freedom from Passion, Tranquility, and Right Conduct. Finally, he attains a Resemblance to the Divine and a Consciousness of Performing Duties like unto the Divine.

"Yoga is skill in action."

Bhakti Yoga

The Sādhanā of the Bhakti yogin consists of Upāsana of his Guru or his Ishṭa-Devatā, such as Vishṇu in the forms of Rāma or Kṛishṇa in the case of Vaishṇavas, Śiva or one of his forms in the case of Śaivas, and one of the Devīs, such as Sarasvatī, Lakshmī, Kālī, Durgā, Chaṇḍī, Umā or Gāyatrī, in the case of Śāktas.

Through Sat-Saṅga and Śaraṇāgati he develops Viśva-Prema and Śraddhā, and destroys his Saṁskāras, Tṛishṇā and Ahaṁkāra, and brings about Antarmukha-vṛitti. He thirsts for the Darśana of his Īśvara, and increases his Bhakti through Śravaṇa of the Līlās of Bhagavān, with Kīrtana and Saṁkīrtana, Smaraṇa, Pādasevana, Archanā, Vandanā, and Ātma-nivedana.

Pratīka-Upāsanā is Dhyāna on some Pratimā like the Śāligram of Vishṇu or the Lingam of Śiva or the image of one's Ishṭa-Devatā. Further, by Japa with Mālā, Bhajan, and the Svādhyāya of the Bhakti Sūtras by Ṛishi Śāṇḍilya and Nārada, he experiences the Nārāyaṇa Bhāva. According to the Bhakti's Svabhāva, one of the five Bhāvas is chosen; the Śānta, Dāsya, Sākhya, Vātsalya, or Mādhurya Bhāvas.

The Upāchāra for Pūjā are : Āsana, Svāgata, Pādya, Arghya, Āchamana, Madhuparka, Snāna, Vastra, Bhūshaka, Gandha, Pushpa, Dhūpa, Dīpa, Naivedya, Tāmbula, Namaskāra.

When the Bhakti attains the Loka of Bhagavān, he enjoys Sālokya-Mukti, Sāmīpya-Mukti, and Sāyujya-Mukti. Then his Mahāprema for Bhagavān is fulfilled.

Some of the famous mantras of the Bhakti yogin are : Om Namo Bhagavate Vāsudevāya, Om Hari Om, Śivoham, Om

Namo Nārāyaṇāya, Om Śrī Rām Jaya Rām, Jaya, Jaya Rām. Every name of God or mantra is filled with Achintya Śakti. Om.

Yoga of Devotion

The Spiritual Practice of the One seeking Union with God through Devotion consists of Worship of his Teacher or his Chosen Deity, such as Vishṇu, in the forms of Rāma or Kṛishṇa in the case of Worshippers of Vishṇu, Śiva or one of his forms in the case of Worshippers of Śiva, and one of the Goddesses, such as the Goddess of Creative Arts, the Goddess of Love and Harmony, the Goddess of Power, the Inaccessible Goddess, the Demon-destroyer Goddess, the Goddess of Light, or the Goddess of the Sun in the case of Devotees of the Power of God.

Through the Company of the Holy and Surrender to God he develops All-embracing Love of God and Faith and destroys his Karmic results, Thirst for life, and Egotism, and brings about a Turning-within. He thirsts for the Vision of his Lord and increases his Devotion through Listening to the Plays of the Lord, Singing Praises of the Lord, Singing together of the Praises of the Lord, Remembering the Lord, Service at the feet of the Lord, Offering lights and flowers, Honoring, and Dedication to the Lord within.

Symbol-worship is Meditation on some Sign like the Special Stone of Vishṇu, or the Phallus of Śiva, or the image of one's Chosen Deity. Further, with Repetition of God's Name, with Rosary, Song of Devotion, Study of the Aphorisms of Devotion by Sage Śāṇḍilya and Nārada, and Experiences the State of Loving God in Man. According to the Devotee's Essential Nature, one of the five States is chosen : God as Purified Ascetic, God as Servant, God as Friend, God as Chiid, and God as Lover.

The Materials and Acts of the worship are : Offering a seat for the image, Welcoming the God, Water for the feet, Water offering, Water for sipping, Honey-ghi-milk-curd, Bathing water, Garments, Jewels, Perfume, Flowers, Incense, Lights, Food, Betelnuts, etc., Prayer and Salutation.

When the Devotee attains the World of the Lord, he enjoys the Liberation in the same Plane as the Lord, Liberation with Nearness to the Lord, Liberation of Union with the Lord. Then his Great Love for the Lord is fulfilled.

Some of famous Words of Power of the Devotee of Devotion to the Lord are : Om Honor to the Lord Kṛishṇa, Om God Om, I am Śiva, Om Honor to the God in man, Om Lord Rāma Victory Rāma Victory Victory Rāma. Every name of God or Phrase of Power is filled with Unimaginable Power.

Jñāna Yoga

The Sādhaka of Jñāna Yoga must remove Avidyā and realize Parāvidyā or Brahmavidyā. He develops Viveka, Vairāgya, the Shaṭ-Sampatti: Śama, Indriyaṇigraha, Uparati, Titikshā, Samādhāna, and Mumūkshatva. He listens to the Śrutis from a Guru who is Śrotriya and Brahmaṇishṭha. He practices Manana, Dhyāna on Brahma, and thus finally knows and becomes Brahma, is a Jīvanmukta, and attains Sāyujya-Mukti. Moksha comes through his Brahma-Jñāna and the Union of the Jīvātman with the Paramātman. Then the Jīva rests in his own Sachchidānanda-Svarūpa.

The Yoga of Wisdom

The Spiritual Disciple of the Yoga of Wisdom must remove Ignorance and realize the Higher Wisdom or God Wisdom. He develops Discrimination, Dispassion, the Six Excellences: Tranquility, Control of the Senses, Renunciation, Endurance, Concentration, and Yearning for Liberation. He listens to the Scriptures of Revelation from a Spiritual Teacher who is Learned in the Spiritual Teachings and is Devoted to God. He practices Reflection, Meditation on the Divine, and thus finally knows and becomes the Divine, is a Liberated Soul while Living, and attains Union and Absorption in the Divine.

Liberation comes through his Divine Wisdom and the Union of the Individual Self with the Highest Divine Self. Then the Individual Life-Being rests in his own Pure Reality-Consciousness-Bliss-Own-Form.

Rāja Yoga

The Sādhanā of Rāja Yoga consists of the Ashtānga Yoga : 1. Yama; 2. Niyama; 3. Āsana; 4. Prānāyāma; 5. Pratyāhāra; 6. Dhāranā; 7. Dhyāna. These lead to 8. Samādhi and Chitta-vrittinirodha.

Yama includes Ahimsā, Asteya, Brahmacharya, and Aparigraha. Niyama includes Śaucha, Santosha, Tapas, Svādhyāya, and Īśvara Pranidhāna. Other Gunas to be developed are Maitrī, Karunā, Muditā, Śraddhā, and Vīrya. The Yogin should seek Satsanga and learn holy Ślokas and Stotras.

The first five types of discipline are the Bahiranga Sādhanā. The last three are the Antaranga Sādhanā.

The two stages of Samādhi are : 1. Samprajñāta, with its Savitarka, Savichāra, Sānanda, and Sasmita, 2. Asamprajñāta, sometimes called Nirvikalpa-Samādhi, brings Adhyātma Prasāda, Samyama, and the Yogin becomes a Jīvanmukta and attains Kaivalya-Mukti.

King of Yogas

The spiritual discipline of the King of Yogas consists of the Eight-limbed methods of obtaining union with God : 1. Self-control; 2. Religious observances; 3. Physical postures; 4. Breath-control; 5. Withdrawal of sense-consciousness; 6. Concentration; 7. Meditations. These lead to 8. the Super-conscious state and Control of the workings of the mind.

Self-control includes Non-injury, Not stealing, Continence in thought and act, Non-covetousness in thought, word, and deed. Religious observances include Cleanliness, Contentment, Austerity, Study of religious scriptures, Devotional meditation and surrender to the Highest Lord of Perfection. Other Qualities to be developed are Friendship, Compassion, Sympathetic Joy, Faith, and Dauntless energy. The Divine Seeker should seek Company of the Holy, to learn Holy verses and Hymns of Praise.

The first five types of discipline are the External Spiritual Disciplines. The last three are the Internal Spiritual Disciplines.

The two stages of Spiritual Consciousness are 1. Subject-Object Consciousness with its Deliberation, Reflection, Joy, and Smiling consciousness; 2. a High Consciousness above Subject-Object Distinction, sometimes called Superconsciousness beyond Time brings the Grace of the Highest Self, Perfect Self-control and the Seeker of the Divine becomes a Liberated Soul while living and attains Absolute Liberation from Further Transmigration.

The main scripture of Rāja Yoga is Patañjali's Yoga Sūtras in which a detailed description of the processes involved in controlling and freeing the mind are given.

Japa or Mantra Yoga

The Sādhaka of Japa or Mantra Yoga must do Japa of Ishta-Mantra or Guru-Mantra in the right Bhāva. All Mantras can lead to Brahma-Samādhi and Mantra Siddhi for there is an Achintya and Daivī-Śakti in all Mantras. By Puraścharana of the Mantra one may realize the glory of Brahma-Nāma and may have Darśana of the Ishta-Devatā. One should use a Rudrāksha or Tulasi Mālā of 108 beads. There are three kinds of Japa : Mānasika Japa, Upāṁśu Japa, and Vaikhari Japa and Likhita Japa.

The *Purāṇas* say that in this Kali Yuga Japa is the easy way to Brahmavidyā. Kṛishṇa says in the *Bhāgavad Gītā*, "Among Yajñas I am Japa Yajña."

Some of the famous Mantras that have come down through

the Guruparamparā and have been given in Mantra-Dīkshā
are:

Om namo Nārāyanāya
Om honor to the God in man

Om Hari Om
Om God Om

Om namaḥ Śivāya
Om honor to Śiva

Om namo Bhagavate Vāsudevāya
Om honor to the holy Kṛishṇa, God of spiritual wealth

Om Śrī Rāma jaya Rāma jaya jaya Rāma
Om Śrī Rāma victory Rāma victory victory Rāma

The Yoga of Repeating of God's Name or Holy Words

The devotee of union with God through repetition of God's
Name or some Holy Words must do the repeating of God's
Name, or the Chosen Holy Words, or the Holy Verse Given by
his Guru, in the right State of Consciousness. All Holy Verses
can lead to a Divine High Consciousness and the Power of Holy
Words for there is an Unthinkable and Divine Power in all Holy
Words. By Repetition of the Holy Words one may realize the
Glory of the Name of God and may have Vision of his Chosen
Deity. One should use a Rosary or Garland of 108 beads made
of Sacred Basil. There are three kinds of Repetition of God's
Name: Mental, Humming, Aloud, and Written Repetition of
God's name.

The Legendary Histories of India say that it is in this
Dark Age that the Repetition of God's Name is the easy way
to God Wisdom. Kṛishṇa says in the *Holy Song*, "Among
Sacrifices, I am the Sacrifice of Repetition of God's Name."

Some of the famous Holy Words that have come down
through the Line of Gurus Following One Another and have
been given in the Holy Word Initiation are:

Om Hari Om

Japa is a vehicle for Power to descend into one's being.

Kundalini or Tantra Yoga

The first step for the Sādhaka of Kundalini or Tantra Yoga is the Śuddhi of the Nādīs of the Linga Śarīra. This is attained through Prāṇāyāma. The Yoga Nādīs carry the Sūkshma Prāṇa to all parts of the Sūkshma Śarīra as the Sthūla Prāṇa or Breath is carried through the nerves to all parts of the Sthūla Śarīra. The Nādīs spring from the Kāṇḍa at the base of the spine.

Man is a Kshudra Brahmāṇḍa. The Meru-Daṇḍa is the axis of the Sthūla Śarīra as Mount Meru is the axis of the Jagat. Within the Meru-Daṇḍa are the Shaṭ Chakras or Padmas corresponding to the nerve plexuses along the spinal column of the Sthūla Śarīra.

The Shaṭ Chakras of the Linga Śarīra are Mūlādhāra, Svādhishṭhāna, Maṇipura, Anāhata, Viśuddhi and Ājñā, and above them at the top of the head is the seventh and most important Chakra, the Sahasrāra. Each Chakra has its Bīja, its Tattva, Guṇa, Deva, Devī, and its Nādīs called petals whose vibrations are distinguished as different sounds of the Sanskrit alphabet. Each letter denotes the Mantra of the Devī Kundalini or Divine Śakti as She passes upward to the Sahasrāra to unite with Śiva. (See Table attached for all these correspondences.)

The Lokas correspond respectively to the higher Chakras in the trunk and head, and the Talas correspond to the Chakras below the trunk.

The Sushumnā Nādī extends from the Mūlādhāra Chakra to the Brahmarandhra. Within the Sushumnā Nādī there is the Vajra Nādī, radiant like the Sun and with Rājasika Guṇa. Again within the Vajra Nādī is the Chitrā, pale like the Moon and of the Sāttvika Guṇa. Then within this Chitrā Nādī is the Brahma Nādī which corresponds to the Canalis Centralis of Vaidya Śāstra. Through the Brahma Nādī the Kundalini passes upwards awakening each Chakra in turn, causing intense activity and opening many layers of mind and knowledge, and manifesting various Siddhis. When the Kuṇḍalinī reaches the top of head it unites with Śiva and Mukti and Bhukti are attained, and the Sādhaka becomes a Brahmavid-Varishtha.

The Iḍā and Piṅgalā Nāḍīs are on the left and right sides of the spine respectively and carry the Sūkshma Prāṇa to all parts of the body. These two Nāḍīs correspond to the left and right sympathetic nervous systems. Iḍā flows through the left nostril and Piṅgalā through the right. Iḍā is cooling like the Moon, and Piṅgalā heating like the Sun. The lower extremity of the Chitrā Nāḍī is called the Brahmadvāra, and it rises and terminates in the Cerebellum.

Some of the Siddhis attained through the rising of the Kuṇḍalinī through the Chakras are: Dardura, Mṛityuñjaya, Pātāla Siddhi, Bhūchari, Kāya, Khechari, Trikāla-Jñānī, and Ichchā-Mṛityu.

When Kuṇḍalinī sleeps man awakes to the world. When Kuṇḍalinī awakes man awakes to the light in all things and feels one with all. Kuṇḍalinī can be awakened by Prāṇāyāma, Āsanas, Mudrās, Dhāraṇā, Bhakti, Samarpaṇa, Brahmajñāna, Mantra, and by Guru Kṛīpā through touch, sight or mere Saṅkalpa.

Some of the signs of the awakening of the Kuṇḍalinī are freedom from anger, desire, passion, hate, the attainment of the balance of mind, cosmic love, fearlessness, and various Siddhis. For the Kuṇḍalinī to continue to rise higher and higher Deha-Śuddhi, Nāḍī-Śuddhi, Manas-Śuddhi, and Buddhi-Śuddhi are needed.

When the Kuṇḍalinī unites with Śiva, Amṛita flows from the Brahmarandhra to the Mūlādhāra, flooding the Linga and the Sthūla Dehas, satisfying the Devas and Devīs of the Chakras and hence flooding the being with Paramānanda and Brahma-Vidyā-Śreshtha. The Sādhaka thus attains Asaṁprajñāta Samādhi.

Chaṇḍī is one of the most sacred and popular scriptures of the

Chakras	Planet Bija	Nerve Plexus and Place	No. of Petals and Letter		Animal & God	Principles & Metals	Tattvas Elements & Senses	Body Part & Activity
Mūlādhāra (root center) Brahmā Rajas	lam	Sacro-Coccygeal bottom of spine Eliminative Center	4	vam, śam, sham, sam	Elephant Ganeśa Dākinī	Anna lead	earth smell	cohesion obstruction bone
			Fire					
Svādhishṭhāna (own place)	vam	Prostatic generative òrgans Generative Center	6	bam, bham, mam, yam, ram, lam	Makara Brahmā Rākinī	Prāṇa brass	water taste	motion contraction sinew
Maṇipura (full of rays)	ram	Solar navel Digestive Center junction of Iḍā & Piṅgalā	10	ḍam, ḍham, ṇam, tam, tham, dam, dham, nam, pam, pham	Rām Vishṇu Lākinī	Manas tin	fire sight	expansion earth motion flesh
			Sun					
Anāhata (soundless sound)	yam	Cardiac heart Respiratory Center	12	kam, kham, gam, gham, nam, cham, chham, jam, jham, ñam, ṭam, ṭham	Antelope Lākinī Kākinī	Vijñāna gold	air touch	transverse motion in space blood

Viśuddhi (purity)	ham	Laryngeal throat base Broadcasting system, external mind	16 Moon	am, ām, im, īm, um, ūm, ṛim, ṛim, lṛim, lṛim, em, aim, om, aum. am, aḥ	Om Agni Shākinī	Ānanda copper	ether hearing	non-obstructive motion, all direction skin.
Ājñā (command of guru) Rudra Tamas	om	Cavernous between eyes on brow, Control Room of Motor Activity	2	ham, ksham	Vāyu Hākinī	Chit quicksilver silver	mahat spiritual mind	oneness marrow
Sahasrāra (thousand-petalled) Abode of Śiva		top of head Master Switch-board		all letters		Sat		

Tāntrikas. It is the quintessence of Tantra as the *Bhagavad Gītā* is of Vedāntic thought. It consists of thirteen chapters from the *Mārkaṇḍeya Purāṇa*.

Explanation of Special Tantric Terms
(Not Explained Elsewhere)

Nāḍī	Astral channel corresponding to a nerve of the physical body.
Sūkshma	Fine or subtle.
Sthūla	Gross or physical.
Kāṇḍa	Corresponding to the Kānda equini of the physical body.
Kshudra Brahmāṇḍa	The little egg of God, or the microcosm.
Meru	The mythological Olympus.
Meru Daṇḍa	Spinal column.
Shaṭ Chakras	The Six wheels or sacred centers of the inner body.
Padma	Lotus.
Sthūla Śarīra	Physical body.
Sushumnā Nāḍī	The astral channel within the spinal cord.
Brahmarandhra Brahmadvāra	The divine opening at the top of the head, anterior fontanelle. Dvāra is the door to the Divine.
Vajra Nāḍī	The astral channel within the Sushumna Nāḍī.
Chitrā Nāḍī	The astral channel within the Vajra Nāḍī.
Brahma Nāḍī	The astral channel within the Chitrā Nāḍī corresponding to the Canalis Centralis of the physical body.

Vaidya Śāstra	Medical scripture of the Vedas.
Brahmavid-Varishṭha	A full-blown knower of the Divine, or the very best of Divine knowers.
Iḍā Nāḍī	The astral tube on the left side of the spine carrying the Prāṇa through the left nostril.
Piṅgalā Nāḍī	The astral tube on the right side of the spine carrying the Prāṇa through the right nostril.
Siddhi	Occult faculty and power.
Dardura	Ability to rise from the ground.
Mṛityuñjaya	Conquest of death.
Pātāla Siddhi	Ability to acquire hidden treasures.
Bhūchari	Ability to fly over the earth.
Kāya Siddhi	Ability to enter the body of another.
Khechari	Ability to fly in the sky.
Trikāla-Jñānī	Knower of past, present and future.
Ichchhā-Mṛityu	Power to die at will.
Guru Kṛipā	Grace of the teacher.
Śreshṭha	The best.
Asaṁprajñāta Samādhi	A high state of consciousness where all sense of separateness disappears, and self and God are one.

Pūrṇa Yoga — Integral Yoga

The Sādhaka of Pūrṇa Yoga must first make the Saṅkalpa of Ātmasamarpaṇa to the Parātpara Purusha and Ādyā Śakti. Then he must observe their Līlā. The soul is Nityamukta, therefore the aim of Pūrṇa Yoga is not only personal Moksha but the Mukti and Transformation of the whole Manushya on this Jagat, and to bring the Satyayuga here. God's Śakti will work it out, only Anumati, Smṛiti and Śraddhā are the Dhṛiti and

Utsāha needed. When Pramāda comes, be Dhīra, Apramatta and Nitya Anusmaraṇa with Bhoga. The *Sanatsujātīya* says four things are necessary for Siddhi: Śāstra, Utsāha, Guru and Kāla. Seek Satsanga and purify the Ādhāra. Ahaṁkāra and Kāma must be blotted out.

The Sādhaka must be the ever-present Yajamāna who sees the Yajña offered by Iśvara as Śakti or Kālī to Śrī Krishṇa. Kartṛi-tvābhimāna, Niḥspṛiha, and freedom from Saṁskāras must be sought, and the Dvandvas, such as Rāgadvesha, Pāpa or Puṇya and Sukṛita or Dushkṛita, must be renounced. One must be Triguṇātīta and perform the Kartavyam Karma with Sarva-karmaphalatyāga. The Prakṛiti, though using the three Guṇas, will be free from Bandha. Sattva will become pure Prakāśa and Jyoti, Rajas will become pure Tapas, and Tamas will become Śama or Śānti. Then, attaining the Buddhi Bhāva, one must seek to be no longer Sushupta but Jāgrata in Vijñāna and Ānanda, the seat of Satyadharma.

The Sādhaka must perceive "Sarvam eva Brahma", see the Sad-Ātman as "Śāntam Alakshaṇam" and "Ātmānam sarva-bhūteshu sarvabhūtāni chātmani", know Krishṇa as "Avyakto vyaktāt paraḥ", as Ananta and Śānta Iśvara, the Śiva, the Nārā-yaṇa, the Purushottama who is One with Rādhā or Parāprakṛiti. One comes to know Vāsudeva as Viśva or Virāt, Hiraṇyagarbha or Taijasa, or as Prajñā or Viśva or Virāṭ, Hiraṇyagarbha or Taijasa, or as Prajñā or Iśvara, and Aparārdha of the Cosmos as Manas, Prāṇa, and Anna, and the Parārdha as Sachchidānanda. These are the important Kriyās and Siddhi of this Yoga.

The Sādhaka comes to know the various parts of his being: the highest — Ātman, or Jīvātman, or Kāraṇa-Purusha; then the Antarātman or Purusha behind the Heart; then the Chaitya-Purusha; then the personal self of Ahaṁkāra. One learns that all humans have an Antarātman, but all have not developed the Chaityapurusha, a necessary Kriyā in Pūrṇa Yoga before Vijñāna can prevail.

Each Avatāra has revealed one of the major or minor cords of the harmonious make-up of man's being in evolution: Rāma awakened the Sattva Guṇa; Śankara reached the Transcendental Heights; Buddha awakened the Heart of Compassion and demonstrated a New Way of Life; Christ revealed the Power of Love and Charity; Rāmakrishna revealed the Unity of All Paths Leading to God; Krishna revealed the Joy and Many-powered Blessings of a fully developed Overmind; Śrī Aurobindo, through his Pūrṇa Yoga, was the pioneer of Vijñāna which will lead to Divine Unity and to the Daivyam Janam on this Jagat.

The Divine, through his Śakti, is behind all action, but is veiled by his Yoga Māyā and works through the Ego of the Jīva in the Lower Nature. Many are the Vibhūtis and Śaktis of Purushottama-Parāprakriti, Īśvara-Śakti, and Purusha-Prakriti. (See Table attached.)

The Four Requisites for the work of perfection are: Śakti, Vīrya, Daivī Prakriti, and Śraddhā. The Four Perfections of the body are : Mahattva, Bala, Laghutā, and Dhāraṇa-Sāmarthya. The Four Perfections of the heart are : Saumyatva, Tejas, Kalyāna Śraddhā, and Prema-Sāmarthya. The Four Perfections of Prāṇa are : Pūrṇatā, Prasannatā, Samatā, and Sarvabhogasāmarthya. The Four Perfections of Buddhi are : Viśuddhi, Prakāśa, Vichitrabodha, and Sarva-jñāna-sāmarthya.

The final Artha of Pūrṇa Yoga is to evoke Vijñānamaya-purusha and thus create the Daivyam Janam (see Ṛig Veda X, 53, 6). Śrī Krishna with his Līlāmāyā draws all to himself by his love. Krishna's Abhaya Vachana, "Na me bhaktaḥ praṇaśyati," must be remembered.

Become Brāhmī-Sthiti

The Saṁyama of Rāja Yoga, the most developed Prāṇāyāma of Haṭha Yoga, the most ecstatic Bhakti, and the purest Karma Yoga are indeed efficacious, but these are human methods — something more powerful is needed along with them to take us not only to limited goals but to the freedom of the Infinite : the potency of God's capacity. To sail this ship of Brahmavidyā,

Purushottama — Supreme Person

Become two:	Īśvara — Divine Father		Śakti — Divine Mother	
Become four:	Mahāvīra — Maheśvarī;	Balarāma — Mahākālī;	Pradyumna — Mahā-lakshmī;	Aniruddha — Mahā-sarasvatī.
	Knowledge	Strength	Love	Skill in work
Four Castes:	Brāhmaṇa Large wisdom Wide comprehension Vast Consciousness	Kshatriya Force Dynamism Power	Vaiśya Harmony Beauty Mutuality	Śūdra Perfect execution Thoroughness in detailed working, Order and arrangement
Heavenly Gods Svar:	Varuṇa	Aryaman Rudra	Mitra Bhaga Soma	Ribhus—artisans of Divinity
Purāṇas:	Brahmā	Śiva	Vishṇu	Indra
Human Manifestations:	Homer Vālmīki	Napoleon Dante Byron Michelangelo	Christ Chaitanya Virgil Petrarch Shelley Tagore Raphael Titian	Caesar Colbert (statesman) Louis XIV Horace Racine Kālidāsa Tintoretto Leonardo da Vinci

utter Ātmasamarpaṇa to God and His Śakti, often considered as Divine Mother, are demanded.

We must escape from the Māyā of Avidyā, not from Life. Līlā includes the idea of Māyā and exceeds it. God is One but not bounded by His unity. He is One and Many. Outside His manifestation, He is Anirdeśyam. The Upanishad says He is "Ekamevādvitīyam" i.e., "One without a second".

The Vedānta of Śaṅkara is the Sādhanā of Purusha with an inactive stress. Tantra is the Sādhanā of the Prakṛiti with a dynamic aspect. The Vedānta of Śaṅkara teaches that Truth is Stability, Peace, and Joy of Union with the inactive Purusha. Tantra teaches that Truth is infinite power and dynamis. Ādyā-Śakti or Parāprakṛiti is the Mother of the Universe and its Up-holder. Prakṛiti and Māyā are particular and comparatively gross forms of Ādyā-Śakti. By attaining Śakti one attains Śiva. Mukti and Bhukti, are both experienced when Kuṇḍalini Śakti and Parama-Śiva are united. This is a bolder and larger system and synthesis than the Vedānta of Śaṅkara. In the Dakshiṇa Mārga of Tantra, knowledge is predominant while in the Vāma Mārga enjoyment is predominant, but both worship Śakti.

Ādyā-Śakti or Parāprakṛiti of Pūrṇa Yoga has not only created all Jīvas but has entered into each of them as its own Prakṛiti sleeping in our inconscience. Further, in Pūrṇa Yoga, Śrī Aurobindo teaches that not only Mukti and Bhukti must be attained, but a full descent of the Divine Śakti in the Jīva or individual. A new race free from disease, decay, and death shall be a consummation of the terrestrial evolution because there shall be an integral transformation of human nature into the Divine.

Further Aims of Pūrṇa Yoga

Pūrṇa Yoga requires a threefold process : Psychicisation, Spiritualisation, and Transformation.

Note that in English 'psychic' is usually used to point to something deeper than the external life, something occult or supraphysical; but in Śri Aurobindo's Pūrṇa Yoga the words 'psyche' or 'psychic' is used in the pure Greek sense of 'soul', the Divine Spark containing all the potentialities of the Divine to be unfolded.

As the mental life uses and perfects the material, so will the spiritual use and perfect the material, vital, and mental as instruments of the divine nature.

Sri Aurobindo in an article called "The Brain of India" says, "To raise up the physical to the spiritual is Brahmacharya, for by the meeting of the two the energy which starts from one and produces the other is enhanced and fulfils itself." He further relates in the same article of the transmuting process of sperm-fire to Spiritual Force or Vīrya. The refinement takes place successively as follows : Sperm-fire (retas) is refined from water (jala) to fiery energy (tapas), then to electricity (vidyut), then radiant energy (ojas) which fills man's whole being with all types of power and strength, and lastly Ojas creates Spiritual Force or Vīrya. It is this Vīrya, Spiritual Force and dauntless energy, which leads man to spiritual unfoldment along with all its concomitant wondrous faculties.

Sri Aurobindo speaks of Divine love as the crown of all Being and leads from the suffering of division into the bliss of perfect union.

Pūrṇa Yoga includes the essence and many processes of the other older Yogas. Its newness is its aim : a change of life and existence, not a departure out of the world and life into heaven or Nirvāṇa. The object is a cosmic one, not only a supercosmic one. It is to make Vijñāna or Supermind directly active in the earth nature. Transformation means a bringing down of this Divine Consciousness, static and dynamic, into all parts of the being, and changing them for Divine use.

All Yogas are special psychological processes founded on a fixed truth of nature, and the development of these to extraordinary powers beyond the normal. As material life with all its servitude to machinery and its victorious artificiality has its disadvantages, so Yoga in its inward turn, has lost hold of common existence, and attained an inner freedom by an outer death. An incompatibility has grown between life in the world and spiritual growth and perfection.

Though the ideal is a victorious harmony between inner and outer life it has been little exemplified. So Yoga has come to imply escape from life, but no synthesis of Yoga can be satisfying that does not reunite God and nature in a perfected human life.

King Janaka, the ideal Karma-yogin of ancient lore, attained to perfection by equal and desireless works done as a sacrifice, without the least egoistic aim or attachment. So works can be continued after liberation in a large Divine spirit, with a calm high nature of a spiritual royalty.

Yogas That Deal with Perfecting the Physical Body

Kuṇḍalinī Yoga is the highest Yoga in which a perfect Samādhi is gained by the union with Śiva of both mind and body.

Haṭha Yoga deals with the physical body, its power and functions, and affects the subtle body through the gross body.

Mantra Yoga is specially concerned with forces and powers at work outside, though affecting the body.

Laya Yoga deals with the supersensible centers, forces, and functions of the inner world of the body.

Tantra Yoga refers to immortality being possible by the return of Kuṇḍalinī awakened, but does not develop it. It cures the ravages of disease and wrinkles and man becomes long-lived until as Jīvanmukta at the end of life he attains Kailāsa or the world of Ānanda.

Sri Aurobindo's Pūrṇa Yoga teaches that the descent of Śakti can completely conquer disease and death, and a divine life be started on earth. The Yoga of Tantra is the Yoga of dissolution through Śakti, at least that is the stress. Sri Aurobindo's Yoga is the Yoga of creation through Śakti. The Integral Transformation of all Prakṛiti is the Supermind's own Dharma (see Advent Magazine pp. 136-140 on the Yoga Centres beneath Mūlādhāra).

Om Śrī Mirāravindāya Namaḥ Om
Om Honor to Sri Aurobindo and Mother Mira Om

Adhyātma Yoga

"Adhyātma Yoga is, in knowledge, the realization of all things that we see or do not see but are aware of, — men, things, ourselves, events, gods, titans, angels, — as one divine Brahman, and in action and attitude, an absolute self-surrender to the Parātpara Purusha, the transcendent, infinite and universal Personality who is at once personal and impersonal, finite and infinite, self-limiting and illimitable, one and many, and informs with his being not only the Gods above, but man and the worm and the clod below. The surrender must be complete. Nothing must be reserved, no desire, no demand, no opinion, no idea that this must be, that cannot be, that this should be and that should not be; — all must be given. The heart must be purified of all desire, the intellect of all self-will, every duality must be renounced, the whole world seen and unseen must be recognized as one supreme expression of concealed Wisdom, Power and Bliss, and the entire being given up, as an engine is passive in the hands of the driver, for the divine Love, Might and perfect Intelligence to do its work and fulfil its divine Līlā. Ahaṅkāra must be blotted out in order that we may have, as God intends us ultimately to have, the perfect bliss, the perfect calm and knowledge and the perfect activity of the divine existence." (From Sri Aurobindo's *The Yoga and its Objects*)

Pūrṇa Yoga — Integral Yoga
Sanskrit Terms Used in Pūrṇa Yoga
(Only Terms Not Used Elsewhere)

Saṅkalpa   Determination.

Ātmasamarpaṇa   Self-surrender.

Parātpara Purusha	Higher than the Highest Spirit.
Līlā	The Play of the Divine.
Nityamukta	Always free.
Manushya	Man.
Anumati	Sanction.
Smṛiti	Remembrance.
Dhṛiti	Spiritual patience.
Utsāha	Perseverance, constant alertness — a quality of the vital will.
Pramāda	Cloudiness.
Dhīra	Self-composed.
Apramatta	Without losing oneself.
Nitya Anusmaraṇa	Always remembering.
Bhoga	Enjoyment.
Sanatsujātiya	A chapter in the Mahābhārata.
Kāla	Time.
Satsaṅga	Company of the holy.
Ādhāra	The containing system composed of the five sheaths of the five principles constituting the physical, vital, mental, supramental and spiritual being.
Yajamāna	One who performs a sacrifice.
Kartṛitva-abhimāna	Idea of self as doer.
Niḥspṛiha	Without any hankering.
Saṁskāra	Fundamental tendencies, habitual impulsions.
Rāgadvesha	Desire and hate.

Pāpa   Sin.

Puṇya   Merit.

Sukṛita   That which is well done.

Dushkṛita   That which is badly done.

Kartavyam   The action that is to be done; duty.
  Karma

Buddhi Bhāva   Higher mental state.

Sushupta   Deep Sleep.

Jāgrata   Awake.

Ananta   Infinite.

Viśva   The All.

Hiraṇyagarbha   The Golden Egg; the Universe.

Taijasa   The Shining One.

Prajñā   Fore-knowledge or perfect wisdom.

Aparārdha   The lower half.

Parārdha   The upper half.

Mahattva   Greatness of sustaining force.

Bala   Abounding strength of outgoing and managing
                         force.

Laghutā   Lightness, swiftness, and adaptability of the
                         nervous and physical being.

Dhāraṇa-   A holding and responsive power in the whole
  Sāmarthya   physical machine.

Saumyatva   Gentleness, benevolence.

Tejas   Fiery spirit.

Kalyāṇa-   Excellent faith.
  Śraddhā

Prema-Sāmarthya	Power of Love.
Pūrṇatā	Fullness of strength, and tireless drive of radiant energies.
Prasannatā	Crystal purity and gladness.
Samatā	Harmonious equality.
Sarvabhoga-sāmarthya	Power of illimitable possession and enjoyment.
Viśuddhi	Perfect purity.
Prakāśa	Radiance.
Vichitrabodha	Manifold wisdom.
Sarva-jñāna-sāmarthya	Power of all wisdom.
Daivyam Janam	The divine race.
Lilāmāyā	The illusion of the Play of God.
Abhaya Vachana	Words of fearlessness.
Brāhmī-Sthiti	Center of Divine radiation.
Anirdeśyam	Indescribable.
Parama Śiva	The highest Śiva, or the Divine of the Tantra.
Dakshiṇa Mārga	The right-hand path.
Vāma Mārga	The left-hand path.
Bhukti	Enjoyment.
Vīrya	Dauntless spiritual energy.
Retas	Sperm-fire.
Jala	Water.
Tapas	Fiery energy.
Vidyut	Electricity.

Ojas   Radiant.

King Janaka   An ideal Karma-yogin of ancient India.

Adhyātma   The Yoga of the Self beyond.
  Yoga

"Sarvam eva Brahma"
   All indeed (is) the Divine.

"Śāntam Alakshaṇam"
   Peaceful without feature.

"Ātmānam sarvabhūteshu sarvabhūtāni chātmani"
   Self in all beings and all beings in the Self.
   (You will see) the Self in all existing things and all existing
   things in the Self.

"Avyakto vyaktāt paraḥ"
   Unmanifest than the manifest higher.
   Higher than the manifest and unmanifest existence.

VOCABULARY
(Terms Not Used Elsewhere)

Abhaya-Vachana	Arghya
Āchamana	Asamprajñāta
Achintya-Śakti	Asamprajñāta Samādhi
Ādhāra	Āsana
Adhyātma	Ashṭāṅga-Yoga
Adhyātma Yoga	Asteya
Anirdeśyam	Ātma-Bhāva
Aniruddha	Ātma-nivedana
Antaraṅga	Ātmasamarpaṇa
Antarmukha-Vṛitti	Bala
Anumati	Bahiraṅga
Aparārdha	Balarāma
Aparigraha	Basti
Apramatta	Bhajan
Archanā	Bhakti-Sūtras

Bhoga
Bhūchari Siddhi
Bhūjangāsana
Bhukti
Bhūshaka
Brahmacharya
Brahma-jñāna
Brahma-nāḍī
Brahma-nāma
Brahmanishtha
Brahmarandhra
Brāhmīsthiti
Brahmavid-Varishtha
Chakrāsana
Chaṇḍī
Chitrā-nāḍī
Daivī-Śakti
Daivyam Janam
Dakshiṇa Mārga
Dardura-Siddhi
Dāsya
Dhanurāsana
Dhāraṇā
Dhāraṇa-Sāmarthya
Dhauti
Dhīra
Dhṛiti
Dhūpa
Dīpa
Durgā
Dushkṛita
Dvesha
Gandha
Guru Kṛipā
Halāsana
Hiraṇyagarbha
Ichchhā-Mṛityu Siddhi

Iḍā Nāḍī
Indriyaṇigraha
Īśvarārpaṇa
Jala
Janaka
Japa
Kaivalya-Mukti
Kāla
Kalyāṇa-Śraddhā
Kāṇḍa
Kartavyam Karma
Kartṛitva-abhimāna
Kāya Siddhi
Khechari Siddhi
Kīrtana
Kriyā
Kshudra Brahmāṇḍa
Kumbhaka
Kuṇḍalinī
Laghutā
Likhita-Japa
Līlā
Līlāmāyā
Madhuparka
Mādhurya
Mahālakshmī
Mahāprema
Mahāśakti
Mahāsarasvatī
Mahattva
Mahāvīra
Maheśvarī
Maitrī
Mālā
Manana
Mānasika Japa
Manushya

Matsyāsana

Matsyendrāsana

Māyurāsana

Meru

Merudaṇḍa

Mṛityuñjaya-Siddhi

Muditā

Mudrā

Mumukshatva

Nāḍī

Naivedya

Nārada

Nauli

Neti

Niḥspṛiha

Nirvikalpa-Samādhi

Nitya Anusmaraṇa

Niyama

Nityamukti

Ojas

Padahastāsana

Pada-sevana

Padmāsana

Pādya

Pāpa

Parama Śiva

Parārdha

Parātpara Purusha

Parāvidyā

Paśchimottānāsana

Pātāla Siddhi

Piṅgalā-nāḍī

Pradyumna

Prajñā

Pramāda

Prāṇāyāma

Praṇidhāna

Prasannatā

Pratīka

Pratyāhāra

Prema

Prema-Sāmarthya

Pūjā

Puṇya

Pūrṇatā

Puraścharaṇa

Pūrvaka

Pushpa

Rāga

Rechaka

Retas

Ṛishi Śāṇḍilya

Rudrāksha

Sadāchāra

Sakhya

Śalabhāsana

Śāligrām

Śama

Samādhāna

Samprajñāta

Saṁyama

Sānanda

Sanatsujātiya

Saṅkalpa

Saṅkīrtana

Śānta

Śānta-Īśvara

Śaraṇāgati

Sarvabhogasāmarthya

Sarva-jñāna-sāmarthya

Sarvāṅgāsana

Sasmita

Satya-dharma

Saumyatva

Śavāsana
Savichāra
Savitarka
Sāyujya-Mukti
Shaṭ Chakra(s)
Shaṭ Sampatti
Siddhāsana
Śīrshāsana
Śivo'ham = Śivaḥ aham
Śloka
Smṛiti
Snāna
Śravaṇa
Śreshṭha
Śrotriya
Stotra
Sukṛita
Sūrya Namaskāra
Sushumnā Nāḍī
Svāgata
Svarūpa
Taijasa
Tāmbula
Titikshā
Trāṭaka

Trikāla Jñāna Siddhi
Trikoṇāsana
Ṭrishṇā
Tulasī Mālā
Umā
Upāchāra
Upāṁśu Japa
Uparati
Utsāha
Vaidya Śāstra
Vairāgya
Vajra Nāḍī
Vāma Mārga
Vandana
Vāsanās
Vastra
Vātsalya
Vichitrabodha
Vidyut
Vaikhari-Japa
Viśuddhi
Viśva
Viśva Prema
Yajamāna
Yama

QUOTATIONS

Om Hari Om

Om Namo Bhagavate Vāsudevāya

Om Namo Nārāyaṇāya

Om Namaḥ Śivāya

Om Śrī Rāma Jaya Rāma Jaya Jaya Rāma

Samatvam Yoga Uchyate

Śāntam Alakshaṇam

Sarvam Eva Brahma

Ātmānam Sarvabhūteshu Sarvabhūtāni Chātmani

Avyakto Vyaktāt Paraḥ

Yogaḥ Karmasu Kauśalam.

Na me bhaktaḥ praṇaśyati. My devotee does not perish.

Ekamevādvitīyam. Eka-eva-advitīyam. One, verily, not two.

CHAPTER IX

THE VEDA — ITS SPIRITUAL MEANING

Ekam	sad	viprā	bahudhā	vadanti
(one)	(Truth)	(wise)	(variously)	(speak)

Truth is one: the Wise speak of it in many ways.

Sri Aurobindo's Interpretation of the Vedas

Sri Aurobindo, the greatest 'scholar-mystic' of recent years, in a series of articles called "The Secret of the Veda",[1] "Hymns of the Atris"[2] and "Hymns to the Mystic Fire"[3] has revealed in a cogent manner that the Vedas are the ancient psychological and spiritual wisdom of India expressed in a symbolic language which took the visible phenomena of nature, the sun, sky, wind, rain, lightning, dawn, etc., so familiar to every man and employed them for Gods and their activities because these were more revelatory of great truths, more luminous and enduring in their connotation than abstract words.

Hence the Vedas are shown to have a double meaning presented in a system of parallelisms of internal and external deities. But Sri Aurobindo declares that the Veda was primarily a record of spiritual enlightenment. It is secret words for awakened and purified souls. The extraordinary incoherence so puzzling to most translators following Sāyaṇa's exoteric interpretation disappears when this inner interpretation is adopted. A thread of sense exists through the Vedas when this inner meaning is followed, thus showing that the Vedas were primarily meant for the illumined down the ages and that its external meaning which was the secondary meaning was for the worship of the populace. Thus he has justified and substantiated the widely accepted tradition in India that the Vedas are the supreme font of divine knowledge.

---

[1][2][3] : From *Ārya* magazine 1916-1921.

The intricate Vedic ritual is shown to be representative of both the outer and inner sacrifice, the outer ritual and mantra bringing about the benefits in the here and the hereafter, and the inner sacrifice and prayers the spiritual ascension, the complete transmutation of the whole being for a Divine Life on Earth. It teaches that the greater surrender gives the greater right. Coomaraswamy in his essay "Ātmayajña"[1] (Self-Sacrifice), also declares that: "Just as Christianity turns upon and in its rites repeats and commemorates a Sacrifice, so the liturgical texts of the Ṛigveda cannot be considered apart from the rites to which they apply, and so are these rites themselves a mimesis of what was done by the First Sacrificers who found in the Sacrifice their Way from privation, to plenty, darkness to light, and death to immortality." The Upanishads, the essence of Veda, refer to this higher sacrifice as the true Wisdom.

Before the time of Sāyaṇa, the Vedic Commentator, whose ritualistic and naturalistic interpretation of the Vedas which has been so widely accepted in the West as well as by Indians trained in Western scholarship, there was prevalent in India among all schools of traditional commentators such as Yāska, Skandasvāmī, Durga, Udagitha, Venkaṭa Mādhava, Ānanda Tīrtha, Madhva, etc., the knowledge of a triple meaning to be found in the Ṛiks: the *Ādhibhautika* or external worship and ritualistic sense, the *Ādhidaivika*, the cosmogonical, giving the knowledge of the Gods, and the *Ādhyātmika* or spiritual, yielding the knowledge of the Self, of man's inner life in its journey from the mortal to the immortal. Yāska in his *Nirukta*, I, 4, 6, referring to these three interpretations says: "The *Yājñic* or sacrificial is the flower and the *daivic* or that pertaining to the Gods is the fruit or the *daivic* is the flower and the *ādhyātmic* or that pertaining to the supreme self is the fruit".

These other two senses spoken of gradually became obscure and after Upanishad times it seemed that the Vedas were for the priests and the Vedānta or Upanishads, which were a more

---

[1] Harvard Journal of Asiatic Studies, Vol. 6, February 1942.

direct expression of spiritual truth, were for the sages.

But the tradition of Vedic revelation has continued in India. Radhakrishnan says in his *Hindu View of Life*, p.17, "The Vedas register the intuitions of the perfected souls. They are not so much dogmatic dicta as transcripts from life. They record the spiritual experiences of souls strongly endowed with sense of reality. They are held to be authoritative on the ground that they express the experiences of the experts in the field of religion. If the utterances of the Vedas were uninformed by spiritual insight, they would have no claim to our belief. The truths revealed in the Vedas are capable of being re-experienced in compliance with ascertained conditions."

And Yāska clearly mentions that the true sense of the Veda cannot be perceived by the ordinary mind, but can be recovered directly by meditation and *tapasyā* (*Nirukta*, II, 11; XIII, 13). We find similar passages in the Ṛig-Veda (Ṛig-Veda V, 81, 1) and Shaunaka's *Bṛihad Devatā* (VIII, 129; VIII; 130-137).

So Sri Aurobindo, the great Seer and Yogin of India, after undergoing his spiritual discipline and attaining divine realization writes in his Vedic commentaries, "The Secret of the Veda":

"All this Vedic imagery is easy to understand when once we have the key, but it must not be taken for mere imagery. The Gods are not simple personifications of abstract ideas or of psychological and physical functions of Nature. To the Vedic seers they are living realities; the vicissitudes of the human soul represent a cosmic struggle not merely of principles and tendencies but of the cosmic Powers which support and embody them. These are the Gods and the Demons. On the world-stage and in the individual soul the same real drama with the same personages is enacted.

"The development of all these godheads is necessary to our perfection and that perfection must be attained on all our levels — in the wideness of earth, our physical being and consciousness; in the full force of vital speed and action and enjoyment and nervous vibration, typified as the Horse which must be brought forward to up-bear our endeavour; in the perfect gladness of the heart of emotion and a brilliant heat and clarity of the mind through our intellectual and psychical being; in the coming of the supramental Light, the Dawn and the Sun and the shining Mother of the herds, to transform all our existence; for so comes to us the possession of the Truth, by the Truth the admirable surge of the Bliss, in the Bliss infinite Consciousness of absolute being."

In India this higher meaning of the Vedic ritual and worship will aid the country both religiously and economically. Instead of the clarified butter and various food being thrown into the outer Fire, the inner sacrifice or the holy action of feeding or quickening the Divine Immortal spark in man, Agni, the Fire God, will be acted out by kindling the divine fire with the purified and clarified mind, symbolized by the *ghi* and the physical or outer manifestation of the divine in life, symbolized by food or *annam*. Agni, thus invoked, calls and invites other Gods to share in the fruits of the sacrifice and in turn each brings blessing, or interpreted, means that once the God in man is awakened, it reveals its powers and aspects as the flame of his presence is sustained in life.

Then *Indra*, God of the Firmament, the Illumined mentally, appears and is represented as constantly struggling and battling with *Vritra*, the Serpent Adversary who covers with his darkness all divine activity and who hides the cows, the rays of truth-light in the caves of the Panis or the sense-life. *Indra* is often aided in his fight by *Rudra* and his hosts of *Maruts*, the great Destroyer and the storm gods, symbolical of the Breaker of old molds and the powers of will and nervous or vital Force. The *Ribhus*, the Seasons, who accompany them are symbolical of the artisans of the Gods who help one repeat man's divine achievements.

Gradually *Ushas*, the Dawn of higher truth, comes escorted by the *Aśvins*, the Horsemen of the Sun, representing the swiftness and effectiveness of action in the great journey to Truth and illumination, the Sun.

With the glorious Sun of Truth come his goddesses or aspects: *Sāvitrī*, Divine Grace which manifests the immortal in the mortal; *Mitra*, the Friend of the Gods, the luminous power of love leading to harmony in thought, impulse and action; *Varuṇa*, the Vast Expanse, the oceanic wideness and unity of infinite Truth; *Aryaman*, the Chief of the Milky Way, the immortal puissance of clear-discerning aspiration leading beyond.

Then follows *Ṛita* and *Ṛitachit*, Truth in action and Truth-Consciousness with their goddesses or powers: *Mahī* or *Bhāratī*, the Vast Word or greatness of Wisdom that brings us all things out of the Divine source; *Iḷā*, Goddess of Truth vision or revelation; *Saraswatī*, Goddess of streaming inspiration; *Saramā*, the hound of heaven, intuition; and *Dakshiṇā*, Goddess of divine discernment.

Soma, the God of immortal nectar is the consummation of beatitude, the wine of immortality and divine ecstasy.

Thus in the Vedas is portrayed richly the psychological science of the transformation of the human into the Divine, the mental into the Supermental, the falsehood into the Truth, darkness into Light, mortality into Immortality.

A specialized study, following along the lines of any one of these keys given would enrich the science of higher psychology. Excluding a few Christian mystics, Western Science is a babe in respect to the supernormal psychology so minutely and beautifully presented in the Vedic *śāstras*. Sri Aurobindo shows that *Ṛitachit* or Truth-Consciousness of the *Vedas*, is a promise to those who make the inner Yajña or sacrifice. The how of this sacrifice is fully unfolded by the unveiling of the symbol-language of Veda. Thus Sri Aurobindo, the fine flower of the Renaissance of the Sanātana Dharma or Perennial Truth, has shown that the poetic hymns of the Ṛishis of old India were both intuitive of, and a psychological and spiritual guide to a Divine Life on Earth.

But the Veda warns: "To enter into the very heart of the mystic doctrine, we must ourselves have trod the ancient paths and renewed the lost discipline, the forgotten experience. Who will have the strength to recover the light of the Forefathers or soar above the two enclosing firmaments of mind and body into their luminous empyrean of the infinite Truth?

"Who will free the radiant herds of the Sun imprisoned in the darkling cave of the Lords of the sense-life? When will the Maruts again drive abroad and when the Hound of Heaven once again speed down to us from beyond the rivers of Paradise and break the seals of the heavenly water and the caverns be rent and the immortalising wine be pressed out in the body of man by the electric thunder stones?

"Till this happens the secret of the Veda, even when it has been unveiled, remains a secret." (Sri Aurobindo, *Secret of the Veda*)

Sri Aurobindo's hints and leads to a higher understanding and use of the Veda have not passed into the ethers with him, but are bearing rich fruit in India today. Sri T. V. Kapāli Śāstri, one of the great and illumined Sanskrit Pandits of South India, recognizing Sri Aurobindo as the 'Recoverer of the Lost Lights of the Vedas', has taken the symbolic keys given by Sri Aurobindo in his translations and commentaries and worked them out in full detail in a systematic and scholarly and penetrating commentary into Sanskrit, a Ṛig Veda Bhāshya entitled *Siddhāñjana* or "Mystic Collyrium".

M. P. Pandit, a young and devoted disciple and brilliant Sanskrit scholar of the Sri Aurobindo Ashram, recently published this work and says, regarding the title, that the name of the commentary signifies that it "gives us the vision clear and direct which pierces straight into the heart and real nature of the Ṛig Veda undeflected by the coverings of dogma and prejudice which have accumulated through the ages and reduced the ancient tradition of the revealed character of the Veda to a mockery. For the word *Veda* means Knowledge and it was as such that the country's tradition dating back to the Upanishads regarded the Veda. The Vedas were regarded as the supreme fount of divine knowledge and were looked up to as the Parent-Arbiter by every characteristic school of thought and philosophy in the land.

"...We are fortunate that a work of such a capital importance has been undertaken by Śrī Śāstrī who is singularly qualified for the task by reason of his intimacy with the facts and truths of the life spiritual to which he has devoted himself with exclusive preoccupation.

"This work is not only the life-time's work of an individual but is a crowning glory of achievement of our national quest for ages. The author has plunged himself into the profundities and depths of a past age and has brought out the result of his labours in this literary and scholarly contribution. It is at once subtle and deep, yet lucid and easily understandable.

"Transcending, yet benefitted by all the previous authorities like Yāska or Sāyaṇa, the present work takes us to an age that is prehistoric and concretises in our personal experience the truth of a rich spiritual living retrieved from the trammels of Time..." (From a circular sent out by M. P. Pandit on Kapāli Śāstrī's *Siddhāñjana*).

For further works in English, summarizing the information given in the Sanskrit commentary of Kapāli Śāstrī, see the same author's *Lights on the Vedas, Lights on the Upanishads, Lights on the Teachings, Lights on the Fundamentals*.

See also the article by Kapāli Śāstrī in *Sri Aurobindo Mandir Annual* 1950: "Anjah-Save or The Rapid Rite of a Seer-Priest" and articles by M. P. Pandit in the *Sri Aurobindo Mandir Annual* 1949: "Legend of Shunah Shepa" and in *Sri Aurobindo Circle* 1950: "Vedic Study: Need for a New Approach."

A divine word that came vibrating out of the Infinite to the inner audience of the prepared one, the self-cultured one; the direct hearing of the word of Truth; a faculty of the Super-

mind. *Śruti* is a rhythm not composed like ordinary poems by
the intellect, but a creative word that thrilled out
Śruti of the Infinite Bliss of Self-realization. It is a
record of the Soul-experience of Sons of Light and Truth first
seen within and then poured out into the entrancing Spirit's
hymn of Life Divine. *Śruti* is inspired writing, revelation,
scripture, revealed by the Spirit.

'That which has been heard', the Word. The Word may
come to us from within; it may come to us from without. But
in either case, it is only an agency for setting the
Śruta hidden knowledge to work. The word within may
be the utterance of the inmost soul in us which is always open
to the Divine or it may be the word of the secret universal
Teacher who is seated in the hearts of all. The Word from
without, representative of the Divine is ordinarily needed as an
aid in the work of self-unfolding, and it may be either a word
from the past or the more powerful word of the living *Guru*.
Written scripture is some word from the past which embodies
the experience of former Yogins. All written *Śāstra*, however
great its authority or however large its spirit, cannot be more
than a partial expression of the Eternal Knowledge. In the end,
one must live in his own soul beyond the written Truth:
Śabdabrahmātivartate (He should go beyond the word of God).
He must become a *sādhaka* of the Infinite (*śru* — to hear).

Honor; worship; adoring submission to the deity by prostration of the body; inward prostration, the act of submission or
surrender to the deity. In *Veda*, internal and ex-
Namas ternal obeisance; symbol of submission to the
divine Being in ourselves and in the world. It is the offering of
that completest submission and the self-surrender of all the
faculties of the lower egoistic human nature to the divine Will-
force, *Agni*, so that, free from internal opposition, it may lead
the soul of man through the truth towards a felicity full of
spiritual riches (*nam* — to bow, to bend).

Rich (Rig, Rik) Verse. Hence Rig-Veda. Verses of Wisdom.

The Seer, the truth-seer, those who saw the true law of things, directly by inner vision. *Vedic Ṛishis* never attained to Super-

Ṛishi   mind for the earth or perhaps never made the attempt. They tried to rise individually to the supramental plane, but did not bring it down and make it a permanent part of the earth-consciousness. (Verses in the Upanishad: "It is impossible to pass through the gates of the Sun (symbol of Supermind) and yet retain the earthly body.") Names of *Ṛishis* in the *Veda* have significance. They represent certain spiritual victories which tend to be constantly repeated in the experience of humanity:

Shunaḥ Shepa   *Shunaḥ Shepa* — Bliss-ray.

Gavishṭhira   *Gavishṭhira* — Steadfast in the Light.

Atri   *Atri* — General name of *Ṛishis*: Eater or traveller.

"Out of devouring desire, experience and enjoyment of the forms of the world he advances to the liberated truth and delight of the soul in the possession of its infinite existence.

"The *Ṛishis* of old India were knowers of the Divine as well as *Kavis*, poet-seers who revealed the eternal truths of the universe that they intuitively perceived in poetic hymns now known as the *Ṛig-Veda*. The *Ṛishis'* work for humanity was not only to know God, but to know the world and all aspects of life and to reduce this high knowledge to a form understandable to man's mind and yet keep it alive through the ages with the purity and vitality of truth so that it would always appeal and awaken man's higher consciousness. These *Ṛishis*, instead of using abstract language and symbol took the visible phenomena of nature, the sun, sky, wind, rain and lightning, etc. so familiar to every man and employed them for Gods and their activities because these were more revelatory of great truths, more luminous and enduring in their connotation than words." (Sri Aurobindo, *Secret of the Veda*)

Seer, poet of God-vision. The *Kavi* in Vedic thought indicated the divine supra-intellectual knowledge which by direct

vision and illumination sees the reality, the principles, and
the forms of things in their true relation. *Svayambhū*
Kavi   sees or comprehends Himself in the essence of the
Fact as *Kavi*. The Lord appears to us first, in the relative notion
of the process of things, as the *Kavi* who sees the Truth in itself,
in its becoming, in its essence, possibilities and actuality. He
contains all that is in the Idea, the Vijñāna, called the Truth and
the Law — *Satyam Ritam*. He contains it comprehensively, not
piecemeal; the Truth and Law of things is the *Brihat*, the Large.

The true thought (*man* — to think). The singing of the Rik,
the hymn of illumination. The *Satya Mantra* is the true
thought expressed in the rhythm of the truth; the
Mantra   hidden light is found and the Dawn brought to
birth.

A large collection of hymns containing spiritual and psychological knowledge concealed in figures and symbols. The Source
of Knowledge for both the profane and initiated,
Rig-Veda   the book of outer and inner sacrifice: the outer
worship for the profane and the inner discipline for the initiate.
The thread of sense in this inner meaning is a Divine Algebra
which repeats throughout the same phrases and terms for ini-
tiates down the years; not primitive but well thought out. The
direct words of the Upanishads caused the mystic Vedic symbols to be forgotten.

Gāyatrī   A meter and verse of the Rig-Veda (III, 62, 10)
used as a sacred formula for initiation of the Sacred
Thread.

Om bhūr bhuvah svah!
Tat savitur varenyam
Bhargo devasya dhīmahi
Dhiyo yo nah prachodayāt.

1	2	3		1	2	3
Om bhūr bhuvah svah!				Earth, Midworld, Heaven!		

4	5	6		9		4
Tat savitur varenyam				Let us meditate on that most		

7	8	9		6	7	8	5

Bhargo devasya dhīmahi   Excellent light of the divine Sun,

11	10 12	13		10	13	12 11

Dhiyo yo naḥ prachodayāt.   That it may illumine our minds.

Amṛito	
martveshu	An immortal awakened to truth in mortals.
ṛitāvā	

Tad Ekam Tat	The vast mightiness of the Gods: That One
Satyam	concealed by this truth is That Truth of You.

Satyam Ṛitam	The True, the Right, the Vast, Character of
Bṛihat	the supramental consciousness.

Arka	Hymn of illumination.

VEDIC GODS

Notes from "Hymns to the mystic Fire" and "On the Veda" by Sri Aurobindo.

A God; a power or personality of the universal Godhead. The Gods represent each some essential puissance of the Divine Being. They manifest the cosmos and are manifest in it. Children of Light, Sons of the Infinite, they recognize in the soul of man their brother and ally and desire to help and increase him by themselves increasing in him so as to possess his world with their light, strength and beauty. The Gods call man to a divine companionship and alliance; they attract and uplift him to their luminous fraternity, invite his aid and offer theirs against the Sons of Darkness and Division. Man in return calls the Gods to his sacrifice, offers to them his swiftnesses and his strengths, his clarities and his sweetness — milk and butter of the shining Cow, distilled juices of the Plant of Joy, the Horse of the Sacrifice, the radiant coursers. He receives them into his being and their gifts into his life, increases them by the hymn and the wine and forms perfectly, as a smith forges iron (says the Veda) their great and luminous godheads. As the Gods have built the series of the cosmic worlds, even so they labor to build up the same series of ordered states and ascending degrees in man's consciousness from the mortal condition to the crowning immortality. To what gods shall the sacrifice be offered? Who shall be invoked to manifest and project in the human being this increasing godhead? The Gods are conquerors and givers of the Cows or rays of light, and the Horses or divine energies, and the divine riches.

Fire; the Vedic God of Fire, Symbol of Divine Will, and the fire of human aspiration. The fire of sacrifice is no material flame. It is the Brahman-word energy, inner Agni, priest of the sacrifice, into which the offering is poured; it is "The fire of self-control or it is purified sense-action, or it is vital energy in that discipline of the control of the vital being through the control of breath which is common to Rāja Yoga and Haṭha Yoga, or it is the fire of self-knowledge, the flame of the supreme sacrifice" (Sri Aurobindo, *Essays on the Gita* I, 108). *Agni* is the Flame of Divine Force, Illumined Will, Divine Will, Fire of Human Aspiration.

He is divine force which manifests first in matter as heat and light and material energy, and then taking different forms in other principles of man's consciousness, leads him by a progressive manifestation upwards to the Truth and the Bliss.

The flame of *Agni* is the seven-tongued power of the Will, a Force of God instinct with knowledge. This conscious and forceful will is the immortal guest in our mortality, a pure priest and a divine worker, the mediator between earth and heaven. It carries what we offer to the higher Powers and brings back in return their forces and light and joy into our humanity.

Agni, the fire-purifier, devours all the forms of material existence and enjoyment in order to reduce them to their divine equivalent.

In Truth Will is in harmony with truth of things, therefore effective of Divine Will. Will is first necessity, the chief actualizing force. When man turns towards great aims consciously and offers his enriched capacities to the Sons of Heaven and seeks to form the Divine in himself *Agni* is first and chief.

Agni, the truth-conscious Seer-Will, is the principal godhead who enables us to effect the sacrifice; he leads us on the path of the Truth, he is the warrior of the battle, the doer of the work, and his unity and universality in us comprehending in itself all other godheads is the basis of immortality.

Aditi   Infinite consciousness; Infinite Mother of the gods. She is the source of all the cosmic forms of consciousness from the physical upwards.

Āditya(s)   Sons of *Aditi*, the Mother of the Gods; the solar deities, variously enumerated as seven or eight or twelve; they are the sons of Infinite Consciousness.

Color like the sun, descriptive of the light of *Purushottama* (the highest Spirit). This light is seen visually by the *sūkshma dṛishṭi*, the subtle vision. It is a fact of spiritual experience.

Ādityavarṇa

The universal *Agni* or universal Divine Will who contains in himself all the gods and all the worlds, upholds all the universal workings and finally fulfils the godhead, the immortality; He is the worker of the divine Work.

Agni Vaiśvā-
nara

Airāvata   Chief of elephants churned from the ocean. A name of Indra's (Illumined Mind) elephant, symbolic of the power and plenitude of the luminous world of the Divine Mind.

The *Angirasas* are the seven Ṛishis or sages, descendants of Angiras, the author of the ninth book of Ṛig Veda. They represent aspiring humanity, the sun's flames, bringers of the Dawn, powers of *Agni*, rescuers of the Sun out of darkness. Divine seers who assist in the human working of the Gods and their earthly representatives. Powers of the seer-will, the flame of the Dawn-Force instinct with victorious knowledge. They may have been human and then deified by their descendants or may have been divine beings humanized as the Fathers of the race and dis-

Angirasas
(Plural)
Angiras
(Singular)

coverers of Wisdom. *Agni* is the fire and the *Aṅgirasas* are the burning coal. The *Aṅgirasas* are the radiant lusters of Agni. The Aṅgirasas' function is to bring the divine Dawn into mental nature. They are at once divine and human seers, the path, and the goal.

Waters; the waters of being, the Mothers from whom all forms of existence are born. In the Vedic sense, the symbol for the

Āpas   seven cosmic principles and their activities: Physical (*anna*), vital (*prāṇa*), mental *manas*, Divine Truth (*vijñāna*), Divine Bliss (*ānanda*), Divine Will and consciousness (*chit*) and Divine Being (*sat*).

Apām-Napāt   'Son of the Waters', (Lightning form of *Agni*), an epithet of *Agni*. The Divine element in aspiring man is born of the waters or principles of being.

An immortal puissance of clear discerning aspiration and endeavour; the aspiring power and action of the Truth; light of the

Aryaman   divine consciousness working as Force; the lord of aspiration and upward labour.

Arjuna   'The White One'; usually an epithet of Dawn in the *Veda*; symbolic also of the *sāttvic* or purified and light-filled soul.

'The two riders on the horses', *Nāsatya* and *Dasra*. They are the lords of nerve and vital power, the enlighteners, the twin

Aśvins   physician gods, the name of two divinities who appear in the sky before dawn in a golden carriage drawn by horses or birds. They bring treasures to men and avert misfortune and sickness, the enlighteners and healers of every malady. They are givers of a happy and enlightened and unmaimed condition of mind, vitality and body. The *Aśvins* are wedded to the daughters of Light, drinkers of honey, bringers of perfect satisfactions, healers of maim and malady. They occupy our parts of knowledge and parts of action and prepare our mental, vital and physical being for an easy and victorious ascension.

The *Aśvins*, like Castor and Pollux, represent powers that carry over the *Rishis* as in a ship or save them from drowning in the ocean. The great change from the inner obscuration to the illumination is effected by the *Aśvins*, lords of the joyous upward action of the mind and the Vital powers, through the immortal wine of the *Ānanda* poured into the mind and body and there drunk by them. They mentalize the expressive Word, they lead us into the Heaven of pure Mind beyond this darkness and there by the Thought they set the powers of Delight to work. But even over the heavenly waters they cross, for the power of *Soma* helps them to dissolve all mental constructions, and they cast aside even this veil; they go beyond Mind and the last attaining is described as the crossing of the rivers, the passage through the heaven of the pure Mind, the journey by the path of the Truth to the other side. Not till we reach the highest supreme *paramaparavat*, do we rest at last from the great human journey.

This all indicates that the *Aśvins* are twin divine powers whose special function is to perfect the nervous or vital being in man in the sense of action and enjoyment. They are powers of Truth, of intelligent action. They bring in their chariots ripe and perfected satisfactions to man, they are the creators of beatitude. They carry man in their ships to the other shore beyond thoughts and states of the human mind to the supramental consciousness. *Sūrya* mounts on their car. They are powers of the Aryan journey, lords of the great human movement.

Barhishad   Lunar ancestors, symbolic of the personal self or lower mind.

The Divine Enjoyer in Man (*bhaga* — enjoyment). The Divine in its pure bliss and all-seizing joy, who dispels the evil

Bhaga   dream of our jarring and divided existence and possesses all things in the light and glory of *Aryaman's* power, *Mitra's* light and life, and *Varuṇa's* unity. These four functions of the soul (*Varuṇa, Mitra, Aryaman* and *Bhaga*) must be firmly established in our mortal nature to open the way for *Surya*. *Bhaga* is a happy spontaneity of the right enjoyment of all things dispelling the evil dream of sin and error and suffering.

The Vast Word that brings us all things out of the divine source: Wisdoms' Vastness; the largeness of the Truth-consciousness, which when drawing on man's limited mind, brings with it the two sister puissances of *Sarasvatī*, truth-audition, and *Iḷā* truth-vision. The three together bring *Mayas* or Bliss to man.

Bhāratī

Expression of heart or soul of man; prayer. *Brahman* in the *Veda* means the *Vedic* Word or mantra in its profoundest aspect as the expression of the intuition. It is a voice of the rhythm which has created the worlds and creates perpetually. *Brahman* in the *Veda* is the soul or soul-consciousness emerging from the secret heart of things, but more often the thought, inspired, creative, full of the secret truth, which emerges from that consciousness and becomes thought of mind, *manma*, or the soul itself. *Brahman* is an expression of the soul: voice of the rhythm perpetually creating the world.

Brahman

The Vedic *Brahmā*, one of three great Gods, the origin of the *Purāṇic Trimūrti*, Father of the World, the evoker of the worlds. The Creator; by the word, by his cry he creates — that is to say, he expresses, he brings out all existence and conscious knowledge and movement of life and eventual forms from the darkness of the Inconscient (*Rudra* and *Vishṇu* are the other two of the trinity). He calls light and the visible cosmos out of the darkness of the inconscient ocean and forms speech which is the formation of conscious being upward to the supreme goal.

Brahmaṇas-pati

Creator of the Word, he gives the word of knowledge, the potency of word-power, the creative rhythm of expression. He is the Fashioner of the 'calling of the Gods'. *Brihaspati* conquers and slays the foe by the hymns of illumination. The host and troop of *Brihaspati* are the *Aṅgirasa Rishis* who by the true mantra help in the great victory. The

Brihaspati

seven-mouthed *Brihaspati* are the seven *Angirasas* who repeat the divine word which comes from the seat of power or *Svar* and of which he is the lord (hence *Brahmanaspati*).

Chitraratha — The king of the *Gandharvas*, musicians of the gods, the king of a tribe of vital beings (*chitra* — variegated, *ratha* — cart).

Dadhikravan — The divine war-horse, a power of Agni.

Daityas — Beings of the intermediate planes.

Daksha — Intuitive discrimination, the understanding mind (*daksh* — to be able).

Dakshina — The discerning knowledge that comes with the Dawn of the spirit; the separative intuitional discrimination. The fifth power of the *Ritachit* or Truth-consciousness, her function is to discern rightly, to dispose the action and the offering and to distribute to each godhead its portion of the sacrifice of the aspirant. *Dakshina* is the goddess of divine discernment, a form of the Dawn herself. She presides over the right-hand powers of the sacrifice and distribution of the offering (*daksh* — to be able).

Diśaḥ — The quarters of directions of Space (*diś* — to point to).

Gopati — Master of the herds, a title of *Indra*.

Gomati — A description of Dawn as 'full of light', entirely possessed of the Light, implying richness of mental illumination (*go* — cow; *mati* — thought).

Gandharvas — Musical ministrants of the upper air, the musicians of the gods, powers of the vital world that preside over artistic activities.

Indra — God of the Firmament with his thunderbolt. *Indra* has a wealth of cows and horses, light and energy, which man covets. *Indra* is the Puissant, the power of pure existence self-manifested as the Divine Mind. As Agni is one pole of Force instinct with knowledge that sends its current upward from the earth to heaven, so Indra is the other pole of Light instinct with force which descends from heaven to earth. He comes down into our world as the Hero with the shining horses and slays darkness and division with his lightnings, pours down the life-giving heavenly waters, finds in the trace of the hound, Intuition, the lost or hidden illuminations, makes the Sun of Truth mount high in the heaven of our mentality. He is:

Vajriṇaḥ — thunderarmed

Dhanasput — winner of wealth

Vṛitrahari — slayer of *Vṛitra*

Vṛishabha — bull of the herds

Indra is the king of all the gods in heaven; the Lord of the Illumined Mind, the luminous Mind, the *Ṛishi* of life-powers, the slayer of *Vṛitra*, the Coverer. *Indra*, when full of *Soma*-ecstasy, is sure to give light, that is, when *Soma*-drunk he is cow-giving or light-giving. When *Indra* is intoxicated with *Soma*, which is his strength, he conquers cows. *Indra's* right and left hands are his two powers of action in knowledge.

Iḷā	Goddess of Truth-vision or revelation. She is the vision of knowledge, the strong primal word of the Truth who gives us its active vision. The Word of Truth, the Teacher of knowledge, she is full of energy (*suvīra*). *Iḷā* is the vision of the seer which attains the truth.
Indu	The moon, symbolic of mind-power.
Iśāna	A ruler, one of the older names of *Śiva-Rudra* (*īś* — to own, be master of).
Kandarpa	Eros, the God of Love.
Kārtikeya	God of war, Mars.
Kubera	The God of riches and treasure.
Kumāra	The pure Male, the soul of Man revealed in its universality.

Lokapāla(s)	Guardians of the eight points of the compass.		
1. Indra	East	Airāvata	Abhramu
2. Agni	Southeast	Puṇḍarīka	Kapilā
3. Yama	South	Vāmana	Puṅgalā
4. Sūrya	Southwest	Kumuda, Nirṛita	Anupamā
5. Varuṇa	West	Añjana	Añjanavatī
6. Vāyu	Northwest	Pushpadanta	Śubha-dantī
7. Kuvera	North	Sārva-bhauma	
8. Soma	Northeast	Śiva(s) Īśāna	Su-pratīka

Maghavan An epithet of *Indra*, the 'Great'.

The great sages: *Marīchi, Atri, Aṅgiras, Pulastya, Pulaha, Kratu, Prashṭas, Vasishṭha, Bhrigu* and *Nārada* (*mahā* — great; *rishi* — seer). The seven ancient Great Seers are intelligence-powers of that divine Wisdom which Maharshi(s) has evolved all things out of its own self-conscious infinitude, developed them down the range of the seven-principles of its own essence. These *Rishis* embody the all-upholding, all-illuminating, all-manifesting seven Thoughts of the *Veda, sapta dhiyaḥ*.

Mahas 'The Great', the infinity of Truth, the supramental or Truth-consciousness, the large consciousness where separateness disappears.

Mahī or Bhāratī The greatness of Wisdom, Wisdom's vastness, the vast Word that brings us all things out of the divine source, the luminous vastness of Truth like a branch covered with fruit. *Mahī* is one of the five powers of *Rita-chit*.

Marīchi Chief of the *Maruts*, the storm-gods.

The Storm-Gods, *Indra's* helpers, powers of will and nervous or vital Force that have attained to the light of thought and the voice of self-expression. They are behind all Maruts thought and speech as its impellers and they battle towards the Light, Truth and Bliss of the supreme Consciousness. The *Maruts* are powers of thought that break old molds, Energies of mind, Friends of Truth, Creators of Light, Destroyers of obstacles. They are not the settled truth, but the movement, the search, the lightning-flash, and when Truth is found, the many-sided play of its separate illuminations. They are *Rudra's* children, who make light for themselves by violence. The *Maruts* are singers of the World, of the prayer of *Brahman*, they are the Life-Powers that support by their nervous or vital energies the action of the thought in the attempt of the mortal consciousness to grow and expand itself into the immortality of the Truth and Bliss.

Mātariśvan   The life-breath, the life that grows in the Mother (*mātari* — in the mother; *śva* — to grow).

Lord of love and light, the all-embracing harmony of Truth, the Friend of all Beings who takes all our activities of thought and feeling and will, links them into a Divine harmony, charioteers our movement and dictates our works. *Mitra* is a luminous power of love and comprehension leading and forming into harmony all our thoughts, acts and impulses. When the Divine Will or *Agni* is entirely delivered and fulfilled out of the envelope of the world's crookedness, this deity of flame and force is revealed as the solar godhead of love and harmony and light, *Mitra*, who leads men towards the truth. *Agni* unfolded becomes *Mitra*, the Lord of Love, who introduces the principle of harmony into the workings of the divine effort in us and thus combines all the lines of our advance, all the strands of our sacrifice until the work is accomplished in the supreme unity of Knowledge, Power and Delight. *Mitra* is Force and Love united, and both illumined by knowledge, fulfill God in the world.

Parjanya   The rain-cloud, the giver of the rain of heaven.

Pāvaka   The 'Cleanser', an epithet of *Agni*, the 'purifying flame' (*pū* — to purify).

Pavana   Wind, air.

The Cosmic Person, Lord of the Universe becoming, or coming into existence in front of the consciousness at a parti-

Prabhu   cular point as a particular object or experience. *Soma* emerges into the consciousness concentrated at some particular point, *prabhu*, or as some particular experience and then pervades the whole being as *Ānanda prabhu*.

Prachetas   The conscious thinker, conscious observation (*pra* — before; *chit* — be conscious).

Prajāpati   Lord of creation, the father of creatures, lord of becoming.

Purushas   Male gods, active divine souls or powers. *Agni* is the Divine *Purusha*.

Pūshan   A name for the Sun; the Fosterer, Increaser; Symbol of the Truth that effects the enlargement of the divided self-perception and action of will into integral will and knowledge. He is sole seer, and replacing other forms of knowledge by his unifying vision, enables us to arrive finally at oneness.

Rātrī   Goddess of the starlit night.

Ribhukshan   The skilful Shaper of Knowledge.

Rudra   The *Śiva* of the *Purāṇas*; the third deity of the Hindu Trinity: the destroyer of the world, as *Brahmā* is the creator and emanator and *Vishṇu* the Preserver. He is the Violent and Merciful and Mighty One who presides over the struggle of life to affirm itself, the power of God that lifts forcibly all that errs and resists, heals all that is wounded and suffers and complains and submits. *Rudra* leads upward evolution of conscious being, his force battles against all evil, smites the sinner and the enemy, intolerant of defect and stumbling, he is the most terrible of the Gods.

Saramā   The Fleet One, the hound of heaven, intuition, who descends into the cavern of the subconscient and finds there the concealed illuminations. *Saramā* leads in the search for the radiant herds and discovers both the path and the secret hold in the mountain. *Saramā* is the Forerunner of the

Dawn of Truth in the human mind; the traveller and seeker on the path of Truth and finds what is lost. The knowledge comes to *Saramā* before vision, springing up instinctively at the least indication and with that knowledge she guides the rest of the faculties and divine powers that seek. *Saramā* is the fourth power of Ṛitachit.

Ṛibhu(s)   Artisans of the gods, human powers which by the work of sacrifice and their brilliant ascension to the high dwelling-place of the Sun have attained immortality and help mankind to repeat the achievement. They form things by the mind and build up immortality by works; they are the artisans of immortality.

Śachī   The wife of *Indra*, who symbolizes the Divine Mind.

Sādhya(s)   A class of celestial beings. Their world is said to be above the sphere of the Gods. Differently interpreted through the ages, they are symbolic of the Overmind status.

Śankara   One of the *Rudras*.

Saptarshi(s)   The Seven Seer-Sages of the *Vedas* (*sapta* — seven; *ṛishi* — sage). The *Saptarshis* are the seven original Seers, the intelligence powers of the Divine Wisdom which has evolved all things out of its own self-conscious infinitude, and developed them down the range of the seven principles of its own essence.

Sarasvatī   'She of the stream' (*saras* — stream), the flowing movement, Truth-audition, Divine Word, the streaming current and word of Truth's inspiration; she of wisdom's flowing inspiration. Later in the *Purāṇas* she is Goddess of Learning, Speech and Poetry. She has become now the Muse and Goddess of Learning. *Sarasvatī* is the word, the inspiration that comes directly from the Truth-consciousness. She is the Impeller of happy truths, an awakener of the consciousness to right thinking. She is the mother of the *Rayi*, the herds of the Sun. *Sarasvatī* brings into active consciousness in the human being the great flood, the Truth-consciousness itself, illumines with it all our thoughts. She is the secret self of *Indra*, hence the inspiration of the supramental plane of Truth on the illumined mind (*Indra*). *Sarasvatī* gives the full flood of knowledge; she awakens the great stream (*maho'rṇah*) and illumines with plenitude (*viśva-dhiyo virajati*). She is the third power of *Ṛitachit*.

Savitṛi (masc.) The Sun, the Truth as Creator, God of illumination, God of Creation, the material Sun which illuminates the solar System and is the creator and sustainer of the physical world.

One who is descended from the sun, hence symbolically 'Divine Grace'. Sāvitrī manifests in this mortal world the state of Immortality and dispels the evil dream

Sāvitrī (fem.) of egoism, suffering, and transforms life into the immortality, the good, the beatitude.

Also another name for the Vedic hymn known as the Gāyatrī (q.v.). Sāvitrī is derived from the verb root *su* — 'to give birth to'. The word Soma or 'Divine Nectar' symbolizing 'spiritual ecstasy' is also from the same verb-root.

In Sri Aurobindo's Epic poem of "Sāvitrī" based on a legend in the Mahābhārata Sāvitrī is a princess who embodies Divine Grace descended in human birth to work out with the aspiring soul of humanity his divine destiny. Satyavān whom she marries represents 'Truth' or 'one who has the Truth'.

Wine of delight; wine of immortality, symbolic of divine beatitude. The "Lord of Ānanda — true creator who possesses

Soma the soul and brings out of it a divine creation"

Amṛita ambrosia, Amṛita (*amṛita* — wine of immortality). It is the figure for the Divine *Ānanda* or Bliss. The wine of his ecstasy is concealed in the growths of earth, in the waters of existence; even here in our physical being are his immortalizing juices and they have to be pressed out and offered to all the gods; for in the strength these shall increase and conquer.

The *Taittirīya Upanishads* says that the Secret of Delight is the basis of existence and its sustaining atmosphere and almost its substance. Without this bliss nothing could remain in being.

Soma is the divine delight hidden in all existences which, once manifest, supports all life's crowning activities, and is the force that finally immortalizes the mortal.

Indra, as Intelligence, feeds on *Soma*. Its action becomes an intoxicated ecstasy of inspiration by which the rays of light come pouring abundantly and joyously in.

Soma is pressed out of the rock of inert material. The *Soma*-wine symbolizes the replacing of our ordinary sense enjoyment by the divine *Ānanda*. Therefore, a *Soma*-wine offering is symbolic of the surrender of sense-enjoyment. The drinking of the *Soma*-wine, as the means of strength, victory and attainment, is one of the pervading figures of the *Veda*. It is the great force by which men have the power to follow the path of Truth.

Soma, in its impersonal aspect, is *Ānanda*. In its personal aspect, he is the Divine Person, the supreme Personality, the high and universal *Deva*, or God (symbolized by the dappled Bull). He is the Generator of the world leading to the existence of delight. He fertilizes the force of consciousness, Nature, symbolized by the Cow, and produces the worlds of delight. *Soma* is also a *Gandharva*, the Lord of the hosts of delight.

In the *Aitareya Upanishad*, *Soma* is described as a lunar deity, born from the sense-mind in the Universal *Purusha*, and when man is produced, expresses himself again as sense mentality in the human being. For delight is the *raison d'être* of sensation, or sensation is an attempt to translate the secret delight of existence into terms of physical consciousness.

In the *Purāṇas*, *Soma* has become the God of Moon.

Description of the *Soma* Sacrifice in its Outer Form

The Soma stalks (*aṁśu*) are pressed between stones (*adri* or *gravan*) by a priest and the juice or *rasa* is passed through a sieve (*pavitra*) made of sheep's wool and it comes out flowing clear and is bright in color (*śukra* or *śuchi*). The strained juice flows into a jar (*kalaśa*) or a large vessel (*droṇa*) where it is mixed with barley (*yava*) or milk (*dugdha*) or curds (*dadhi*). This *āśir* or mixture was then offered to the Gods on the altar (*vedī*), to *Indra* or *Vāyu*. It is sweet (*madhu*) and the color is either brown (*babhru*), ruddy (*aruṇa*), or tawny (*hari*). It was then drunk by the worshippers and had the power to elevate the spirits and produce a temporary frenzy. They also found in it something divine, so the process of preparing it was a holy sacrifice and the instruments used therefore were sacred.

Inner Meaning of the Soma Sacrifice from *The Vedic Soma* by M. P. Pandit.

The *Rishis* give a great importance to the extraction and offering of this very cream of life from their being to the higher Powers and Gods and they developed the necessary inner discipline to achieve the object. For, quoth they.

"He tastes not that delight who is unripe and whose body has not suffered the heat of the fire; they alone are able to bear that and enjoy it who have been prepared by the flame." *Rig Veda* IX, 83, I.

A physical system which has not been subjected to the purifying fire of an ardous *tapasyā* is like a raw earthen vessel, insufficiently baked, which splits and spills what is poured into it. It is only when the body of man, the *mortar*, has received enough of the 'benign blows' of the *grava* or *adri*, the *vajra* weapon of God above that the hold of *tamas* and other opposing forces of darkness on him loosen and crack, making it possible for it to be supple enough to yield the *rasa*, the delight of all experiences, for the offering to the Gods. A dynamic and enlightened life-force stimulates the extraction of this sap with every vibrant movement of its own and sets in current a stream of the Wine of delight flowing towards the eager hosts of Gods or pours it into the purifying sieve, *pavitra*, of the higher psycho-emotional and higher mental layers awakened to knowledge and light, whence purified of dregs, it is strained into the *chamasa* (jar) or *kalaśa* of the being of the worshipper and kept ready for the delectation of *Indra*, the Lord of the Divine Mind who rejoices at the gift. Strengthened and contented by this nectar of delight, *Indra*, the monarch of the Gods, pours fresh strengths and Waters of conscious-energy into the *Yajamāna* (sacrificer), and himself grows into the person of the latter and (with hosts of other Gods who partake of the Cup in the measure of their share) prepares him to transcend his humanity, and eventually admits him into companionship in the realms celestial.

Soma Terms

Adri	Stones for pressing the *Soma* plant.
Aṁśu	The shoot of the *Soma* plant.
Amṛita	Draught of immortality.
Aruṇa	Ruddy, color of *Soma*.
Āśir	Mixture.
Babhru	Brown, color of *Soma*.
Barhis	Sacred grass (*Kuśa* — grass).
Dadhi	Sour milk.
Droṇa	Vats where *Soma* is mixed with water and milk and thus sweetened.
Go	Cow.
Gravan	Stones for pressing the *Soma* plant.
Hari	Tawny, color of *Soma*.
Indu	The bright drop.
Kalaśa	Jars for the *Soma*.
Madhu	Sweet draught.
Mṛij	To add water and milk to *Soma*.

Pavamāna	Flowing clear (*Soma*).
Pavitra	Sieve through which *Soma* is strained.
Rasa	*Soma*-juice.
Sadhasthu	Three abodes of *Soma*.
Somapā	*Soma*-drinker.
Śuchi	Bright.
Śuddha	Pure.
Śukra	Bright.
Ulūkhala	The mortar out of which the *Rasa* or *Soma*-juice is pressed, symbolic of the material body.
Vanaspati	Epithet of the mortar, 'lord of the forest'; wood is always symbolic of the body.
Yava	Barley or corn.

Soma-plants symbolize that growth or element behind all sense-activities and enjoyments which yields the Divine Essence. It has to be distilled, purified and intensified until it has grown luminous, full of radiance, of swiftness and energy, *gomat, āśu,* and *yuvaka*. It becomes the chief food of the gods, who called to the *Soma* oblation, take their share of the enjoyments and in the strength of that ecstasy increase in man, exalt him to the highest possibilities and make him capable of the supreme experience. Those who do not give the delight in them as an offering to the divine Powers, preferring to reserve themselves for the sense and the lower life, are adorers not of the gods, but of the Paṇis, *lords of the sense-consciousness,* traffickers in the limited activities, they who press not the mystic wine, give not the purified offering, raise not the sacred chant. It is the Paṇis who steal from us the Rays of the illumined consciousness, those brilliant herds of the sun, and pen them up in the cavern of the subconscient, in the dense hill of matter, corrupting even *Saramā,* the hound of heaven, the luminous intuition, when she comes on their track to the cave of the Paṇis.

Soma is the true creator who possesses the soul and brings out of it a divine creation. For him the mind and heart, enlightened, have been formed into a purifying instrument; freed from all narrowness and duality, the consciousness in it has been extended widely to receive the full flow of the sense-life and mind-life and turn it into pure delight of true existence, the divine, the immortal Ānanda. (Sri Aurobindo *On the Veda*, page 406)

The Sun, Truth, the Illuminator. The Sun is the master of the supreme Truth, the truth of being, truth of knowledge, truth of process, act, movement and functioning. He is, therefore, the creator or rather manifester of all things, for creation is outbringing, expression by the Truth and Will — and the father, fosterer, enlightener of our souls. The illuminations we seek are the herds of this Sun who come to us in the track of divine Dawn and release and reveal in us night-hidden world after world up to the highest beatitude. In the inner sense of the *Veda*, the Sun God represents the divine Illumination of the *Kavi* which exceeds mind and forms the pure self-luminous Truth of things.

Sūrya

His principle power is self-revelatory knowledge, termed in the *Veda* "Sight". His rays are the thoughts that proceed luminously from the Truth, the Vast, the Symbol of Supreme Truth, self-luminousness, the Illuminator, symbol of the Gnosis, vision of essence and image at once, of totality and contents, the Self-vision and the all-vision.

As *Sūrya* represents Divine Light, *Vāyu* represents Divine Energy, and *Agni*, Divine Will, directs that energy.

The Triple Effectivity, the mystic Dragon of Foundations, who on the third plane of existence consummates our triple being. There on that rare level he takes the high flaming force of the Divine will or *Agni* and forges it into a weapon of sharpness that shall destroy all evil and ignorance in the physical, vital, and mental being.

Trita Āptya

Fashioner of the worlds and things; the Divine as the Fashioner of things pervades all that He fashions both with His immutable self-existence and with that suitable becoming of Himself in things by which the soul seems to grow and increase and take on new forms. By the former He is an indwelling Lord and Maker, by the latter He is the material of His own works.

Tvashtri

Dawn; the arising of the Sun of that higher Truth, the Bringer of Truth. She is the outshining of Truth. New openings of divine illumination alternate with night. Darkness is mother of light and always Dawn comes to reveal what the black-browed Mother has prepared. She is the illumination of divine knowledge breaking on the mental man, the Mother of the Cows or radiances.

Ushas

Ushas awakens to vision, perception, right movement; she discovers speech for all that think. Dawn can release life and mind into their fullest wideness. *Ushas* is accompanied by cows, horses and heroes. She is the inner dawn which brings to man all the various fullnesses of his widest being, force, consciousness, and joy. She is accompanied by all sorts of powers and energies. She gives man the full force of vitality so that he can enjoy the infinite delight of that vaster existence. The Dawn is new openings of divine illumination after the black night of preparation.

Speech; the creative Goddess, the expressive Power of *Aditi*, Infinity, of the Supreme *Prakriti* (*Parāprakriti*) who is spoken of as the Cow just as the *Deva* or *Purusha* is described in the *Veda* as *Vrishabha* or *Vrishan*, the Bull. *Vāch* is the Word wide-based in the Vasts above, a power of Indra, sometimes called his *Vajra* or thunderbolt weapon. The power of *Vāch* is called *ūrdhva-budhna* or the 'vasts above' when its function causes its vibrations to blow the din and dust off the lower triple body of mind, life, and matter, and it illumines the mind, energizes the life-force, drives out the inertia from the physical body and softens it so that it releases the *rasa* of all experiences it earned through the life, heart and mind.

Vāch or Vāk

Lord of the Vast Consciousness, a vast purity and clear wideness destructive of all sin and crooked falsehood. He represents

Varuṇa the ethereal purity and oceanic wideness of infinite Truth. He is the All-pervading vastness and purity of Divine supporting and perfecting the world. *Varuṇa* is called *ṛishidāsa* (servant of the sages) because he destroys all hurters or enemies that interfere with the growth of the Truth-consciousness in man's mind.

Varuṇa is the Indian Poseidon, the Lord of the Oceans.

A group of eight gods whose chief is *Agni*; powers of plenitude, of material and spiritual wealth. These wise call

Vasu(s) our fathers *Vasus*, our paternal grandfathers *Rudras*, and our paternal great-grandfathers *Ādityas*.

Apa — Water	Anila — Wind
Dhruva — Pole-star	Anala — Fire
Soma — Moon	Prabhāsa — Light
Dharā — Earth	Pratyūsha — Dawn

33 Deities, 8 Vasus, 12 Ādityas, 11 Rudras and 2 Aśvins are included in the over 300,000,000 gods and goddesses.

The Wind-God, a vital force; the Master of life, who links earth and heaven together in the mid-air, the region of vital

Vāta

Vāyu force. *Vāyu* is the Inspirer of *prāṇa* and man's nervous and vital activities; Force with mind makes the sacrifices.

Vāyu is often called *Mātariśvan*, that is "He who extends himself in the Mother or the container" whether that be the containing

Mātariśvan mother element, Ether, or the material energy called Earth in the *Veda* and spoken of there as the Mother. It is a Vedic epithet of the God *Vāyu*, who, representing the divine principle in the Life-energy, *Prāṇa*, extends himself in Matter and vivifies its forms. In the *Īśa Upanishad* it signifies the divine Life-power that presides in all forms of cosmic activity.

Veṇa   A musician; the master of mental delight of existence, creator of the sense mind.

Vira   A hero, a divine energy. *Vīravat*: with conquer-
Viravat   ing energies. *Ushas* is accompanied by *Vīra(s)* or horses in the army of *Agni* or Divine Will.

The Wide Moving One. *Vishnu* of the vast pervading motion holds in his triple stride all these worlds; it is he that makes a
Vishṇu   wide room for the action of *Indra* in our limited mortality; it is by him and with him that we rise into his highest seats where we find waiting for us the Friend, the Beloved, the Beatific Godhead.

Vishṇu has three strides or movements, earth, heaven, and the supreme world of which Light, Truth, and the Sun are the foundation. He is said in the *Purāṇas* "to sleep on the folds of the snake *Ananta* upon the ocean of sweet Milk". That is, God rests on the coils of the Infinite in the blissful ocean of Eternal Existence.

Viśva   The All; the Sun-God, Creator and Lord of knowledge.

Viśvadeva(s)   All the gods; the universal collectivity of the divine powers, fosterers or increasers of man and upholders of his struggle, labor and effort of work and the sacrifice.

Viśvakarman   All-Creator, Divine Creative Architect of Gods; sometimes identified with *Prajāpati*, the Lord of Creatures.

Originally a form or appelation of the Sun, and then later one of the twin children with Yamī of the wide-shining lord of
Yama   Truth. He is the guardian of *dharma*, the law of the Truth which is the condition of Immortality, therefore himself the guardian of immortality.

The so-called hymn of Death (*Ŗig-Veda* X, 14) is indeed not a hymn of Death so much as a hymn of Life and Immortality.

Later, *Yama* was considered as the God of Death, the Ordainer or Controller who assures the law, the *dharma*.

Yama is *Āditya*, the Sun of Truth in the *Ṛig-Veda*, or as in the *Kaṭha* text, son of *Vivasvan* (Sun), the Law, born of the Truth, *Dharmarāja* (King of the Law).

Yamī   One of the twin children, *Yama* and *Yamī*, of *Sūrya*.

The *Asuras*, the Undivine Beings.

The titans, dividers of our unity and completeness of being and sons of the Mothers of Division, who are powers of the nether cave and the darkness. The *Asuras* are the powers of the circumscribing Night, the hostile beings of the mental world who ascend from the obscurity and the vagueness, angry to the struggle. Their instincts call for a visible, tangible mastery and sensational domination. To be able to coerce, exact, slay, overtly, irresistibly fills them with a sense of glory and dominion, for they are sons of division and strong flowering of the Ego.

Asura

These hostile powers try to break up the unity and completeness of our being and are those from whom the riches which rightly belong to us have to be rescued. Sri Aurobindo says: "All hostile energies or *Asuras* that attack the soul of man possess certain riches which he needs and has to wrest from them in order to arrive at his perfect plenitude."

Daityas   Children of division.

Dānavas   Sons of *Danu*, sons of the Mother of division; plunderers, harmful powers, enemies of the gods and man in his progress.

Diti   Mother of *Vṛitra* and the *Dānavas*, the enemies of man's progress; divided consciousness, ignorance.

The destroyer; the *Dasyus* are the enemies of spiritual light, the natural enemies, the Dividers who hack and cut up the growth and unity of the soul and seek to assail and destroy

Dasyu(s)   its divine strength, joy and knowledge. They are the powers of Darkness, the sons of *Danu* or *Diti*, the divided being.

The *Dasyus* are haters of the sacred word; they are those who give not to the gods the gift of the holy wine, who keep their wealth of cows and horses (light and energy) and find other treasures for themselves and do not give to the seers; they are those who do not sacrifice. They are powers of physical or spiritual darkness, Lords of Division and evil in the realms of troubled rapidities and intensities.

The light of the Sun is called the *Aryan* light in contradistinction to the *Dasa* — darkness.

Namuchi   Symbol of weakness, who fights man with his weaknesses.

Lords of the sense-life, spiritual enemies, miser traffickers in the sense-life. The *Panis* are an impious host who are jealous of their store and will not offer sacrifice to the Gods. Panis   These are much more than the personifications of our ignorance, evil and weakness and many limitations. They make constant war upon man, encircle him from near, shoot their arrows at him from afar or even dwell in his gated house with their shapeless stammering and their insufficient breath of force to mar his self-expression. They must be expelled, overpowered, slain, thrust down into their nether darkness by the aid of the mighty and helpful deities.

The *Panis* are powers that prevent the Truth from emerging out of the subconscient condition and that constantly try to steal the illuminations (Cows) from man and throw him back into the night. They are withholders of the thoughts of Truth and dwellers in the darkness without knowledge, sons of the Inconscient and their front is falsehood. For the world as we see it has come out of the darkness concealed in darkness, the deep and abysmal flood that covered all things, the inconscient ocean.

Rākshasas   A giant or titan; a hostile being of the middle vital world. He is not a being as yet in the evolution but he has a psychic being hidden by virtue of his latent humanity.

Śambara   The name of a demon, the power of circumscribing night, a foe of the God of Love in epic poetry; the wily *Asura*.

Sūshṇa   A false force that distorts knowledge and action; the impure and ineffective force of *Sūshṇa* afflicts us.

Vala   The encircler, he who holds back the light, the miser, the stealer and concealer, the withholder of the higher Light which he can only darken and misuse. *Indra* is called *Valahan*, the slayer of *Vala*, the enemy who keeps for himself the Light.

Vala is the chief of the *Paṇis*, who dwells in a hole (*bila*) in the Mountains and the Gods have to pursue him there and force him to give up his wealth of cows from the pen-cave. He withholds the seven rays.

Vala's body is made up of light, his hole or cave is a city full of treasures; that body must be broken up, the city rent open, and those treasures seized.

Vṛitra   The Serpent, the grand Adversary; he obstructs with his coils of darkness all possibility of divine existence and divine action. He must be slain by the cow or light in order to release the seven rivers of our being, the possession of our complete divine consciousness which must be delivered from all falsehood by the free descent of the truth-light. *Vṛitra* is the darkened cloud of adverse force, ignorance and inertia.

Vṛitra(s)   The titans, subconscient powers who hold the light and the force in themselves, in their cities of darkness and illusion, but can neither use it rightly nor will they give it up to man, the mental being. Their ignorance, evil and limitation have not merely to be cut away from us, but broken up and made to yield up the secret of light and good and infinity.

Out of this death immortality has to be conquered. Pent up behind this ignorance is a secret knowledge and a great light of truth; prisoned in this evil is an infinite content of good; in this limiting death is the seed of a boundless immortality.

SYMBOLS

Immortality; an accomplished self-possession in the infinite and the power to live and move in firm vastnesses, *Amṛita* is the nectar of immortality. It is the nature of the Higher Existence which is free from Birth or Death.

Amṛita

Anna

Food; symbolic of the physical reality of *Brahman*; matter.

Apas

Waters, the outpourings of the luminous movement and infinity of the Divine. Also *Apodivyāḥ*, the Divine Waters.

The horse; life's swiftness, the full force of vital speed and action and enjoyment and nervous vibration, which must be brought forward to upbear our endeavour. Our life is a horse that, neighing and galloping, bears us onward and upwards. The vital powers are the motive forces that bear us on our journey and are therefore symbolized by the horse. *Aśva* is the symbol of Force, especially of vital force, and is variously the *Arvat* or war-steed in the battle and the *Vājin*, the steed of the journey, which brings us in the plenty of our spiritual wealth. *Aśva*, the Steed of Life, is a figure of *Prāṇa*, the nervous energy, the vital breath, the half-mental, half-material dynamism which links mind and matter. Its root is capable, among other senses, of impulsion, force, possession and enjoyment. *Āśu aśvyān* — the swift horse-power.

Aśva
Arvat
Vājin

Dhenu(s.)
Dhenavaḥ (pl.)

Cows yielding milk-rivers; the waters of vital dynamics or kinesis, the *Prāṇa* which moves and acts and desires and enjoys. *Dhenu* meant a fosterer, a nourisher, and therefore a cow, from *dhā*, to suck.

Dhī (s.)   Thought-mind, the intellect in Vedic psycholo-
Dhiyaḥ (pl.)   gy; the *nous* of the Greeks, the subtlety and
swiftness of thought conception, *Buddhi*. Plural:
Dhiyaḥ, thoughts.

Father and Mother correspond to heaven and earth.

Clarified butter, the clarified mind, purified discernment,
richly bright understanding; symbolizes a rich and bright state
Ghṛita   of activity of the brain power. The offering of
clarified butter, the yield of the cow in a sacred
ceremony is symbolic of surrendering a purified mind. *Ghrita*
or illumination, clarity of mind, is hidden in the Cow; the triple
clarity of *Ghṛita* is *Indra*, *Sūrya* and *Soma*. It is the formed
light of conscious knowledge. *Soma* releases the divine light
from the sense-mentality, *Indra* from the dynamic mentality,
and *Sūrya* from the purely reflective mentality.

Ghi   Clarified butter from the udder of the shining
Cow of infinitude, symbol of the rich clarity that
comes to the mind visited by the light.

Cow, a ray of truth, light; the physical force of higher
thought, spiritual illumination. The *gāvaḥ* rays are the brilliant
herds of the Sun, the divine cows. The ruddy cow
Go(s.)   is the dawn, spiritual readiness. The cow is also
Gāvaḥ (pl.)   a symbol of consciousness in the form of know-
Usra   ledge. The figure of the Cow stolen and hidden by
the *Paṇis* is constant in the *Veda*. The Cow is
Aditi, the infinite consciousness hidden in the subconscient.
Cows of the dawn are symbols of Light. *Usra* means also both
cow and ray of light.

Herds of cattle or herds of light; the illuminations of the
Truth, shining troops of Light recovered by the Gods from the
Gāvaḥ   *Paṇis* and *Vala*. The herds are the illuminations
Netṛi gavām that come to us from the supramental Truth, herd-
ing rays of the Sun of Light. The herds are the
trooping rays of the divine Sun, herds of the luminous Con-

sciousness. *Ushas*, Dawn, is said to be the *Netri gavām*, 'Leader of the herds' or 'radiances'.

The swan; the soul of man soaring past the shining firmaments of physical and mental consciousness towards the ascending path of the Truth where God is to be found.

Haṁsa The mental being or this soul is pictured as the upsoaring swan or the falcon that breaks out from a hundred iron walls and wrests from the jealous guardians of felicity the wine of the *Soma*.

Hiraṇya Gold, the light of truth, the shining wealth of a divine Sun: the True Light.

Hiraṇyavat The substance of truth.

Hiraṇya- The *Aśvins* are asked to drive downward their
rūpa chariot on a path that is radiant and golden. *Hiraṇyarūpa* is 'gold form'.

Hotā *Hotri* is the invoker. *Agni* is the *Hotri*, the priest
Hotri of the sacrifice, he who performs the offering. Therefore, it is the power of *Agni* to apply the Truth in the work, *karma*, symbolized by the sacrifice.

Honey; the *Soma* sweetness, divine beatitude. It is the wine of *Ānanda*, the ecstasy of the Gods. The well of honey which is

Madhu opened by *Brihaspati* is the divine beatitude of the supreme threefold world of bliss, the *Satya*, *Tapas* and *Jñāna* worlds of the *Purāṇas* based on three supreme principles of *Sat*, *Chit-Tapas* and *Ānanda*; their base is *Svar* of *Veda* and *Mahar* of the *Upanishads* and *Purāṇas*, the World of Truth.

Nādyaḥ Flowing rivers, organ pipes carrying the breaths (*Maruts*).

Pāśa Bonds of ropes and knots; the triple bonds of ignorance which hold us to the lower body, life and mind.

Paśu   The passion mind and the animal being. The
paśus, animal impulses, become the *Gāvaḥ* or rays,
the brilliant herds of the sun, the divine cows of the *Veda*.

Priest; every shining godward Thought that arises from the
secret abysses of the heart is a priest and a creator and chants a
Purohita   divine hymn of luminous realization and puissant
fulfilment. We seek for the shining gold of the
Truth; we lust after a heavenly treasure. Conscient offering is
Agni in front, hence *Puro-hita*, 'set in front', 'before'.

Pṛithu-budhna   Vast-base, descriptive of *Vāch*, the divine Word.

Juice, sap of delight; *Soma* is the Lord of *Rasa*. It is the
essence in sense-experience, in the plants and growths of earth-
nature. *Rasa* represents the essence of all experi-
Rasa   ences and movements which the individual being
has derived and accumulated in his venture on the field of life,
and it forms his means of subsistence, urge for growth and seed
for rebirth. And as the most priceless possession of man it is the
choicest gift that could be offered to the Gods whose presence
is invoked by him.

The pressing of the sap or *rasa* of the *Soma*-stalks is symbolic
of the essence or delight of sense-experience being pressed out
by the force of *Yoga* or the Divine and then offered to the Gods.
Then the *Vṛitras* or the darkened clan of adverse forces and ignorance and inertia vanish so that the body loses its hardness,
becomes plastic, free from *Tamas*, inertia and its brood of
adverse conditions.

Ratha   Chariot; movements of energy. By the advanc-
ing chariots of the gods we conquer our divine
possessions.

Night and day, the symbols of the alteration of the divine and
human consciousness in us. The Night of our ordinary consciousness holds and prepares all that the Dawn
Rātri-diva   brings out into conscious being.

Satyam in action, Truth of the Supramental plane. It is right

Ṛita

truth of divine being regulating right activity of both mind and body. *Ṛita* is *brihat*, universal truth proceeding directly and uninformed out of the Infinite.

Ṛita-chit

Truth-consciousness, or *Vedānta's vijñāna*.

Sachchidānanda

Sat-Chit-Ānanda.

The triple divine worlds, the supreme and rapturous abodes of the Godhead. Substance of being, light of consciousness and active force and possessive delight are the constituent principles of existence.

Samudra

Ocean, infinite and eternal existence; floods of higher consciousness pouring upon mortal mind from the place of immortality.

Sūryadvāra

The gate or door of the Sun; the Sun as the door to supreme realization represents here the spiritual illumination.

Svayambhū

Self-becoming. All objective existence is self-becoming by the force of the Idea within it.

Ūrdhva-budhna

Vasts or bases above (*ūrdhva*), symbolic of the luminous mind of heaven, of the higher consciousness, descriptive of *Vāch*.

Usra

Bull, the illumined power of truth. The four horns of the Bull are *Sat, Chit, Ānanda* and Truth. The four-horned bull is *Agni*, the Divine *Purusha*.

Vajra
Pāpman

The thunderbolt of *Indra*, his weapon or voice. A blow from *Vajra* destroys *pāpman* or evil. The *Vajra* is the *Vāch*, the word wide-based in the Vast above.

Vṛika

The wolf, the tearer. The Gods are called *avṛika*, 'not wolf'.

Vṛishṭi

Rain, the raining of the world of light, a downpour of luminous mind. *Indra* is called *Vṛishabhu*. *Vṛishṭi* is the descent of the superconscient into our life; spiritual abundance.

Vyāhṛiti(s)   The three symbolic words of the Mantra: *"Om Bhūr bhuvaḥ svaḥ"*: Earth, Midworld, Heaven. The fourth *vyāhṛiti* is *Mahas*, the Supermind.

Yajña   Sacrifice, a rite, symbolic of action. The outer sacrifice or ritual was meant to turn the mass of men's minds to godly things. To the Initiate it served as a kind of scaffolding for the inner development. To the *Ṛishis* the inner sacrifice was the sole means of opening out to God.

Antaryajña   Inner sacrifice, which is presided over by Agni or aspiration.

Yajamāna   One sacrificing, the giver of sacrifice.

A Summary of the Victory of Light over Darkness (notes from "On the Veda" by Sri Aurobindo).

We shall find in the *Vedas* the summary of that great hope which the Vedic mystics held ever before their eyes; that journey, that victory, is the ancient primal achievement set as a type by the luminous Ancestors for the mortality that was to come after them. It was the conquest of the powers of the circumscribing Night (*rātri paritakmya*), *Vritras*, *Sambaras* and *Valas*, the Titans, Giants, Pythons, subconscient Powers who hold the light and the force in themselves, in their cities of darkness and illusion, but can neither use them aright nor will give them up to man, the mental being. Their ignorance, evil and limitation have not merely to be cut away from us, but broken up and made to yield up the secret of light and good and infinity. Out of this death immortality has to be conquered. Pent up behind this ignorance is a secret knowledge and a great light of truth; prisoned by this evil is an infinite content of good; in this limiting death is the seed of a boundless immortality. *Vala*, for example, is *Vala* of the radiances, *valam gomantam*, his body is made of the light, *govapusham valam*, his hole or cave is a city full of treasures; that body has to be broken up, that city rent open, those treasures seized. This is the work set for humanity and the Ancestors, *Aṅgiras*, have done it for the race that the way may be known and the goal reached by the same means and through the same companionship with the gods of Light.

Sri Aurobindo translates the prayer in the Veda:

"Let there be that ancient friendship between you gods and us as when with the *Aṅgirasa* who spoke aright the word, thou didst make to fall that which was fixed and slewest *Vala* as he rushed against thee, O achiever of works, and thou didst make to swing open all the doors of his city."

At the beginning of all human traditions there is this ancient memory. It is *Indra* and the serpent *Vṛitra*, it is Apollo and the Python, it is Thor and the Giants, Sigurd and Fafner, it is the mutually opposing gods of the Celtic mythology; but only in the *Veda* do we find the key to this imagery which conceals the hope or the widom of a pre-historic humanity.

Life is the condition from which the Will and the Light emerge. It is said in the *Veda* that *Vāyu* or *Mātariśvan*, the Life-principle, is he who brings down *Agni* from *Sūrya* in the high and far-off supreme world. Life calls down the divine Will from the Truth-consciousness into the realm of mind and body to prepare here, in Life, its own manifestation. *Agni*, enjoying and devouring the things of Life, generates the *Maruts*, nervous forces of Life that become forces of thought; they, upheld by *Agni*, prepare the action of *Indra*, the luminous Mind, who is for our Life-powers their *Ṛishi* or finder of Truth and Right. *Indra* slays *Vṛitra*, the Coverer, dispels the darkness, causes *Sūrya* to rise upon our being and go abroad over its whole field with the rays of the Truth. *Sūrya* is the Creator or manifester, *Sāvitrī*, who manifests in this mortal world the world or state of immortality, dispels the evil dream of egoism, sin and suffering and transforms life into the immortality, the good, the beatitude. The Vedic gods are a parable of human life emerging, mounting, lifting itself toward the Godhead.

To use the figures of the Vedic seers: by Yoga *Varuṇa* is born in us, a vast sky of spiritual living, the Divine in his wide existence and infinite truth; into that wideness Mitra rises up, Lord of Light and Love, who takes all our activities of thought and feeling and will, links them into a Divine harmony, charioteers our movement and dictates our works; called by this wideness and this harmony *Aryaman* appears in us, the Divine in its illumined power, uplifted force of being and all-judging effective will; and then there comes the indwelling *Bhaga*, the Divine in its pure bliss and all-seizing joy who dispels the evil dream of our jarring and divided existence and possesses all things in the light and glory of *Aryaman*'s power, *Mitra*'s love and light, *Varuṇa's* unity. This divine Birth shall be the son of our works.

YAJÑA SACRIFICE (notes from Sri Aurobindo)

Self-sacrifice is the sacrifice of oneself by oneself to one's Self, 'This Self's immortal Self'. (*Muṇḍaka Upanishad* III 2)

Veda recongnizes an Unknowable, Timeless Unnameable above all things not seizable by the mind. Impersonally it is *Tat*, That, the One Existence; to the personality it reveals itself out of the deep secrecy of things as God or *Deva*, nameless though he has many names, immeasurable and beyond description, though he holds in himself all description of name and knowledge and all measures of form and substance, force and activity. God is both the original cause and the final result, the builder of worlds, lord and begetter of all things, Male and Female, Being and Consciousness, Father and Mother of worlds and beings, and also their Son and ours; for he is the Divine Child born into the Worlds who manifests himself in the growth of the creature. He is the wise and liberating Son born from our works and sacrifice, the Hero in our warfare, and the Seer of our knowledge, the White Steed who gallops towards the Upper Ocean. God is *Rudra, Vishṇu, Prajāpati, Hiraṇyagarbha, Sūrya, Agni, Indra, Vāyu, Soma, Bṛihaspati, Varuṇa* and *Mitra, Bhaga* and *Aryaman*, all the Gods.

The soul of man soars as the Bird, the *Haṁsa*, past the physical and mental consciousness to the heaven of Truth to find God waiting, leaning down helpfully, always the Friend and Lover of man, the pastoral Master of the Herds who gives us the sweet milk and the clarified butter from the udder of the shining Cow of the infinitude. He is the source and outpourer of the ambrosial Wine of divine delight and we drink it drawn from the sevenfold waters of existence or pressed out from the luminous *Soma*-plant on the hill of being and uplifted by its raptures we become immortal.

Such are some of the images of this ancient mystic adoration. Our sacrifice is the offering of all our gains and works to the powers of the higher existence. The whole world is a dumb and helpless sacrifice in which the soul is bound as a victim self-offered to unseen gods. The liberating word must be found and his life be a conscious and voluntary offering in which the soul is no longer the victim, but the master of the sacrifice. The illuminating hymn must be framed in the heart and mind, the all-creative and all-expressive Word that shall arise out of his depths as a sublime hymn to the Gods. Man can achieve all things. He shall conquer. Nature shall come to him as a willing and longing bride, he shall become her seer and rule her as her King.

Dawn comes after a starlit Night and the arising of the Sun of Truth brings with it the effective sacrifice. The luminous herds are rescued from the darkling cave of the *Panis*; by the sacrifice the rain of the abundance of heaven is poured out for us and the sevenfold waters of the higher existence descend impetuously upon our earth because the coils of the enfolding and obscuring and withholding serpent *Vritra* have been cloven asunder by the God-Mind flashing lightnings; in the sacrifice the *Soma* wine is distilled and uplifts us in the streaming of its immortalizing ecstacy to the highest heavens.

By the hymn of prayer and God-attraction, by the hymn of praise and God-affirmation, by the hymn of god-attainment and self-expression, man can house in himself the Gods, build in this gated house of his being the living image of their deity, grow into divine births, form within himself vast and luminous worlds for his soul to inhabit.

The new dawn will repeat the old, the hidden Sun will be recovered. The soul is a battle-field full of helpers and hurters, friends and enemies.... We create for ourselves by the sacrifice and by the word shining seers, heroes, to fight for us, children of our works. The *Rishis* and the Gods find for us our luminous herds; the *Ribhus* fashion by the mind the chariots of the gods and their horses and their shining weapons. Our life is a horse that, neighing and galloping, bears us onward and upward; its forces are swift-hooved steeds, the liberated powers of the mind are wide-winging birds; this mental being or this soul is the up-soaring Swan or the Falcon that breaks out from a hundred iron walls and wrests from the jealous guardians of felicity the wine of *Soma*. Every shining godward Thought that arises from the secret abysses of the heart is a priest and a creator and chants a divine hymn of luminous realization and puissant fulfilment. We seek for the shining gold of the Truth; we lust after a heavenly treasure.

Mind-born and mind-yoked is the ever-recurrent simile of the chariot, i.e., the bodily vehicle in which the solar spiritual Self takes up its stand as a passenger for so long as the chariot lasts, the sense organs are the steeds and the reins are held by the directing mind on behalf of the passenger. When the horses willingly obey the rein, the chariot conducts the passenger to his proper destination; but if they pursue their own ends, the natural objects of the senses and the mind yield to them, the journey ends in disaster (mind is twofold: bound by senses or independent of them).

The soul of man is a world full of beings, a kingdom in which armies clash to help or hinder a supreme conquest, a house where the gods are our guests and which demons strive to possess; the fulness of its energies and wideness of its being make a seat of sacrifice spread, arranged and purified for a celestial session. The *Ṛig-Veda* becomes thus the high-aspiring Song of Humanity; its chants are episodes of the lyrical epic of the soul in its immortal ascension.

The *Vedas* are the outer worship for the profane, but inner discipline for the Initiate. Sāyaṇa, a great Indian commentator, and Orientalists make it nature worship. They are secret words for purified and awakened souls. The extraordinary incoherence disappears with the inner interpretation. A thread of sense exists with the inner meaning. These rhythmic hymns, called *Srutis*, 'that which is heard', were not composed by the intellect, but a divine word that came vibrating out of the Infinite to the inner audience of a man who had previously made himself fit for impersonal knowledge; they were formed from the intuitive illumined mind. These hymns are also called *Mantras*, for they are full of spiritual power. These *mantras*, though written in nature-images, have both an inner and an outer sense, for these seer-poets were also occultists who knew that the inner as well as the outer results could be obtained by the secret power of thought and words, and so these hymns came to have a dual use and meaning. Human phenomena as well as divine noumena could be brought into being by the power of these *mantras*. The outer or external meaning, the apparent interpretation of the images and happenings of physical nature that were used became the basis of all the orthodox ceremonial practices of the Indian civilization known as the *Karmakāṇḍa*, the ceremonial or 'works' portion of the *Veda*, and which was later interpreted and promulgated by the *Pūrva Mīmāṁsā* philosophy. The whole science of Vedic sacrifice and worship which is used even to this day for obtaining of desires spiritual and material in all affairs of Indian life is based on this occult knowledge contained in these outpourings of the inspired Vedic *Rishis*. But it is the luminous Truth of the Spirit, the inner meaning, which is the basis of the tradition that the *Veda* is the sacred book of wisdom, containing the true law of nature which can lead man to a higher consciousness and understanding. The perfect and intricate rhythms, the diction, the refined and noble and beautiful poetry of the *Veda* are evidences that they are a creation of a high culture. Such excellence in beauty, truth and art are only consonant with highly developed minds in tune with the heart's eternal truths and the Infinite Reality.

The Greek Mysteries, Orphic and Eleusinian, prepared rich soil for Pythagoras and Plato but the *Veda* is the basis of the Greek Mysteries. The *Veda* is the ancient psychological wisdom. For the Āryas, the word was *Arata*, out and push forward in other fields. For the Greeks, it was *arete*, virtue.

The *Upanishads'* real work was to found *Vedānta* rather than to interpret *Veda*. The true use of *mantra* and sacrifice was displaced by a leaning towards asceticism and renunciation. So the external use of *mantra* and ritual was exaggerated to hold its own. So it came to be the *Veda* for the priests and the *Vedānta* for the sages. An Age of Intuition passed into an Age of Reason. The direct words of the *Upanishads* caused the mystic symbols of the Veda to be forgotten from lack of use among sages. Buddhism completed the rift. It sought to abolish the *Veda* and used the popular tongue. The Brahmins, to counteract this, produced new tenets of religious worth, simpler, which were the *Purāṇas*. The *Veda* went from the priest to the scholar where it lost its true value and sanctity in meaning, but the scholars have kept the text in perfect condition to be taken up again by the intuitive.

Sāyaṇa's naturalistic interpretations of the *Veda* are the bases of European Comparative Mythology studies. The dominance of Sāyaṇa's ritualistic interpretation has deprived India of the living use of its greatest scripture, but it will also be the springboard from which we leave to penetrate the Vedic Secrets, for the *Veda* has a double meaning in a system of parallelisms. There are internal and external deities. The *Veda* is primarily for spiritual enlightenment and self-culture. The *Purāṇas*, legendary histories, and the *Itihāsas*, epics, may have been parts of Vedic culture before their present forms were evolved.

Coomāraswāmī, writing on the Vedic Sacrifice, says:

"The Gods and the Titans were both the children of *Prajā-pati*, both alike devoid of any spiritual Self and consequently mortal: only *Agni* was immortal. Both parties set up their sacrificial Fires. The Titans performed their rite externally (profanely); but the Gods then set up that Fire in their inward self and, having done so, became immortal and invincible and overcame their mortal and vincible foes. SB II, 2, 2, 8-20.

"In the same way now the sacrificer sets up that Fire (sacrificial) within him, he thinks, 'Herein will I sacrifice, here do the good work.' Nothing can come between him and *this* Fire; 'Surely, as long as I live, that Fire that has been set up in my inward self does not die down in me.' He feeds that flame who utters right (*satyam*), and more and more becomes his own fiery-force (*tejas*); he quenches it who utters wrong (*anṛitam*), and less and less becomes his fiery-force. Its service is just 'right'.

"The sacrificer must apprehend *Agni* in himself; for it is from himself that he brings him to birth. The true *Agnihotā* is, in fact, not a rite to be merely performed at fixed seasons, but within you daily. A distinction is clearly drawn between mere performance and the understanding of what is done, performance as such and performance as the support of contemplation; and between an objective performance on stated occasions and a subjective and incessant performance.

"The observation in SB IX 5.1.42 that the building of the Fire(-altar) includes all kinds of works (*viśva karmāni*) assimilates the sacrificer to the archetypal sacrificer, *Indra*, who is preeminently the 'All-worker'! It is just because the Sacrifice, if it is to be correctly performed (and this is quite indispensable), demands the skilled co-operation of all kinds of artists that it necessarily determines the form of the whole social structure. So there is in traditional society no real distinction of sacred from profane operation; rather, each operation is sacred. Thus the needs of the body and the soul are satisfied together.

"It will be as true of every agent as it is for the king that whatever he does, he does of himself unsupported by any spiritual reason will be to all intents and purposes 'a thing not done'. The true sacrifice is to be performed daily and hourly in each and every one of our functionings.

"So Buddha said: 'I pile no wood for an altar fire; I kindle a flame within me, the heart is the hearth, the flame thereon the dominated self.' Thus he who has slain his *Vritra*, i.e., dominated self, and is thus a true autocrat (*svarāj*) is liberated from the law according to which the Sacrifice is factually performed.

"In the sacrificial interpretation of life, acts of all kinds are reduced to their archetype and so referred to Him from whom all action stems; when the 'notion that I am the doer' (*ahaṅkāra*) has been overcome, and acts are no longer 'ours', when we are no longer anyone, then we are no longer 'under the law', and what is done can no more affect our essence than it can His whose organs we are. It is in this sense only, and not by vainly trying to do nothing that the causal chain of fate (*karma* with its *phalāni*) can be 'broken'; not by any miraculous interference with the operation of mediate causes, but because 'we' are no longer part and parcel of them. The reference of all activities to their archetypes is what we ought to mean when we speak of rationalizing our conduct; if we cannot give a true account of ourselves and our doings it will mean that our actions have been 'as you like it', reckless and irregular, rather than to the point (*sādhu*) and in good form (*pratirūpam*).

" 'I am crucified with Christ, nevertheless I live; yet not I, but Christ liveth in me; and the life which I now live in the flesh I live by the faith of the Son of God, who loved me, and gave himself for me.' (Faith is the daughter of *Sūrya*) 'I do not frustrate the Grace of God: for if righteousness come by the law, then Christ is dead in vain.' (The Bible, Galatians, II, 20-23). In the Vedic period the sacrificial operation involved all kinds of works and the acts of the carpenter, doctor, fletcher and priest had all been regarded as ritual operations (*vratāni*). The Eucharistic meal is of extreme importance in the sacrifice. The essential and only indispensable part of the victim is the heart. It is basted with *Ghi* on a spit and so made to be that living food of which the Gods partake, that 'very self of the victim'.

"*Indra's* defeat of *Ahi Vṛitra* and Buddha's conquest of Māra are relations of one and the same universal mythos.

"The Bible, Luke XIV, 26: 'And if any man come to me, and hate his father, and mother, and wife and children and brethren and sisters, yea and his own life also, he cannot be my disciple. And whosoever doth not bear his cross, and come after me, cannot be my disciple.' Ephesians IV, 13: is fine about the coming into the full stature of Christ, the perfect man in all works.

"It is not pacification (due to force), that we want in our being but the foe to repent and willingly to submit to the bonds into which he enters, not a peace imposed on an enemy. *The consent of the sacrificial victim is always secured.* Then the peace is really an agreement, the *śānti* (peace) is really a *sanjñāna* (perfect wisdom). The victim is killed. In this case the enemy is really resurrected as a friend, or in other words, it is not himself, but his evil that is killed.

"Thus in India it is only the peace by agreement that is real and that can endure; and it is for this reason that Gandhi would rather see the English relinquish, i.e., sacrifice, their hold on India of their own free will than to see them compelled to do so by force. The same applies to the holy war of the Spirit with the carnal soul; if there is to be 'unity in the bond of peace' the soul must have 'put itself to death', and not simply have been suppressed by a force composed of violent asceticism and penances."

Ānanda K. Coomāraswāmī says on *Ātmayajña*, Self-Sacrifice: "Just as Christianity turns upon and in its rites repeats and commemorates a Sacrifice, so the liturgical texts of the *Ṛig-veda* cannot be considered apart from the rites to which they apply and so are these rites themselves a mimesis of what was done by the First Sacrificers who found in the Sacrifice their Way from privation to plenty, darkness to light, and death to immortality.

"The Vedic Sacrifice is always performed for the Sacrificer's benefit, both here and hereafter (for the winning of both worlds), 'that life's best that has been appointed by the gods to men for this time being and hereafter.' (Plato, Timaeus 90 d). The immediate benefits accruing to the sacrificer are that he may live out the term of his life (the relative immortality of 'not dying' prematurely) and may be multiplied in his children and in his possessions; the Sacrifice insuring the perpetual circulation of the "Stream of Wealth" (*vasor dhārā*), the food for the Gods reaching them in the smoke of the burnt offering, and our food in return descending from heaven in the rain and thus through plants and cattle to ourselves, so that neither the Sacrificer nor his people shall die of want. On the other hand, the ultimate benefit secured to the sacrificer who thus lives out his life on earth in good form is that of deification and an absolute immortality. These distinctions of temporal from eternal goods correspond to that which is sharply drawn in the *Brāhmaṇas* between a mere performance or patronage of the rites and a comprehension of them; the mere participant securing only the immediate, and the Comprehensor (*evamvit, vidvān, viduḥ*) both ends of the operation (*Karma, vrata*). This is likewise the well known distinction of the *karma kāṇḍa* and the *karma mārga* from the *jñāna kāṇḍa* and *mārga*; a division of *viae* that is ultimately resolved when the whole of life is sacrificially interpreted and lived accordingly.

"To know *Indra*, oneself, it is only by an understanding of verification of what is done in the sacrifice that he can be found. Here, we ask, not what is enacted outwardly, but what is accomplished inwardly by the understanding sacrificer?

"The victim of the sacrifice is the sacrificer himself. In accordance with the universal rule that initiation (*dīkshā*) is death and rebirth, it is explicit that 'the initiate is the oblation' (*Havir vai dīkshitaḥ*, TS. VI, 1, 4. 5, cf. AB. II, 3), 'the victim' (*paśu*) substantially is the sacrificer himself. This was to be expected, for it is repeatedly emphasized that 'We (the sacrificers here and now) must do what was done by the Gods (the original sacrificers) in the beginning.' It is, in fact, himself that the God offers up, as may be seen in the prayers 'O Agni, sacrifice thine own body'. To sacrifice and to be sacrificed are essentially the same. 'For the God's sake he chose death, for his offspring's (the same as 'God') sake chose not immortality: they made *Brihaspati* the Sacrifice, *Yama* gave up his own dear body.' ṚV. X, 13.4.

"The sacrificer's offering up of himself is ritually enacted in various ways. The *prastara* (grain-seed), for example, which represents the sacrificer, is thrown into the Fire, he only saving himself from actual immolation by an invocation of the Fire itself. If one does not expressly make this renunciation of himself, the Fire would deprive him of it.

"The Bible, Mark VIII, 35: 'For whosoever will save his life shall lose it; but whosoever shall lose his life for my sake and the gospel's, the same shall save it.' So in the SB. VII, 216, to insure his rebirth in heaven the sacrificer casts himself in the form of a seed (represented by grains of sand) into the household Fire (*Ātmānam...retobhūtam siñchati*).

"The Comprehensor of this doctrine, making the Burnt Offering (*agnihotra*) has therefore two selves, two inheritances or births, human and divine; but one who offers, not understanding, has but one self, one inheritance, viz., the human. The Bible, John III, 6: 'That which is born of the flesh is flesh; and that which is born of the Spirit is spirit.' With the sowing of oneself as seed into the Fire and the quickening of this seed by the Breath, cf. the Bible, Romans, VI, 4f. : 'We are buried with him by baptism into death: that like as Christ was raised up from the dead by the glory of the Father, even so we also should walk in newness of life...our old man is crucified with him, that the body of sin might be destroyed....Now if we be dead with Christ we believe that we shall also live with him....'

"The mind is said to be twofold, clean and unclean (*śuddhaṁ chāśuddham eva*); unclean by connection with wanting (*kāma*), clean when dissevered from wanting....The mind, indeed is for a human being the means alike of bondage and freedom, of bondage when attached to objects, and of release when detached therefrom. And hence, for those who do not perform the *Agnihotra* (do not make burnt offerings), who do not build the Fire, who do not know and do not contemplate, the recollection of *Brahma's* empyrian abode is obstructed. So the Fire is to be served with offerings, to be edified, lauded and contemplated. Muṇḍ. I, 2.3. Hence the many hymns to *Agni* in the *Veda* and the many sacrificial Fire Rites in the Brahmanical tradition.

"The real Soma Sacrifice is the bruising of the soma-shoot, the breaths, the elemental self; one withdraws these breaths and sacrifices them into the Fire (*prāṇān uddhṛitya agnaujuhoti*). All the gods are in me; they make their home in me. They are neither in heaven nor on earth, but in breathing creatures. Their forms are the powers of the soul, Gods and Titans competing in these worlds for possession of them; the sense organs of speech, scent, hearing, vision and thought originally sang for the Gods all fruition and for themselves whatever was beautiful, until the Titans infected them with evil, that is whatever was done by any of them informally (without ceremony or prescribed form). Only the Breath remained immune to this infection and he translates the senses, striking off their evil, their mortality, so that each becomes its macrocosmic equivalent, speech becoming *Agni*, smell *Vāyu*, vision the Sun, hearing the Quarters of heaven, mind the Moon. The Breath then shares out the nourishment that it sings for itself (the Breath is the organ-blower, the breaths of the *Maruts* that move in the body-organ 'Pipes' *nādyaḥ*) into which they have been 'put', playing the part of host to the breaths that take up their places round about him as a regiment of the King's Own that at the same time form his body-guard and is fed by him. The Breath is identified with *Agni*.

"The Breath is the Spiritual Power in which the Temporal Power inheres. It is in this sense that the gods were originally mortal and only by *Agni's* counsels, or by the sacrifice, or by making *Brahma* their own, attained their present dignity, immortality and victory. That is to say that when the sacrificer, in whom these powers are immanent, ceasing to use them for improper ends, i.e., the pursuit of pleasure, returns himself with immanent deities to their source, then 'he' becomes an immortal. It is not his personality but his Person that then survives. Self-sacrifice is the sacrifice of oneself by oneself to one's Self, 'this self's immortal Self'. Mu. III, 2". Coomāraswāmī.

"The greater surrender gives the greater right".

(Sri Aurobindo)

GLOSSARY

DEVA(S)

Abhramu	Aśvin(s)
Agni	Barhishad
Aditi	Bhaga
Āditya(s)	Bhāratī
Ādityavarṇa	Brahmā
Agnihotṛi(ā)	Brahman
Agni Vaiśvānara	Brahmaṇaspati
Airāvata	Bhṛigu
Anala	Bṛihaspati
Ananta	Chitraratha
Aṅgiras	Dadhikravan
Aṅgirasas	Dhanasput
Anila	Daitya(s)
Añjana	Daksha
Añjanavatī	Dakshiṇa
Anupamā	Dasra
Āpa	Deva
Āpas	Dhara
Apām Napāt	Dharmarāja
Aryaman	Dhruva
Arjuna	Diśaḥ
Atri(s)	Gandharva(s)

Gomati
Gopati
Hiraṇyagarbha
Iḷā
Indra
Indu
Īśāna
Kandarpa
Kapila
Kārtikeya
Kratu
Kubera
Kuvera
Kumāra
Kumuda
Lokapāla(s)
Maghavan
Mahar
Mahas
Mahī
Marīchi
Marut(s)
Mātariśvan
Mātṛi
Mitra
Nārada
Nāsatya
Parāprakṛiti
Parjanya
Pāvaka
Pavana
Pulaha
Piṅgalā
Prabhu
Prachetas
Prajāpati
Prakṛiti

Prashṭas
Pratyūsha
Pulastya
Puṇḍarīka
Purusha
Purushottama
Pūshan
Pushpadanta
Rātrī
Ṛibhu(s)
Ṛibhukshan
Ṛita
Ṛitachit
Rudra(s)
Śachī
Sādhya(s)
Śaṅkara
Saptarshi(s)
Saramā
Sarasvatī
Satyavān
Sārvabhauma
Savisthura
Sāvitrī
Savitṛi
Shunaḥ Shepa
Śiva
Śiva-Rudra
Soma
Śubha-dantī
Supratīka
Sūrya
Svayambhū
Trimūrti
Tritya Āptya
Tvashṭṛi
Ushas

Vāch

Vāk

Vajra

Vajriṇaḥ

Vāmana

Varuṇa

Vaśishṭha

Vasu

Vāta

Vāyu

Vena

Vīra

Vīravat

Vishṇu

Viśva

Viśvadeva(s)

Viśvakarman

Vivasvan(t)

Vṛishabha

Vṛishan

Vṛitrahari

Yama

Yamī

ASURA(S)

Daitya

Dānava(s)

Danu

Diti

Namuchi

Paṇi(s)

Rākshasa(s)

Śambara(s)

Sūshṇa

Vala(s)

Valohan

Vṛitra(s)

BOOKS

Ānanda Tīrtha

Ārya

Ātmayajña

Devatā

Durgā

Hymns of the Atris

Hymns to the Mystic Fire

Īśa Upanishad

Itihāsa Upanishad

Katha Upanishad

Lights on Fundamentals

Lights on Teachings

Lights on Upanishads

Lights on Veda

Mahābhārata

Maṇḍala

Muṇḍaka Upanishad

Nirukta

On the Veda

Purāṇas

Ṛig-Veda

Ṛig-Veda Bhāshya

Siddhañjana

Sri Aurobindo Mandir Annual

Upanishad(s)

Veda

Vedānta

NAMES OF THE WRITERS

Coomāraswāmī
Kapāli Śastrī
M. P. Pandit
Rādhākrishnan
Sāyana

Śaunaka
Skandasvāmī
Udagitha
Venkaṭa Mādhava
Yāska

OTHER WORDS AND SYMBOLS

Ādhibhautika
Ādhidaivika
Ādhyātmika
Ahankāra
Amrita
Ānanda
Anna
Antaryajña
Anritam
Apas
Apodivya
Arka
Arvat
Ashu aśvyan
Āśu
Aśva
Bila
Brahman
Brihat
Buddhi
Chamasa
Chit
Chit-tapas
Daivika
Daivic
Dasa
Dharma
Dhenu

Dhenavah
Dhī
Dhiyah
Ghi
Ghrita
Go
Gomat
Gāvah
Gāyatrī
Hamsa
Haṭha Yoga
Hiranya
Hiranyavat
Hiranyarūpa
Hotā
Hotri
Jñāna
Karma
Karmakāṇda
Kavi
Kuśa
Madhu
Mahar
Mahas
Mahornah
Manas
Manma
Mantra

Mayas
Mīmāṁsā
Namas
Nirṛita
Netrī gavām
Om bhūr bhuvaḥ svaḥ
Phalāni
Paṇḍit
Pāpman
Parama parāvat
Pāśa
Paśu
Prāṇa
Pṛithu-budhna
Purohita
Pūrva mīmāṁsā
Rāja yoga
Rasa
Ratha
Rātrī
Rātrī-divā
Rātrī paritakmya
Ṛich
Ṛig
Ṛik
Ṛishi
Ṛishidasa
Ṛita
Ṛitachit
Sachchidānanda
Sādhu
Samudra
Sanātana dharma
Sapta dhiyaḥ

Śāstra
Sat
Sāttvic
Satya
Satyāmṛita
Śruta
Śruti
Śuchi
Sūkshma dṛishṭi
Sūryadvāra
Svar
Svara
Svayambhū
Tamas
Tapasya
Tat
Tejas
Ūrdhva-budhna
Usra
Vājin
Vajra
Valam gomantam
Vedī
Vijñāna
Viśvadhiyo virajati
Viśva karmāṇi
Vṛika
Vṛishṭi
Vyāhṛiti
Yajamāna
Yajña
Yoga
Yuvaka

CHAPTER X

SANSKRIT PHILOSOPHICAL SCHOOLS, THEIR EXPONENTS & LITERATURE

GENERAL DIVISION

THE ĀSTIKA SCHOOLS (Orthodox, or those believing in Vedic authority). THE SHAḌ-DARŚANA or 'SIX VISIONS' or Philosophical Schools.

Nyāya, Vaiśeshika Sāṅkhya, Yoga Mīmāṁsā, Vedānta

THE NĀSTIKA SCHOOLS (Heterodox, or those not believing in Vedic authority).

Chārvāka or Lokāyata — Materialistic philosophy.

Jaina — Philosophy derived from the Jaina religion.
4 Schools of Bauddha — Philosophy derived from Buddha's teachings.

Sautrāntika	} Hīnayāna	Mādhyamika	} Mahāyāna
Vaibhāshika		Yogāchāra	

THE SHAḌ DARŚANA

Nyāya — A realistic philosophy based mainly on logical grounds (*ni-i* — to go back; hence an original type, a logical statement or axiom).

Author of the Nyāya-sutra, the basic scripture of the school. Other important works are: Uddyotakara's Nyāya-vārttikā, Vātsāyana's Nyāya-bhāshya, Udadyana's Nyāya-vārttikā-tātparya-pariśuddhi and Kusumāñjali, Vāchaspati's Nyāya-vārttikā-tātparyaṭika, Jayanta's Nyāyamañjarī and Gaṅgeśa's Tattvachintāmaṇi.

Gotama

A philosophy classifying realities and presenting an atomic cosmology (*vi-śish* — to remain apart, distinguish). So called because it elaborately discusses the category of knowledge called *Viśesha* or the eternally distinct nature of the nine substances, earth, water, etc.

Vaiśeshika

Author of Vaiśeshika-Sūtra, the first systematic work of the School. Other important works are Praśastapāda's Padārtha-dharma-saṃgraha, Udayana's Kiraṇāvalī, Śrī-dhara's Nyāya-kandalī, Vallabhāchārya's Nyāya-līlāvatī, Śivāditya's Sapta-Padārthī, Laugākshi Bhāskara's Tarkakaumudī and Viśvanātha's Bhāshāparichchheda.

Kaṇāda

A philosophy of dualistic realism: of the two eternal realities of *Purusha* — Spirit, and *Prakriti* — Nature or primordial matter (*saṃkhyā* — to enumerate). So called because it enumerates the ultimate objects of knowledge.

Sāṅkhya

The originator of this very old system of thought. His original works are lost. Īśvarakrishṇa's Sāṅkhya-kārikā is the earliest available and authoritative text-book. Other important works are Gauḍapāda's Sāṅkhyakārikā-bhāshya, Vāchaspati's Tattva-kaumudī, Vijñānabhikshu's Sāṅk-hyasāra and Sāṅkhya-pravachana-bhāshya.

Kapila

A philosophy leading to the realization of the Spirit as independent and free from all limitations of body, senses and mind (*yuj* — to unite). So called because its object is union of man with the Self, the Divine within.

Yoga

The great Indian sage who was the founder and author of the Yoga-Sūtra. Other important works are Vyāsa's Yoga-bhāshya, Vāchaspati's Tattva-vaiśāradī, Bhojarāja's Vritti and Yogamaṇi-prabhā, and Vijñānabhikshu's Yogavārttikā and Yogasāra Saṃgraha.

Patañjali

A philosophy justifying the Vedic rites and their use (from the wishing-form of the verb *man* — to think; hence to investigate). So called because it investigates into the Vedic scriptures. Other names of this School are:

Mīmāṃsā

Pūrva-Mīmāṁsā or 'Earlier Investigation'.

Karma-Mīmāṁsā or 'Investigation in Actions of Vedic Rites'.

Jaimini's Sūtra is the foundation-work of this philosophy. Commentaries on this work have been written by Sabaraswāmī, Kumārila Bhaṭṭa and Prabhākara.

A philosophy presenting the ultimate wisdom of the Vedas (*veda* — wisdom, *anta* — end or ultimate; hence essence of the Veda or Wisdom Per Se). Other names of the School are:

Vedānta

Uttara-Mīmāṁsā or 'Later Investigation'.

Jñāna-Mīmāṁsā or 'Investigation into the Wisdom of the Veda'.

The Upanishads are regarded as the true authority and source of the Vedānta philosophy. Because of the many approaches to Truth expressed therein Bādarāyaṇa tried to harmonize these various teachings into a systematized form in his Vedānta-Sūtras, usually called the Brahma-Sūtras. But these Sūtras are very brief and hence have been given different interpretations by various sages and Commentators, who in time became the founders of particular schools of the Vedānta. Each of these schools refers to passages from the Upanishads to support their views.

Brahma-Sūtra

Prasthāna-traya

The three famous foundation works of the Vedānta: Upanishads, Bhagavad-Gītā, and Brahma-Sūtras.

The following are the Teachers or Āchāryas of the different Schools of Vedānta with their names, character and chief works:

Śaṅkara (484 A.D.)   Kevalādvaita-Vedānta   Unqualified Non-Dualism

Kevala-Advaita-Vedānta teaches that God or *Brahman* and the Individual Soul or *Jīvātman* are non-different in their transcendental aspects. All else is *Māyā*, illusion, unreal in essence. The Absolute is both personal and suprapersonal, both *Saguṇa* (with qualities) and *Nirguṇa* (without qualities). The world is relatively real to the Individual Soul as long as the separate Soul lasts, but disappearing on becoming one with Brahman. *Moksha* is freedom from birth and individuality and the world. *Jñāna* or Wisdom is the means to this goal. The Many are only manifestations of the One which is Transcendent. Śankarā-chārya was renowned for his learning and his spirituality and as a reviver of *Brāhmaṇism* and was considered as an incarnation of Śiva. He wrote Commentaries or *Bhāshyas* on the Brahma-Sūtras, the 10 principal Upanishads, the Bhagavad-Gītā.

Śankara's original writings are very beautiful and lofty. The most famous are: Ātma-bodha, Ānanda-laharī, Jñāna bodhinī and Maṇiratnamālā. He also wrote Commentaries on the Mahābhārata.

Śankara has many followers all over India. His four famous *Maṭhas* or monasteries are Jaganmaṭh, Kandur, Dvārakā and Badrinath. His disciple Ānandagiri wrote a history of his controversial exploits called Śankara-vijaya or 'Śankara's Victory'.

Rāmānuja (1017-1137)	Viśishṭādvaita-Vedānta	Qualified Non-Dualism

Viśishṭādvaitavāda teaches that the Individual Soul is part of God. The Many are eternal in the One and the world is real, not Māyā. God is *Saguṇa-Brahman* — with qualities, or Universal and is called *Īśvara*. Rāmānuja was a Vaishnava and to maintain the doctrine of Bhakti or 'Love of God' in the face of the Monism and Māyā or 'World-illusion theory' of the Advaita of Śankara he composed a Commentary on the Brahma-Sūtras and another on the Gītā. His other great works were: Vedāntasāra, Vedārthasaṁgraha and Vedāntadīpa. Rāmānuja's followers are numerous in Southern India. He was known for rendering Bhakti as *Upāsana* or the religious meditation prescribed in Upanishad.

Madhva (1208-1279)	Dvaita-Vedānta	Dualism

Dvaitavāda teaches that God and the Individual Soul are eternally separate and that the world is real, not Māyā, an illusion. The One and the Many are eternally different. Madhva was also a Vaishnava and hence wished to establish the doctrine of Bhakti or 'Love of God' on a secure basis so he also wrote a Commentary on the Brahma-Sūtra. He brought into prominence the name of Vishnu as God. He has many followers in the West and South of India. He wrote 37 treatises, the most important of which are Anuvyākhyāna, Bhāratatātparyanirnaya, a gloss on the Bhāgavata, Commentaries on Gītā and Upanishads, and several Prakaranas.

| Nimbārka | Dvaitādvaita-Vedānta | Dualistic Non- |
| (died 1162) | or Bhedābheda | Dualism |

Dvaitādvaitavāda teaches that Brahman is one with All but has three distinct forms: the inanimate world, the individual soul and God. In the religion that associated itself with this belief Vishnu replaced Brahman. He was the founder of the Rādhā-Krishna sect who worship the boy Krishna and Rādhā his beloved. Being a Vaishnava he wished to defend Bhakti worship and hence also wrote a commentary on the Brahma-Sūtra. His other great work is Daśaśloka.

| Vallabha (1479 on) | Śuddhādvaita- | Pure Non- |
| Vishnusvāmī (1250 on) | Vedānta | Dualism |

Śuddhādvaitavāda teaches that the individual soul is not a form of the Supreme or Brahma altered by a third thing being involved in it, such as Māyā or illusive power, but is itself the substance as Brahman with *Ānanda* or the 'Bliss' attribute of Sat-Chit-Ānanda (Brahma) rendered imperceptible. The relation between world and soul are real, not māyā, but a subtle form of God; hence the soul and Brahman are identical in their pristine (śuddha) state. Vallabha's great works are Anubāhya, Siddhāntasahasya and Bhāgavatatīkāsubodhinī.

| Śrī Chaitanya | Achintya Bhedābheda | Unthinkable Dualistic |
| (1485-1533) | Vedānta | Non-Dualism |

Bhedābhedavāda (*bhid* — to divide) teaches that there is both difference and non-difference between all individual souls and Brahman but this dual relation of both difference and non-difference is logically unthinkable. The religious teachings of this great mystic of Bengal are called Gauḍīya Vaishnavism. The record of the life and teachings of Chaitanya are in the *Śrī Chaitanya Charitāmṛita* or 'The Character-Nectar of Chaitanya'. This scripture is the main presentation of this school of thought. Vishṇu, Kṛishṇa and Rādhā are worshipped in this religion. The famous exponents of this school of philosophy after Chaitanya are Jīva Gosvāmī (16th c.) who wrote Satsandarbha, Rūpa Gosvāmī and Sanātana Gosvāmī. Baladeva's Govinda-bhāshya on the Brahma-Sūtras and his Prameyaratnāvalī are also philosophical classics as well as quite popular.

There were many other Vaishṇava sages of the Bhakti movement who followed on through the 16th century and on, but they had no complete system of philosophy to support their beliefs. But in the 20th century we have a unique contribution to Vedānta philosophy in English language but using Vedas, Upanishads and Gītā as authorities:

Śrī Aurobindo (1872-1950)	Pūrṇādvaita-Vedānta	Integral Non-Dualism

Pūrṇādvaitavāda teaches that the Absolute, God, World and Souls are all ONE. Śrī Aurobindo's system is a comprehensive synthesis of all the traditional interpretations of the Vedānta works: God or Brahman has an infinite richness of content. Brahman has three poises of being. It is pure transcendence, cosmic universality, and an infinite plurality of spiritual individuals or Jīvātmans. The last two may be less fundamental and primal but not less real. Brahman or the Absolute is at once Nirguṇa (without qualities) and Saguṇa (with qualities) and hence both static and dynamic. Hence this philosophy combines the *Mukti* or ineffable freedom sought by Vedānta with the endless creativity and dynamism of the Śakti (power of Śiva or 'Divine Mother') of the Tāntrika teachings and the infinite love or *Prema* of Vaishnavism and Mahāyāna Buddhism. It teaches infinite manifoldness in a unity of Brahman or the Supreme Eternal. Śrī Aurobindo's two works in English that reveal his Vedānta doctrine are "The Life Divine", and "The Īśa Upanishad".

ŚAIVA SCHOOLS OF PHILOSOPHY

Śaiva Siddhānta: The philosophy of Southern Śaivism which is similar to Rāmānuja's Qualified Non-Dualism because it does not believe in absolute identity or absolute distinction of God and souls and the world. The Supreme is Śiva with his consort Ambā (the female aspect or Power). They also believe in the reality of the world. The sources of this School are the Vedic conception of Rudra, the Rudra-Śiva cult of the Brāhmaṇas, the Mahābhārata, the Śvetāśvatara Upanishad and the Śaiva Āgamas. Therefore it is based on both Veda and Śaiva-Āgamas, the Aryan and Dravidic Culture. The important works of this school are the Śaiva Siddhānta-Śāstra, Nīlakaṇṭha's Commentary on the Brahma-Sūtra, and Apyaya Dīkshita's Commentary called Śivārkamaṇidīpika.

The philosophical system of Kashmir Śaivism which is based on both Vedas and Āgamas leans more to Advaitism than does the Southern School. Śiva is the only Reality. Pratyabhijñā He is absolutely independent and creates all by his Śakti or female aspect or Power. He makes the world appear in himself as if it were distinct from himself though not so really. God appears in the form of souls and makes objects for their experiences. But Śiva is the infinite pure Self, the basis of the Universe whose activity (*spanda* or vibration) is the cause of all differences. Pratyabhijñā (*prati-abhi-jñā* — to recognize) or Recognition is all that is needed for *Mukti* or Liberation.

The works of this school are called Trika for they represent three distinct kinds of Advaitism or Non-dualism. The most important of these works are Śiva Sūtra, Bhāskara's Vārttikā, Kshemarāja's Vimarśinī, Śivasūtravimarśinī and Spandasandoha,

Vasugupta's Spanda Kārikā with Kallaṭa's Vṛitti, Somānanda's Śivadṛishti, Utpala's Pratyabhijñā Sūtra and Abhinavagupta's Paramārthasāra and Pratyabhijñavimarśinī and Tantraloka.

Śambhava-darśana or Śakta philosophy

The religious philosophy which is the basis of Śaktism or the Tāntrika religion. Śiva is omnipresent, impersonal, and inactive consciousness and Śakti is active personal being including all individual souls. Śiva may be static or dynamic but exists in both states. Śakti is the power latent in Śiva, and is the formative energy of consciousness. The union of Śiva and Śakti cause creation. In reality they are always one. Man is liberated by the knowledge of Śakti or Devī and then Śiva and Śakti become One in unspeakable bliss within man's being. Hence we find the Mother-Goddess in some form or other worshipped by the devotees of this belief. The Tantras or Śakta Āgamas are the basic works of this school.

THE NĀSTIKA OR UNORTHODOX SCHOOLS

Chārvāka or Lokāyata-mata

The materialistic philosophy which holds that matter is the only reality; hence they deny the existence of God and soul. Its name is supposed to be derived from its founder. Also called Lokāyatamata or 'View of the common people'.

The authoritative work, the Bārhaspatya-sūtra, is lost except for some quotations found in other works. References and descriptions of this school may be found in Madhvāchārya's Sarva-Darśana-Saṁgraha and Haribhadra's Shad-darśana-samuchchaya and Dakshiṇarañjan Śāstrī's Chārvāka-Shashṭi.

Jaina philosophy

The philosophy of the Jainas or 'Conquerors', the title given to the 24 teachers or Tīrthankaras through whom their faith is said to have come down from unknown antiquity. The last of these Jaina teachers was Vardhamāna, also called Mahāvīra, 'the great hero', who lived in the sixth century B.C. during the time of the Buddha.

The Jainas do not believe in God, but that all men may become free, perfect, omniscient, omnipotent, and all-blissful by their own efforts inspired by the example of their great teachers. Their philosophy is common-sense realism and pluralism.

The world consists of two kinds of reality, living and non-living. Matter exists but only as something which may become anything. Every living being has a soul, however imperfect its body, therefore they have great respect for life. Another of their unique theories is the many-faced view of reality or the doctrine of Syādvāda, the doctrine of 'it may be' which holds that every judgement is subject to some condition and limitation and hence various judgements about the same reality may be true, each in its own sense and subject to its own condition.

Jaina works are mostly in Prākṛita language but when the Jainas had to defend their theories against the criticism of other philosophical schools they adopted the technical terminology of Sanskrit and thus they developed a Sanskrit literature. The following are some of the more important works: Tattvārthā-dhigama-sūtra by Umāsvāmī, Syādvāda mañjarī by Mellishena, the Dravya Saṁgraha by Nemichandra and the Jaina Sūtras. The Aṅgas are the chief sacred texts of the Jaina religion.

We may observe from the presentation of the different Schools of thought above that no Indian philosophical system is merely speculative as in the West. Each is a Darśana, a vision, an insight; each is based on an original revelation, a divine experience (save for the Chārvāka). So we find that Indian religion and philosophy are not separated, one complements the other. In the West mind is the criterion of philosophy, whereas in the East values are most important, for to an Indian true philosophy should lead to religion, to spiritual action.

Indian philosophical literature is vast as well as tremendous in its scope and detail. Radhakrishnan, the great living exponent of Indian philosophy to the West has shown in his two volumes of Indian philosophy that in their perception of the goal of life, in the acuteness of their reasoning, and in the boldness of their conceptions, the Indian thinkers are second to none. The seed and basis of practically all the philosophies of India can be traced to those early philosophers of the Upanishadic times who were not only formulators of knowledge, but poet-seers and realisers of divine truth. They thought and realised so deeply, so vastly, that all the phases of philosophical thought seem to be suggested in their writings. The Upanishadic philosophy is intuitional whereas the systems of the Darśanas are logical. R. D. Rānade, the great philosophical critic of India points out that the super-rational intuitional method of the Upanishads is not contradictory of the logical one, but subsumptive of it. He further reveals that the problems of contemporary thought in the west have their parallelisms with the thought propounded in the Upanishads (see Rānade's Survey of Upanishadic Philosophy 10-11).

He writes:

"With the advance of knowledge and with the innumerable means for communication and interchange of thought, the whole world is being made one, and the body of Western philosophers could ill afford to neglect the systems of Indian philosophy, and more particularly the Upanishads."

Max Muller speaking of the old Indian sages who were free to meditate on problems of life and all that is nearest to the heart of man said:

"If they were not philosophers, let them be called dreamers, but dreamers of dreams without which life would hardly be worthy living."

PHILOSOPHY-VOCABULARY

Additional philosophical writings and their authors

WRITINGS

Ānanda-laharī	Anuvyākhyāna
Aṇubhāshya	Bārhaspatya-Sūtra

Bhāgavataṭikāsubodhinī
Bhāratatātparyanirṇaya
Bhāshāparichchheda
Chārvāka-Shashṭi
Dravya Saṁgraha
Govindabhāshya
Jñāna bodhinī
Kiraṇāvalī
Kusumāñjali
Maṇi-ratna-mālā
Nyāya-bhāshya
Nyāya-kandalī
Nyāya-līlāvatī
Nyāyamañjarī
Nyāya-vārttikā
Nyāya-vārttikā-tātparya-pariśuchi
Nyāya-vārttikā-tātparyaṭikā
Padārtha-dharma-saṁgraha
Paramārthasāra
Prameyaratnāvalī
Pratyabhijñā Sūtra

Pratyabhijñavimarśinī
Sambhava-darśana
Śaṅkara-vijaya
Sāṅkhyakārikā-bhāshya
Sāṅkhya-pravachana-bhāshya
Sākhya-sāra
Sapta-Padārthī
Satsandarbha
Shaḍ-darśana-samuchchaya
Siddhāntasahasya
Śivadṛishṭi
Śivārkamaṇidīpikā
Śivasūtravimarśinī
Spandasandoha
Syādvāda-mañjarī
Tantraloka
Varttikā
Vedārthasaṁgraha
Vimarśinī
Yogamaṇi-prabhā
Yogasāra Saṁgraha

AUTHORS & COMMENTATORS

Abhinavagupta
Ānandagiri
Apyaya dīkshita
Baladeva
Bhāskara
Bhaṭṭa
Bhojarāja
Dakshiṇarañjan Śāstrī
Gauḍapāda
Gotama
Haribhadra
Jayanta

Jīva Gosvāmī
Kallaṭa
Gaṅgeśa
Kshemarāja
Kumārila
Laugākshi Bhāskara
Nīlakaṇṭha
Prabhākara
Praśastapāda
Rūpa Gosvāmī
Sabarasvāmī
Sanātana Gosvāmī

Śivāditya
Somānanda
Śrīdhara
Tarkakaumudī
Tattvachintāmaṇi
Tattva-kaumudī
Tattvārthādhigama-Sūtra
Tattva-vaiśāradī
Udadyana

Uddyotakara
Umāsvāmī
Utpala
Vāchaspati
Vasugupta
Vijñānabhikshu
Viśesha
Viśvanātha

PHILOSOPHY-VOCABULARY

Achintya-Bhedābheda-
  Vedānta
Āchārya
Advaita
Ānanda
Ambā
Āstika
Ātma-bodha
Aurobindo
Bādarāyaṇa
Badrināth
Bhagavad-Gītā
Bhāgavata
Bauddha
Bhakti
Bhāshya
Bhedābheda
Bhedābhedavāda
Brahman
Brahma-Sūtras
Buddha
Chaitanya
Chaitanya Charitāmṛita
Chārvāka
Darśana

Daśaśloka
Devī
Dvaitavāda
Dvaitādvaitavāda
Dvaitādvaita-Vedānta
Dvaita-Vedānta
Dvārakā
Gauḍīya Vaishṇavism
Hīnayāna
Īśa Upanishad
Īśvara
Īśvarakṛishṇa
Jaganmaṭh
Jaimini
Jaina
Jaina Sūtra
Jīvātman
Jñāna
Jñāna-Mīmāṁsā
Kaṇāda
Kandur
Kapila
Karma-Mīmāṁsā
Kevala
Kevalādvaita-Vedānta

Kṛiśhṇa
Lokāyata
Lokāyata-mata
Madhva
Madhvāchārya
Mādhyamika
Mahābhārata
Mahāvīra
Mahāyāna
Maṭha
Māyā
Mīmāṁsā
Moksha
Mukti
Nāstika
Nimbārka
Nirguṇa
Nyāya
Nyāya-Sūtra
Patañjali
Prakaraṇa
Prākṛita
Prakṛiti
Prasthānatraya
Pratyabhijñā
Prema
Pūrṇādvaitavāda
Purṇādvaita-Vedānta
Purusha
Pūrva-Mīmāṁsā
Rādhā
Rādhākṛishṇa
Rādhākṛishṇan
Rāmānuja
Rudra
Rudra-Śiva
Saguṇa

Saguṇa-Brahman
Śaiva
Śaiva-Āgamas
Śaiva Siddhānta
Śaiva-Siddhānta-Śāstra
Śākta
Śākta-Āgamas
Śakti
Śankara
Śankarāchārya
Sānkhya
Sānkhya-kārikā
Sarva-Darśana-Saṁgraha
Sat-Chit-Ānanda
Sautrāntika
Shaḍ-Darśana
Spanda Kārikā
Siddhānta
Śiva
Śuddhādvaitavāda
Śuddhādvaita-Vedānta
Śvetāśvatara-Upanishad
Syādvāda
Tantra
Tāntrika
Tīrthankara
Trika
Upanishads
Upāsanā
Uttara-Mīmāṁsā
Vaibhāshika
Vaiśeshika
Vaiśeshika-Sūtra
Vaishṇava
Vallabha
Vardhamāna
Vātsāyana

Veda
Vedānta
Vedāntadīpa
Vedāntasāra
Vedānta–Sūtra
Vishṇu
Vishṇusvāmī
Viśishṭādvaitavāda

Viśishṭādvaita-Vedānta
Vṛitti
Vyāsa
Yoga
Yoga-Bhāshya
Yogāchāra
Yoga-Sūtra
Yoga-vārttikā

CHAPTER XI

BUDDHISM

Sanskrit Terms — Pāli forms in parenthesis

Gautama (best on earth) the Buddha (enlightened), also called Siddhārtha (*siddha-artha* — attained goal) was born at Kapilāvastu on the foothills of the Himālayas, north of Bihar in the 6th century B.C. His disciples handed down his conversational instructions in writings.

The three canonical works of Buddhism are called the Tripiṭakas (tipiṭaka or tayo piṭaka) or 'The Three Baskets' which are:

Vinaya-piṭaka — the basket dealing with rules of conduct (*vi-naya* — driving away).

Sutta-piṭaka — the basket containing sermons with parables (*sutta* from Sanskrit *sūtra*, used here for original words).

Abhidhamma-piṭaka — the basket dealing with philosophical problems (*abhi* — special, *dhamma* — doctrine or law; hence the theory of the doctrine).

The followers of Buddha, the Śākya (name of a clan) sage, divided gradually into different schools. The two main divisions based on religious principles were:

The *Hīnayāna* — The original form that Buddhism took after the death of Buddha, the Orthodox, first known as the Theravāda School of Buddhism (*vāda* — belief, *thera* — elders) but later called the Hīnayāna (*hīna* — lesser, *yāna* — vehicle) because it was for the few and stressed individual Nirvāṇa or one's own enlightenment. Hīnayāna flourished in the south of India and its present stronghold is in Ceylon, Burma and Siam. Its literature is vast and is written in Pāli.

The *Mahāyāna* — The Greater Vehicle (*mahā* — great, *yāna* — vehicle) so-called because it took in all men and stressed universal enlightenment. The school broadened the original scope of Buddhism but without contradicting the inner significance of Buddha's teaching. It assimilated other religio-philosophical beliefs within itself and hence met the cultures of many peoples. Its metaphysical beliefs and precepts have their seeds in the Pāli canon nevertheless. The Mahāyāna flourished mostly in the North of India, then went to China and Japan and Tibet where it is still flourishing. In Tibet it became Lamaism.

Some say that the origin of the Mahāyāna lies in the SILEN-CE of the Buddha, his unexpressed spiritual and transcendental wisdom which his disciple Mahākaśyapa recognised and passed on through a line of patriarchs to Bodhidharma who took it to China.

Buddhist religion and philosophy thrived in India for 1,500 years (up to the 11th century A.D.). In the meanwhile it had already spread into many other countries.

Each of these schools broke up into still further divisions as a result of the coloring that was adopted from the original faiths and ideas of the different lands it entered.

Buddha's mission began at Sāranāth near Benaras when he preached his first sermon known as the Dharma-chakra-pravar-tana-sūtra or Dhamma-chakka-pavattana-sūtta in Pāli or 'the sutta of turning the wheel of the doctrine'.

The principal teachings of Buddhism are:

Chatvāri ārya-satyāni (Chatvāri ariya-sachchāni). The four noble truths are:

1. Duḥkha (Dukkha) — Pain and suffering, misery, mental and physical.
2. Duḥkha-samudaya (samudaya-dukkha) — Cause and origin of suffering (*sam-ud-aya* — rise up together).
3. Duḥkha-nirodha (Dukkha-nirodha) — The cessation of suffering (*ni-rodha* — broken down).
4. Duḥkha-nirodha-mārga (Dukkha-nirodha-magga) — the path (*mārga*) to the cessation of suffering.

The 1st Truth teaches that all life is Suffering, in short, all that is born of attachment is Duḥkha and includes *Soka-parideva - daur - mānasa - upāyāsa* (soka - parideva - domanassa - upāyāsa) or sorrow-grief-distress and trouble.

The 2nd Truth teaches of the *Dvādaśa-Nidāna* or Twelve Fetters (*ni-dā* — to bind down) or links in the chain of Karmic causation, the twelve spokes in the Wheel of Existence or Rebirth called *Saṁsāra-chakra* (sansāra-chakka). This doctrine of evolution or the causal chain of causation is also termed *Prātītya -samutpāda* (Patichcha-samuppāda) or 'happening by way of a cause' (*prati-itya* — gone back, hence cause; *sam-ut-pāda* — happening).

The 12 respective links are:

1. Avidyā (Avijjā) — Ignorance, the root of all, the primary cause of existence (*a* — not; *vidyā* — knowledge), causes.
2. Saṁskāra (sankhārā) — Karmic impressions of past existences (*samkṛi* — to fashion together), causes.
3. Vijñāna (viññaṇa) — Initial consciousness, cognition (*vi-jñā* — to discern), causes.
4. Nāmarūpa (ibid) — Name-form or mind and body, the egoic consciousness (*nāma* — name; *rūpa* — form), causes.
5. Shaḍāyatana (saḷāyatana) — The six sense-organs (*shaḍ* — six; *āya-tana* — organs), causes.
6. Sparśa (phassa) — Sense-contact (*sparśa* — touch, contact), causes.
7. Vedanā (ibid) — Sense-experience, feeling (*vid* — to know), causes.
8. Tṛishṇā (tanhā) — Thirst for life, craving to enjoy objects (*tṛish* — to thirst), causes.
9. Upādāna (ibid) — Mental clinging (*upādā* — to acquire, appropriate for oneself), causes.
10. Bhāva (bhava) — State of existence or becoming (*bhū* — to become), causes.

11. Jāti (ibid) — Birth (*jan* — to be born), causes.
12. Jarāmāraṇa (jaramarana) — Old age and death (*jṛi* — to grow old; *mṛi* — to die, causes).

The 3rd Truth teaches of *Nirvāṇa* (Nibbana) — the Supreme Goal, or Liberation from the limitations of existence (*nir-vā* — to blow out from lack of fuel). *Paranirvāṇa* (Paranibbana) is the Complete Liberation from phenomenal existence (*para* — beyond; *nirvāṇa* — liberation). This last state is often called *Śūnyatā* (Suññatā) or Void, meaning unsubstantiality; hence the higher and inner reaches of Reality beyond human thought and expression and hence a seeming abstraction. One attaining Nirvāṇa is an *Arhat* (Arahat) or 'Holy One' (*arh* — to be worthy, or holy). There are 3 *Mārgas* or 'stages' to Arhatship (Arahantship) in the Hīnayāna: (Maggas) (*mṛig* — to trace, track).

1. Srotāpatti-mārga (Sotāpatti-magga) — The stage of entering the stream of liberation (*srota* — stream; *āpat* — enter).
2. Sakṛidāgāmī-mārga (Sakadāgāmi-magga) — The stage of one returning once again (*sakṛid* — again; *āgāmin* — one coming).
3. Anāgāmī-mārga (Anāgāmi-magga) — The stage of never returning, that of an Arhat (Arahat) (*an* — not; *āgāmin* — one coming).

The 4th Noble Truth teaches of the *Ārya-Ashtāṅga-Mārga* (Ariya-atthangika-magga) or 'The Noble Eightfold Path' to Liberation and Enlightenment or Nirvāṇa. The Eight Steps are:

1. Samyagdrishṭi (sammāditthi) — Right view (*samyak* — right; *drishṭi* — view) which corrects *Mithyādrishṭi* (michchhāditthi) or Wrong View (*mithyā* — false).
2. Samyagvāk (sammāvāchā) — Right speech (*vach* — to speak).
3. Samyaksaṁkalpa (sammāsankappa) — Right resolve (*samklṛip* — to resolve).
4. Samyakkarmānta (sammākammanta) — Right conduct (*karma* — action; *anta* — end).

5. Samyagājīva (sammājīva) — Right livelihood (*jīv* — to live).
6. Samyagvyāyāma (sammāvāyāma) — Right effort (*vi-ā-yam* — to strive).
7. Samyaksmṛiti (sammāsāti) — Right recollection (*smṛi* — to remember).
8. Samyaksamādhi (sammāsamādhi) — Right contemplation (*sam-ā-dhā* — to direct, together, unite).

Dharma (dhamma) — The course of right conduct for a man; religion; law; justice; truth (*dhṛi* — to uphold, sustain). The Buddha said his law or Dharma was synonymous with every moral and spiritual Law.

Karma (kamma) — Action. It has come to mean the 'law of causation': the present existence is the effect of the past and the future is the effect of the present. Karma as mere action does not bind to the Wheel of Rebirth; it is only the personal desire for the fruit of action that binds (*kṛi* — to do).

Punarjanman (punabbhava) — Rebirth (*punar* — again; *janman* — birth).

Ahimsā (ahimsa) — Non-injury: the law of compassion in body, mind and spirit (*a* — not; *hins* — to harm, injure).

The three characteristics of all existence are:

1. Duḥkha (dukkha) — Pain, suffering (*duḥ, dur, duś, dus, dush* — bad, difficult; *kha* — condition).
2. Anitya (anichcha) — Impermanence. Nothing is stable but is in a constant state of flux, of becoming (*a* — not; *nitya* — constant).
3. Anātman (anatta) — Non-self: the doctrine that there is no abiding self or ego (*an* — not; *ātman* — self).

The ego is a collection of:

1. *Kāya* (ibid) — body
2. *Manas* (mano) or mana(s) — Mind or *Chitta* (ibid) — disposition, heart; and

3. *Vijñāna* (viññāna) — principle of conscious life. These three break up at death.

Psychologically man is a collection of:

Pañcha-Skandhāḥ (pañcha-khandha) — Five Aggregates or collections:

1. *Rūpa* (ibid) — Body.
2. *Vedanā* (ibid) — feelings.
3. *Sañjñā* (sañña) — Perceptions.
4. *Saṃskāra* (sankhāra) — predispositions from past impressions.
5. *Vijñāna* (viññana) — consciousness.

These *Skandhas* dissolve after death but the result of their experience is assimilated by the character so that the new man is a result of his past thinking and doing.

Saṃsāra (samsara) — Existence; faring on; the continued 'becoming' in recurring cycles of embodied life as contrasted with Nirvāṇa (nibbana) which is 'Being' and freedom from all limited existence (*saṃsṛi* — to wander or pass through).

The three essentials of Buddha's ethical teaching are:

1. Jñāna (ñāna) — Wisdom (*jñā* — to know).
2. Āchāra (ibid) — Conduct, good behavior (*āchar* — to lead hither).
3. Dhyāna (Jhana) — Concentration; meditation; the effort to cease thinking and to attain mental tranquility in order to attain insight into the nature of Reality or *Śūnyatā* (*dhyai* — to meditate).

Pañcha-Śīla (pansil) — The Five Moral Precepts which every Buddhist lay disciple or *Upāsaka* (*Upāsikā*, f.) and every monk or mendicant or *Bhikshu* (bhikkhu) (*Bhikshu-ṇī*, bhikkhuni f.) promise to observe.

These 5 Precepts are Abstinence or *Viramaṇa* (veramanī) from:

1. Prāṇātipāta (pāṇātipāta) — Injuring any living thing (*Prāṇa* — life; *ati-pāta* — injuring, transgressing).
2. Adattanādāna (adinn'ādāna) — Taking that which is not given (*adatta* — not given; *ā-dā* — to take).
3. Abrahmacharya (abrahmachariya) — Incontinence (*a* — not; *brahma* — divine; *charya* — conduct).
4. Mrishāvāda (musāvāda) — False speech (*mrisha* — false; *vāda* — speech).
5. Surā-maireya-majja-pramāda-sthāna (surā-ceraya-majja-pamāda-tthāna) — Intoxicating-drink-sunk-indolence-state.

In short: compassion, honesty, purity, sincerity and temperance.

Other undesirable qualities are: *Dosha* (dosa) meaning darkness or corruption, or fault; *Moha* (ibid) — delusion, dullness of mind (*muh* — to delude); *Rāga* (ibid) — passion, lust, sensuality (*rāj* — to glow, to be excited); the 10 Kleśas (kalesas) — sins of the body, speech and mind (*kliś* — to suffer) and Kāma (ibid) — desire.

Dṛishṭi (ditthi) — belief, dogma, (often) false theory (*dṛiś* — to see).

Avidyā (avijjā) — ignorance, the root of evil and continual rebirth (*a* — not; *vid* — to know).

Ātmavāda (attavāda) — belief in *ātman* (attan) or the self as abiding reality which according to Buddhism is false.

Sakkāyadṛishṭi (Sakkāyaditthi) — false belief in the reality of the body (*sat* — existence, being; *kāya* — body; *dṛishṭi* — belief).

Lobha (ibid) — greed, covetousness (*lubh* — to be greedy).

Māra (ibid) — killing, destroying (*mṛi* — to die). In Buddhism Māra is the personification of Death, the Evil One, the Tempter. Sometimes it is applied to the whole of worldly existence as opposed to Nirvāṇa.

Pāramitās (pāramiyo) — ideals of spiritual perfection that are to be the guide of the disciples on the path to self-realization.

They are to be considered in three stages: first as ideals for the worldly life; secondly, for the mental life; and lastly, for the spiritual and unitive life. The 6 Pāramitās (pāramīs) are:

1. Dāna (ibid) — (1) Charity and love; giving of impersonal gifts; (2) Sympathy and understanding with others; (3) Self-yielding of the hope of Nirvāṇa that all may enjoy it together (*dā* — to give).

2. Śīla (ibid) — (1) Good behavior; (2) Humility, restraint, and self-giving; (3) Spontaneous and effortless actuality of perfect behavior due to the lack of discrimination between the interest of self and the interest of others and between good and evil (*śīl* — to practice).

3. Kshānti (khanti) — (1) Patience, forbearance with external circumstances and the temperaments of other people; (2) Patience with oneself; (3) Patience that is derived from a full knowledge of all things and which is non-attached (*ksham* — to be patient).

4. Vīrya (viriyo) — (1) Zeal, industry and earnestness; (2) Self-control in the task of following the Noble Path and in manifesting the Dharma in one's own life; (3) To exert oneself with energy for the fulfilling of the Dharma every moment of the day and night (*vīr* — to be valiant).

5. Dhyāna (jhana) — (1) Thoughtfulness; (2) Contemplation wherein discriminated meanings and logical deductions and rationalizations will give way to intuitions of significance and spirit; (3) *Samādhi* or that state of tranquility that comes as the mind enters into unity with truth and a perfect love-filled imagelessness which brings *Samāpatti* or transcendental powers, faculties and graces (*dhyai* — to meditate).

6. Prajñā (paññā) — (1) Wisdom, pragmatic and erudite; (2) All-inclusive truth which is Love; (3) Self-realization which is radiant with the potency and freedom of its self-nature and blissfully peaceful with the serenity of Perfect Love (*prajñā* — to foreknow).

Other virtues sometimes added for those of the Mahāyāna are:

Satya (sachcha) — Truth (*sat* — being, from *as* — to be).

Virāga — Indifference.

Adhishthāna (adhitthāna) — Benediction (*adhi-sthā* — to stand over, superintend).

Maitra (mettā) — Love, Goodwill (*mith* — to unite).

Upekshā (upekhā) — Equanimity, purity of contemplation that comes from disinterestedness (*upa-īksh* — to look upon).

The 4 *Brahma-Vihāras* (ibid) — Divine States which are characteristic of one who is a Bodhisattva (Bodhisatta) or a perfectly enlightened and compassionate being are:

1. *Karuṇā* (ibid) — compassion and pity for all being.
2. *Maitra* (mettā) — love.
3. *Upekshā* (upekhā) — equanimity resulting from disinterestedness.
4. *Mudita* (ibid) — sympathetic and appreciative joy in the happiness of others.

In Buddhism *Brahma* is applied to the greatness or power of prayer (of Vedic origin) or the ecstatic mind or holy enthusiasm. It is a state rather than a being.

Upāya (ibid) — skilful means of bringing people to enlightenment (*upa-i* — to employ).

Praṇidhāna (panidhāna) — resolution to help beings to universal-liberation (*pra-ṇi-dhā* — to place in front, direct).

Bala (ibid) — 'power' which must be increased in all faculties and attainments (*bal* — to breathe, live).

Jñāna (ñāna) — wisdom and intellectual knowledge (*jñā* — to know).

All the above qualities fit one to help and free others.

Pratyeka-Buddha (Pachcheka) — The Arhat or 'enlightened one' who attains Nirvāṇa for his own sake (*prati* — toward; *eka* — one).

Bodhisattva (bodhisatta) — One who has attained the very essence of wisdom which is Love for All (*bodhi* — wisdom; *sattva* — essence). A Bodhisattva passes through many existences and many stages of progress before the last birth in which he fulfils his great destiny for all.

The Bodhisattva-Yāna implies the pathway of striving for the enlightenment of all sentient beings. This is the goal and ideal of the Mahāyāna in contrast to the ideal of the Arhat which is individual liberation or Nirvāṇa.

There are 10 stages of the Bodhisattva:

1. Pramudita (ibid) — joy in one's activities (*pra-mud* — to enjoy).
2. Vimala (ibid) — purity in conduct (*vi* — without; *mala* — stain).
3. Prabhākārī(prabhākari) — illumination (*prabhā* — to shine; *kṛi* — to do).
4. Archismati — flaming insight (*archis* — radiance; *mati* — insight).
5. Sudurjaya — Utmost Invincibility in meditation (*su* — truly; *dur* — hard; *jaya* — conquering; hence 'truly hard to conquer').
6. Abhimukti — 'turned-toward Nirvāṇa', the stage of the Arhat (*abhi* — toward; *mukti* — liberation).
7. Dūraṅgama — the 'far-going' (*dūran* — *far*; *gama* — going) skilful wisdom.
8. Achala — the 'Immovable' (*a* — not; *chal* — to move) Divine will-action.
9. Sādhumati — 'good wisdom' in Preaching the Law (*sādhu* — good).
10. Dharmamegha — 'Cloud of the Law' who rains down the Law on earth (*megha* — cloud).

Siddhi (iddhi) — Attainments, powers (*sidh* — to attain).

Sambodhi or Sambodha (ibid) — Supreme enlightenment (*sam-budh* — to know completely).

Samyaksambodhi(sammāsambodhi)— the Perfect Enlightenment of Budha (*samyak* — perfect).

Bodhichitta(ibid) — Wisdom-heart(*chitta* — heart).

Maitrachitta(mettachitta) — Kind heart, loving heart.

Śikshā (sikkhā) — Study, training, discipline (*śiksh* — to wish, to learn).

The 3 Kinds of Knowledge according to Āryasaṅgha are:

1. Parikalpita — 'illusive' for the simple and ignorant people (*pari-klṛip* — to arrange around).
2. Paratantra — 'relative' for the mind and world of philosophers.
3. Paraṇishpanna — 'Absolute' or the Perfect Knowledge of the Buddha.

The 2 Kinds of Knowledge according to Nāgārjuna are:

Samvṛitti-satya — 'Relative' or Conditioned Truth for the unenlightened (*sam-vṛit* — to cover, hide).

Paramārthasatya — 'Transcendent or Absolute Truth' for the enlightened (*parama* — highest; *artha* — aim).

Trikāya (tikāya) — The Three Sheaths of the Buddha:

1. Dharmakāya (ibid) — The sheath of the Law; the One True Self; Reality; the Void; the Absolute; the Highest Being comprising all others; the Universal and Transcendent Buddha. Buddha is not three, but **ONE**.
2. Sambhogakāya — The Sheath of Enjoyment (of both manifest and unmanifest). The Sheath in which the Buddha, or Bodhisattva may dwell on earth or beyond (*sam-bhuj* — to enjoy completely).
3. Nirmāṇakāya (nimmānakāya) — 'Sheath of Creation or Transformation' (*nir-mā* — to mete out, create). The Nirmāṇakāya is the historical human Buddha who walked this earth and preached to his fellow-men. The Universal Buddha manifested in the world of sentient

beings to teach the Śrāvakas or 'Listeners'. Gradually this conception of Nirmāṇakāya became idealized (similar to the Glorified Christ).

Tathātā — 'Suchness' (*tathā* — such; *tā* — ness); 'Things as they are'.

Tathāgata — A title of the Buddha. (One who has 'thus-gone').

Avalokiteśvara — Another title of the Absolute Buddha as the Enlightener of mankind (*īśvara* — lord; *ava-lok* — behold).

Amitābha — 'The Buddha of Unmeasured Splendor' (*amita* — unmeasured; *abhā* — splendor): The Amitābha-Buddha is the Buddha of the three forms: the Dharmakāya as the Absolute and Unconditioned, the Sambhogakāya as Savior of sentient beings, and the Nirmāṇakāya as the historical Buddha who came on earth to teach.

Bauddha Philosophy — The philosophy derived from Buddha's religious teachings. The four principal views are:

1. Pratītyasamutpāda — The theory of dependent origination: everything that exists is dependent on a cause for nothing happens by chance.
2. Karma — The law of cause and effect: the present existence of an individual is the effect of its past and its future will be the outcome of its present existence.
3. The theory of change: whatever exists arises from some condition and is therefore impermanent.
4. Anātman — The theory of the non-existence of the soul. The law of change is universal, therefore there is no abiding principle or soul in man. There is only a continuity of the stream of successive states that compose life.

The essence of the Buddha's teachings are concerning suffering and the path to liberation or Nirvāṇa. Because the Buddha refused to answer metaphysical questions and confined himself to teachings regarding this world and the improvement of our existence here different aspects and interpretations of his philosophy were developed by his followers. Even his silence was interpreted in various ways and other schools developed explaining what they considered his transcendental experience and knowledge of reality.

The 2 main Hīnayāna Schools that rose up in India were:

Bāhyānumeyavāda or Sautrāntika — Critical realism or 're-presentationalism': Both the mental and material are real, but the external reality is only known by inference (*Bāhya* — external; *anumeya* — inference). Called the Sautrāntika because it derives its authority entirely from the *Sutta-piṭaka*.

Bāhyapratyakshavāda or Vaibhāshika (Both these schools called Sarvāstivāda) — Direct realism: both the mental and material are real, and the material world is known by direct perception (*bāhya* — external; *prati-aksh* — to see directly). Called Vaibhāshika because its tenets came from a commentary called *Vibhāshā* (*sarva* — all; *asti* — is; *vāda* — doctrine).

The 2 main Mahāyāna Schools that rose in India were:

Śūnyavāda or Mādhyamika of Nāgārjuna (100-200 A.D.) — So-called Nihilism. There is no reality, mental or material, or is there anything unreal, all is *Śūnya* or 'Void'. Nothing is real apart from the whole. It disposes of all duality and proclaims the oneness of *Saṁsāra* or 'transmigratory existence' and *Nirvāṇa* or 'Liberation from limitation'. This school is not true Nihilism but a theory of Relativity for it teaches that there is a reality which is not describable by any concept, mental or material. Hence being devoid of phenomenal characteristics it is called *Śūnya*, 'Void' or the indescribable real nature of things. Nāgārjuna was the great exponent. His *Mādhyamika-Śāstra* is an authority. Called Mādhyamika or 'Middle' path because it avoids extremes of reality and unreality.

Vijñānavāda or Yogāchāra — Subjective idealism. The mental is real and the material world is void of reality. Only consciousness or *Vijñāna* exists. The sole reality is *Alaya-vijñāna* —

'abode of consciousness' or 'ideation store' which is above subject and object and ego. This school also was called Yogāchāra because it practised Yoga (*āchāra* — practice). Āryasaṅgha and Vasubandhu are the famous leaders of this school.

GREAT CHARACTERS IN THE HISTORY
OF BUDDHISM

Ānanda — The beloved disciple of the Buddha. He attained Arhatship in the early morning of the same day that the Buddhist Council at Rājagṛiha took place in 499 B.C. As he took his seat, it is said, he "shone like the full moon on a cloudless night, like a lotus touched into bloom by the rays of the sun; his face was pure, cleansed, radiant and resplendent as though it were proclaiming his attainment of Arahantiship."

He was entrusted with the handing down of the *Dīghanikāya* of the Buddhist Canon.

Other important disciples who helped to classify and arrange the teachings of the Buddha were:

Sariputta's pupils and Aniruddha (Sāriputra in Sanskrit).

Mahākaśyapa — The intuitive disciple of the Buddha, who, when the Enlightened One silently held up a flower before his gathered disciples, was the only one who understood and smiled at the Buddha in recognition of the Truth he was silently teaching. This inexpressible spiritual treasure Mahākaśyapa passed on to a line of patriarchs. One of these, Bodhidharma, systematised the Mahāyāna and carried it to China.

Aśoka — The Great Buddhist Emperor of India (270-230 B.C.).

Mahendra — King Aśoka's son who introduced Buddhism into Ceylon 236 years after Buddha's death.

Buddhaghosha — 'Voice of Buddha', the name of a notable Buddhist scholar and writer of the 5th century A.D. who translated the Sinhalese Commentaries on Buddhism into Pāli and wrote the *Visuddhimagga* and Commentaries on the whole of the three *Piṭakas*.

Dharmapāla — A South Indian Elder of the Hīnayāna in the 5th century A.D. who wrote Commentaries on the *Piṭakas*.

Aśvaghosha (2nd C.A.D.) — One of the most famous of Buddhist philosophers, poets and writers. He synthesized the essence of the Mahāyāna in the *Mahāyānaśraddhotpāda* and also wrote the *Buddhacharitakāvya*, a poem containing the Life of the Buddha in Sanskrit. He taught that the phenomenal world has its basis of reality which is *tathātā* symbolized by *Amitābha*. He promulgated the faith in the Grace of Amitābha.

Bodhidharma (6th century A.D.) — A famous Indian Buddhist who systematized the Mahāyāna School of *Dhyāna* Buddhism and who went to China where his School became the Ch'an School which later developed the Zen School so well-known in Japan.

Śāntideva (7th century A.D.) — One of the most important writers of the Mahāyāna. He wrote the *Śikshā-Samuchchhaya*, a compendium of the true doctrines of the Māhāyāna, and the *Bodhi-charāvatāra*, consisting of rules of discipline for Mahāyānists.

Padma Sambhava — 'The Lotus Born', a north Indian Buddhist of Nālanda University who established Āryasaṅgha's Yogāchāra Buddhism in Tibet in 747 A.D. which later developed into the *Lamaism* of Tibet.

THE PĀLI LITERATURE OF BUDDHISM

The canonical texts of Hīnayāna Buddhism are divided into three collections called the Tipiṭaka or 'Three Baskets' of teachings.

The Vinaya-Piṭaka is divided as follows:
   (1) Suttavibhanga
   (2) Khandhakas — Mahāvagga, Chullavagga

(3) Parivāra

The Sutta-Piṭaka has five Nikāyas or Collections:

(1) Dīghanikāya
(2) Majjhimanikāya
(3) Samyuttanikāya
(4) Anguttaranikāya
(5) Khuddakanikāya — with its minor works:
    1. Khuddakapāṭha
    2. Dhammapada
    3. Udāna
    4. Itivuttaka
    5. Suttanipāta
    6. Vimānavatthu
    7. Petavatthu
    8. Theragāthā
    9. Theragīthā
    10. Jātaka
    11. Niddesa
    12. Patisambhidāmagga
    13. Apadāna
    14. Buddhavamsa
    15. Chariyāpiṭaka

The Abhidhamma-Piṭaka has seven divisions:

(1) Dhammasanganī
(2) Vibhanga
(3) Kathāvatthu
(4) Puggalapaññati
(5) Dhātukathā
(6) Yamaka
(7) Paṭṭhāna

All these writings have Pāli *Atthakathās* or Commentaries each with their own names. Buddhaghosha and Dhammapāla are the two chief ones.

Bhānakas were the Reciters of Buddha's teachings.

Theras were the Buddhist Elders.

Other important Buddhist literature:

The Dīpavaṁśa — 'History of the Island', relating to the history of Buddhism in India and its propagation in Ceylon.

The Milinda-pañha — The Milinda Questions.

The Visuddhimagga, Buddhaghosha's famous Commentary on the Vinaya Piṭaka.

THE 4 PRINCIPAL SACRED BUDDHIST SHRINES

Lumbinī — the birth-place of the Buddha.

Buddhagayā — the site where Prince Siddhārtha attained enlightenment under the Bodhi (Bo)-tree.

Sāranāth — the site where the Buddha preached his first sermon.

Kuśinara — the site where the Buddha passed away into Mahānirvāṇa.

SOME IMPORTANT SANSKRIT SCRIPTURES OF MAHĀYĀNA BUDDHISM

THE PRAJÑĀPĀRAMITĀ SŪTRAS (dealing with the Emptiness of all things):

> Mahāprajñāpāramitā Sūtra.
> Ashṭasaharika-Prajñāpāramitā.
> Vajrachchhedika.

Saddharmapuṇḍarīka containing the last and supreme teaching before Buddha entered Samādhi (basis of Mahāyāna).

Mahāparanirvāṇa Sūtra — 'The Paradise Sūtra' telling of Nirvāṇa and the Bodhisattva's virtues.

Kumārajīva said that the Prajñāpāramitā exterminates false views, the Saddharmapuṇḍarīka reveals the ultimate truth and the Mahāparaṇirvāṇa preaches the true way. These three Sūtras are the Gates to Liberation.

Avatamsaka — 'The Wreath-Doctrine' or Buddha's supreme mystic doctrine. Important sections of this work are:

Gandavyūha — dealing with religious practice and vows.

Daśabhūmika — the Ten Stages of Enlightenment.

Laṅkāvatāra Sūtra — containing a memorandum of the important teachings of the Mahāyāna.

Samādhi-rāja — dealing with the samādhi of the King.

Tathāgata-guhyaka — dealing with the mystery of Tathāgata.

Lalita-vistara — gives detailed account of the artless and natural acts in the Buddha's life.

Suvarṇa-prabhāsa — dealing with the 'golden light' of the Buddha.

Vimalakīrti Nirdeśa — tells how to find Buddhahood within ourselves.

Vajraśekhara Sūtra — explains the realization of the Buddha.

Brahmajāla Sūtra — contains the Mahāyāna disciplinary precepts.

Sukhavatī-Vyūha — dealing with the problems of after-death.

Suraṅgamasamādhi — explains how Samādhi along with Enlightenment is obtained.

Śrīmaladevī Sūtra — Princess Śrīmala preaches the one vehicle (yāna) for all.

Besides these Sūtras there are other works and many commentaries of great importance.

BUDDHIST VOCABULARY

Abhimukti	Achala
Abrahmacharya	Āchāra

Adattanādāna
Adhishṭhāna
Ahiṁsā
Alaya-vijñāna
Amitābha
Amitābha-Buddha
Anāgāmī-mārga
Ānanda
Anātman
Anitya
Aniruddha
Archismati
Arhat
Ārya-Ashṭāṅga-Mārga
Ātman
Ātmavāda
Avalokiteśvara
Avidyā
Bāhyānumeyavāda
Bāhyapratyakshavāda
Bala
Bauddha
Bhānaka
Bhāva
Bhikshu
Bhikshuṇi
Bodhichitta
Bodhisattva
Bodhisattva-Yāna
Bodhi(Bo)-tree
Brahma
Brahma-Vihāra
Buddha
Buddhism
Chatvāri-ārya satyāni
Chitta
Dāna

Dharma
Dharmakāya
Dharmamegha
Dhyāna
Dosha
Dṛishṭi
Duḥkha
Duḥkha-nirodha-mārga
Duḥkham-samudaya
Dūraṅgama
Dvādaśa-Nidāna
Gautama
Hīnayāna
Jarāmāraṇa
Jāri
Jñāna
Kāma
Karma
Karuṇā
Kāya
Kleśa
Kshānti
Lamaism
Lobha
Mādhyamika
Mahānirvāṇa
Mahāparaṇirvāṇa
Mahāyāna
Maitra
Maitrachitta
Manas
Māra
Mārga
Moha
Mṛishavāda
Muditā
Nāmarūpa

Nirmāṇakāya
Nirvāṇa
Pāli
Pañcha-Śīla
Pañcha-Skandhāḥ
Paramārthasatya
Pāramitās
Paraṇirvāṇa
Paraṇishpanna
Paratantra
Parikalpita
Parivāra
Prabhakarī
Prajñā
Prajñāpāramitā
Pramudita
Prāṇātipāta
Praṇidhāna
Prātītya-samutpāda
Pratyeka-Buddha
Punarjanman
Rāga
Rūpa
Sādhumati
Sakkāyadṛishṭi
Sakṛidāgāmī-mārga
Śākya
Śākyamuni
Samādhi
Samāpatti
Sambhogakāya
Sambodha
Sambodhi
Saṁsāra
Saṁskāra
Saṁsāra-chakra
Samvṛitti-satya

Samyagājīva
Samyagdṛishṭi
Samyagvāk
Samyagvyāyāma
Samyakkarmānta
Samyaksamādhi
Samyaksambodhi
Samyaksaṁkalpa
Samyaksmṛiti
Satya
Sautrāntika
Shaḍāyatana
Siddhārtha
Siddhi
Śikshā
Śīla
Skandha
Śoka-parideya-daurmānasa-
    upāyāsa
Sparśa
Śrāvaka
Srotāpatti-mārga
Sudurjaya
Śūnya
Śūnyavāda
Śūnyatā
Surā-maireya-majja-
    pramāda-sthāna
Suraṅgamasamādhi
Sūtra
Sutta
Tathāgata
Tathātā
Thera
Theravāda
Trikāya
Tṛishṇā

Udāna
Upādāna
Upāsaka
Upāsikā
Upāya
Upekshā
Vaibhāshika
Vedanā

Vibhaṅga
Vijñāna
Vijñānavāda
Vimala
Viramaṇa
Vīrya
Virāga
Yogāchāra

FAMOUS BUDDHIST PLACES

Budhgayā
Kapilāvastu
Kuśinara
Lumbinī

Nālanda University
Rājagṛiha
Sāranāth

FAMOUS BUDDHISTS

Āryasaṅgha
Aśoka
Aśvaghosha
Bodhidharma
Buddhaghosha
Dharmapāla
Kumārajīva

Mahākaśyapa
Mahinda
Nāgārjuna
Padma Sambhava
Śāntideva
Sariputta
Vasubandhu

IMPORTANT BUDDHIST SCRIPTURES

Abhidhamma-piṭaka
Anguttaranikāya
Ashṭasaharika-prajñā-pāramitā
Atthakathās
Avatamsaka
Boddhicharāvatāra
Brahmajāla-Sūtra

Buddhacharitakāvya
Buddhavaṁśa
Chariyāpiṭaka
Chullavagga
Daśabhūmika
Dhamma-chakka-pavatana-
  sutta

Dhammapada
Dhammasanganī
Dharma-chakra-pravartana-
  sūtra
Dhātukathā
Khuddakapātha
Dīghanikāya
Dīpavamśa
Gandavyūha
Itivuttaka
Jātaka
Kathāvatthu
Khandhaka
Chuddakanikāya
Lalita-vistara
Laṅkāvatāra Sūtra
Mādhyamika-Śāstra
Mahāprajñāpāramitā-Sūtra
Mahāvagga
Mahāyānaśraddhotpāda
Majjhimanikāya
Milinda-pañha
Niddesa
Nikāyas
Patisambhidāmagga
Paṭṭhāna

Petavatthu
Piṭaka
Prajñāpāramitā-Sūtra
Puggalapaññati
Saddharmapuṇḍarīka
Samādhi-rāja
Samyuttanikāya
Śikshāsamuchchhaya
Śrīmaladevī Sūtra
Sukhavatī-Vyūha
Suttanipāta
Sutta-piṭaka
Suttavibhaṅga
Suvarṇa-prabhāsa
Tathāgata-guhyaka
Theragāthā
Theragīthā
Tipiṭaka(Tripiṭaka)
Vajrachchhedika
Vajraśekhara-Sūtra
Vimalakīrti-Nirdeśa
Vibhāshā
Vimānavatthu
Vinaya-piṭaka
Visuddhimagga

Om maṇi padme Hum
Om the jewel in the lotus Hum

Chapter XII

SANĀTANA DHARMA — ETERNAL RELIGION (Hinduism)

4	divisions of Dharma	1	Karma Kriyā Ritual Vidhi	2	Nīti — Ethics	3	Pūjā — worship Sādhanā, spiritual self-discipline	4	Darśana — Philoso- phy
4	divisions of Religion	1	Primitive Worship Fetishism, Totemism Nature Worship	2	Ethical Values Hīnayāna Buddhism Jainism	3	Love and Worship of God Mahāyāna Buddhism Vaishṇavism Śaivism Śaktism Sikhism Islam	4	Realization and God-Union Vedānta Mysticism Dhyāna and Zen Buddhism Yoga Sufiism
2	divisions of Scripture	1	Śruti or Revelation			2	Smṛiti or Tradition		

I. Śruti or Revelation (What is heard within)

					Vedas { Ṛig-Veda Yajur-Veda		Sāma-Veda Atharva-Veda		
3	divisions of each Veda	1	Mantras — hymns	2	Brāhmaṇas — exege- sis			3	Upanishad — Spiri- tual Philosophy
3	divisions of the use of Vedic material	1	Karma-kāṇḍa Action-portion Sacrifice	2	Upāsanā-kāṇḍa Worship-portion			3	Jñāna-kāṇḍa Wisdom-portion
	produced		Yajña — Sacrifice Ritual		Pūjā — worship Sādhanā — inner discipline				Vedānta — essence of wisdom
	resulted in		Mīmāṁsā — Vedic ceremonial Karma — Action		Bhakti Movements Love and Devotion to God				Jñāna — Wisdom

2. Smṛiti or Tradition (What is remembered)

1. Dharma-śāstras — Law books — Mānava-dharma-śāstra (Laws of Manu).

2. Itihāsas — Epics — Rāmāyaṇa, Mahābhārata (Bhagavad-Gītā).

3. Purāṇas — Legendary history, Instruments of popular instruction — Vishṇu, Bhāgavata.

4. Āgamas — Manuals of worship for — Vaishṇava (Vishṇu), Śaiva (Śiva), Śākta (Śakti) — Sects.

5. Darśana — Philosophical Schools.

Nyāya	Sāṁkhya	Mīmāṁsā
Vaiśeshika	Yoga	Vedānta

6. Sūtras — Aphoristic Rules — Bhāshyas — Commentaries.

7. Nīti-śāstra — Ethical scriptures — Jātaka (Buddhist Birth Tales), Pañcha-Tantra (Fables), Hitopadeśa (Book of Good Counsil).

Veda — Source of All

Its philosophy leads to Vedānta and Jñāna.

Its meditation and prayer leads to Bhakti Movements.

Its rituals and sacrifice leads to Mīmāṁsā and Karma.

Its accounts of creation leads to Sāṁkhya Cosmology and Psychology.

Its religious and occult experience leads to Sādhanās of Yoga and Tantras.

Its metaphysical reasoning leads to Nyāya and Vaiśeshika.

Its lives of Ṛishis, Kings and Devotees leads to Itihāsas and Purāṇas.

Its social customs leads to Dharma-śāstras and Āgamas.

Sources and Causes of Other Movements and Religions

Protests against sacrifice and religious degradation lead to Buddhism and Jainism.

Modern Developments of Vedic Wisdom

Reform movements leads to Brāhmo-Samāj, Ārya-Samāj.

Integrating East and West leads to Poetic genius of Tagore.

Neo-Vedāntism and Integral Spiritual Illumination lead to Śrī Rāmakṛishṇa, Swāmī Vivekānanda, Śrī Aurobindo.

Freedom movement and Social Regeneration lead to Mahātmā Gāndhi.

The Sanātana Dharma

Sri Aurobindo in his famous Uttarpara Speech tells of his revelation in prison and his *Ādeśa* or Command from God regarding the Sanātana Dharma.

"Then He placed the Gita in my hands. His strength entered into me and I was able to do the sadhana of the Gita. I was not only to understand intellectually but to realise what Sri Krishna demanded of Arjuna and what He demands of those who aspire to do His work, to be free from repulsion and desire, to do work for Him without the demand for fruit, to renounce self-will and become a passive and faithful instrument in His hands, to have an equal heart for high and low, friend and opponent, success and failure, yet not to do His work negligently. I realised what the Hindu religion meant. We speak often of the Hindu religion, of the Sanatana Dharma, but few of us really know what that religion is. Other religions are preponderatingly religions of faith and profession, but the Sanatana Dharma is life itself;

it is a thing that has not so much to be believed as lived. This is the Dharma that for the salvation of humanity was cherished in the seclusion of this peninsula from of old. It is to give this religion that India is rising. She does not rise as other countries do, for self or when she is strong, to trample on the weak. She is rising to shed the eternal light entrusted to her over the world."

"When it is said that India shall expand and extend herself, it is the Sanatana Dharma that shall expand and extend itself over the world. It is for the Dharma and by the Dharma that India exists. To magnify the religion means to magnify the country. I have shown you that I am everywhere and in all men and in all things,..."

"What is this religion which we call Sanatana, eternal? It is the Hindu religion only because the Hindu nation has kept it, because in this Peninsula it grew up in the seclusion of the sea and the Himalayas, because in this sacred and ancient land it was given as a charge to the Aryan race to preserve through the ages. But it is not circumscribed by the confines of a single country, it does not belong peculiarly and for ever to a bounded part of the world. That which we call the Hindu religion is really the eternal religion, because it is the universal religion which embraces all others. If a religion is not universal, it cannot be eternal. A narrow religion, a sectarian religion, an exclusive religion can live only for a limited time and a limited purpose. This is the one religion that can triumph over materialism by including and anticipating the discoveries of science and the speculations of philosophy. It is the one religion which impresses on mankind the closeness of God to us and embraces in its compass all the possible means by which man can approach God. It is the one religion which insists every moment on the truth which all religions acknowledge that He is in all men and all things and that in Him we move and have our being. It is the one religion which enables us not only to understand and believe this truth but to realise it with every part of our being. It is the one religion which shows what the world is, that it is the Lila of Vasudeva. It is the one religion which shows us how we can best play our part in that Lila, its subtlest laws and its noblest rules. It is the one religion which does not separate life in any smallest detail from religion, which knows what immortality is and has utterly removed from us the reality of death."

Sri Aurobindo

INDEX

INDEX
of
PERSONS, BOOKS and PLACES

Pali Vocabulary

Index of the Yoga Chapters of the Bhagavad Gita

Names and Titles Given to Arjuna

Names and Titles Given to Krishna

Index of Proper Names and Their Genealogical Forbears from Chapter I of the Bhagavad Gita

Index of Special Lists and Charts